The CANADIAN
Writer's Handbook

ᴂ Essentials Edition ᴂ

Messenger • de Bruyn • Brown • Montagnes

OXFORD
UNIVERSITY PRESS

OXFORD
UNIVERSITY PRESS

Oxford University Press is a department of the University of Oxford.

It furthers the University's objective of excellence in research, scholarship, and education by publishing worldwide. Oxford is a registered trade mark of Oxford University Press in the UK and in certain other countries.

Published in Canada by
Oxford University Press
8 Sampson Mews, Suite 204,
Don Mills, Ontario M3C 0H5 Canada

www.oupcanada.com

Copyright © Oxford University Press Canada 2012

Library and Archives Canada Cataloguing in Publication
The Canadian writer's handbook / William E. Messenger ...
[et al.]. — Essentials ed.
Includes index.

ISBN 978-0-19-543039-4

1. English language—Composition and exercises.
2. English language—Grammar. 3. Report writing.
I. Messenger, William E., 1931–

PE1408.C353 2012   808'.042   C2011-908063-X

Cover image: © iStockPhoto.com/TheresaTibbetts

This book is printed on permanent acid-free paper ∞.

Printed and bound in the United States of America.

1A 2 3 4 — 15 14 13 12

CONTENTS

PART IV ESSENTIALS OF PUNCTUATION   151

**PART V   ESSENTIALS OF
MECHANICS AND SPELLING   183**

PREFACE

This Essentials edition of *The Canadian Writer's Handbook* is designed to help you work on your writing skills. Improving written communication is an ongoing—even lifelong—project. Whether you are a long-time writer of English seeking to refine your abilities or a writer who is approaching English as an additional language, we hope that the suggestions, examples, and guidelines in this new edition will provide a trustworthy resource that will enable you to write with greater confidence and communicate with greater clarity.

Overview

This handbook contains six parts, each of which addresses an essential aspect of the writing process. We begin with a section on the principles of composition, in which you will learn how to approach your topic and how to structure your writing to achieve your goal. In the next two parts, we explore the essentials of grammar and style, first by examining how sentences work, then by looking at how parts of speech come together to form meaning. In Part IV we discuss the importance of punctuation. Part V addresses issues of spelling and mechanics—for example, how to use abbreviations, which terms to capitalize, and when to use italics. Part VI offers valuable information on how to conduct research and cite sources you reference in your paper. Finally, the appendix provides a checklist that will help you work through the revising, editing, and proofreading stages of your own writing.

How to Use This Handbook

We encourage you to use this handbook as a reference tool that you can consult on particular issues arising from the everyday writing activities, challenges, and questions you encounter. We suggest that you begin by familiarizing yourself with it by seeing what each part has to offer you. Browse through the table of contents and the index. Look up some sections that arouse your interest. Flip through the pages, pausing now and then for a closer look. Note the numbered running heads at the tops of pages and the numbered tabs at the outer edge of each page. These features, together with the part index at the end of this preface, can help you find things in a hurry.

When you sit down to read the text, you may want to start at the beginning and proceed carefully through the book. Note that some points in later sections might not be clear to you unless you understand the material in the early sections.

The text is subdivided into sections and subsections that are numbered consecutively throughout. Cross-references will guide you to related section and subsection. The index will guide you to specific pages related to the topic you are investigating.

PART III
ESSENTIALS OF GRAMMAR AND
STYLE: PARTS OF SPEECH; DICTION

CONTENTS

INTRODUCTION

English words fall traditionally into eight categories called **parts of speech**. Five of these can be inflected (changed in their form) in one or more ways:

- noun
- adjective
- pronoun
- adverb
- verb

The other three are not inflected (that is, they do not change form):

- preposition
- interjection
- conjunction

Note that the term *inflection* applies only to the change of a word's form within its part of speech. That is, when the noun *boy* is inflected to make it plural, the new form, *boys*, is still a noun; when the pronoun *they* is inflected to *them* or *theirs*, the new forms are still pronouns.

Many words can be changed so that they function as different parts of speech. For example the noun *centre* can be made into the adjective *central*, or the noun *meaning* into the adjective *meaningful*, or the verb *vacate* into the noun *vacation*. Such changes are not inflections but **derivations**; a word can be *derived* from a word of a different part of speech, often by the addition of one or more suffixes: *trust*, *trustful*, *trustfully*, *trustfulness*. And many

One can also classify nouns as either **concrete**, for names of tangible items (*doctor*, *elephant*, *utensil*, *book*, *barn*), or **abstract**, for names of intangible things or ideas (*freedom*, *honour*, *happiness*, *history*).

Collective nouns are names of collections or groups often considered as units: *army*, *committee*, *family*, *herd*, *flock*.

6a Inflection of Nouns:
Number; Possessive Case

EAL Nouns can be inflected in two ways: for **number** and for **possessive case**.

1. For number

Most common concrete nouns that stand for **countable** things are either **singular** or **plural**. Most singular nouns are inflected to indicate the plural by the addition of *s* or *es*: *girl*, *girls*; *box*, *boxes*. But some are made plural in other irregular ways: *child*, *children*; *stimulus*, *stimuli*.

Some concrete nouns, however, called **mass** nouns, name materials that are measured, weighed, or divided, rather than counted—for example *gold*, *oxygen*, *rice*, *sand*, and *pasta*. As **uncountable** or **noncountable** nouns, these are not inflected for the plural. Also uncountable are **abstract** nouns and nouns that stand for ideas, activities, and states of mind or being; for example, *honour*, *journalism*, *skiing*, *happiness*.

Some nouns, however, can be either countable or uncountable, depending on the context in which they are used. For example:

The butcher sells <u>meat</u>. (uncountable)

The delicatessen offers several delicious smoked <u>meats</u>. (countable, equivalent to *kinds of smoked meat*)

They insisted on telling the truth as a matter of <u>honour</u>. (uncountable)

Many <u>honours</u> were heaped upon the returning hero. (countable)

6

Help with Polishing Your Work

When you finish a piece of writing, go through the checklist in the appendix. If you find you're not sure about something, follow the cross-references to the sections that will give you the help you need.

Help with Correcting and Revising Your Work

When you get a piece of writing back with marks and comments, look it over alongside the list of marking symbols and abbreviations on this handbook's inside back cover. The information there may be enough to help you make the appropriate changes. But if you need more than a reminder about a specific issue or pattern, look up the relevant topic and study the sections that discuss and illustrate those principles in greater detail. You should then be able to edit and revise your work with understanding and confidence.

Key Terms

Throughout the text, you will find important terms set in boldface. Pay attention to these terms, for they make up the basic vocabulary necessary for the discussion of grammar, syntax, and style.

For Readers and Writers of English as an Additional Language

Our experience as university instructors has given us the opportunity to work with a number of writers engaged in the challenging project of reading and writing in English as an additional language (EAL). At several points in this handbook, we offer information and direction of particular importance to those of you who are approaching English as a relatively new language, and we have designated those relevant sections with the symbol (**EAL**).

Up-to-Date Documentation Guidelines

Part VI offers guidelines that cover the three most popular citation styles used in Canada today: MLA style (the name–page method), APA style (the name–date method), and Chicago style (the note method). To illustrate each method of documentation, we offer an array of examples modelled on the recommendations set out in the most recent editions of each style guide.

Frankenstein family. Victor takes pains to describe him as a man of "honour and reputation . . . respected by all who [know] him for his integrity and indefatigable attention to public business" and "perpetually occupied by the affairs of his country" (Shelley 31). A first-time reader of the novel might well be forgiven for assuming that Victor's narrative will be more a tribute to his father than an account of his own creation of a monster.

Here, the student writer has selected key words and phrases from the opening paragraph of Victor Frankenstein's narrative in order to make a point about the novel's focus. The ellipsis indicates that material has been omitted in the interests of the student's own sentence structure.

37 DOCUMENTATION

To be effective, documentation must be complete, accurate, and clear. Completeness and accuracy depend on careful recording of necessary information as you do your research and take notes. Clarity depends on the way you present that information to your reader. You will be clear only if your audience can follow your method of documentation. Before you begin any research project, investigate the method of documentation you need to use. This section presents three frequently used methods:

1. The *name–page* method, currently recommended by the Modern Language Association (**MLA**) and in wide use in the humanities;
2. the *name–date* method, recommended by the American Psychological Association (**APA**) and used in some of the social and other sciences as well as in education studies; and
3. the *note* method, recommended by *The Chicago Manual of Style* and preferred in some disciplines.

Which method you choose will depend on what discipline (field of study) you are writing in and on the wishes of your audience.

 37a The Name–Page Method (MLA Style)

The name–page method is detailed in the seventh edition of the *MLA Handbook for Writers of Research Papers* (2009). This method of citation is simple and efficient. Using this method, you provide a short, usually **parenthetical** or **in-text reference** to each source as you use it in the body of your paper. Then, you provide complete bibliographical information about all the electronic and non-electronic sources you have used as it in the body of your paper. Then, you provide complete bibliographical information about all the electronic and non-electronic sources you have used as it in the body of your paper, in a list titled "Works Cited," alphabetized by surnames of authors or editors (or title, when no author or editor is named).

The pages that follow illustrate examples of the most common patterns of MLA documentation: each in-text parenthetical reference is accompanied by its works-cited entry. Note that parenthetical references are usually placed at the end of the sentence in which the citation occurs; but if a sentence is long and complicated, a reference may be placed earlier, immediately after the citation itself.

Note also that in an actual paper, the examples that follow would be **double-spaced** rather than single-spaced.

Print Sources

A book by one author (or editor)

IN-TEXT REFERENCE

Today, North Americans do less walking than they did fifty years ago. Even if they are travelling only a short distance, they tend to drive or get a ride to their destination. In fact, a recent survey revealed that many Canadian municipalities "did not provide pedestrian amenities at all, and only half, in any way, encouraged their citizens to reach their destinations by foot" (Friedman 136).

When you don't mention the author by name in your sentence, the parenthetical reference includes the author's surname and a page reference, with *no intervening punctuation*. The closing period follows the parenthesis. If you can include the author's name and credentials in your text,

ACKNOWLEDGEMENTS

As with the previous editions of *The Canadian Writer's Handbook*, this essential edition owes much to the contributions of reviewers, colleagues, friends, fellow writers, and talented and committed editors.

For their determination to strengthen and polish their work and their commitment to grow and change as thinkers and writers, we thank our students. We are especially grateful for their generosity in allowing us to use their questions and insights about writing in this book.

We would also like to thank all of the reviewers whose comments and suggestions have helped shape all editions of *The Canadian Writer's Handbook* over the years.

We deeply appreciate the encouragement, advice, and support we receive from the talented and enthusiastic staff at Oxford University Press—especially from David Stover and Phyllis Wilson. Special appreciation goes to our meticulous, ever-patient editors, Peter Chambers, Eric Sinkins, Janice Evans, Suzanne Clark, and Lisa Ball.

To all of you, many thanks.

Jan de Bruyn, Ramona Montagnes, and Judy Brown
University of British Columbia

ESSENTIALS OF COMPOSITION

I

CONTENTS

INTRODUCTION

Writing is paradoxical, when you think about it. It is, on the one hand, the most commonplace of activities—something many of us do every day of the week, every week of the year. On the other hand, writing is one of the most astonishing and complex acts of communication any of us is asked to undertake in the course of getting an education, doing a job, or living a life.

Writing calls upon us to exercise creativity in generating ideas out of our own experience; it asks us to practise synthesis in entering the world of ideas and in discovering and integrating the ideas of others with insights of our own; it expects us to develop our powers of communication in shaping and presenting our arguments to different audiences of readers; it challenges us to demonstrate our talents for organization, reflection, and revision in working through the writing process from that first idea to the printing of our final draft.

Part I investigates the principles of unity, coherence, and emphasis that apply to the larger units of communication, the essay and the paragraph.

1 THE WRITING PROCESS: PLANNING, WRITING, AND REVISING THE WHOLE ESSAY

A piece of writing is the result of a process. The usual steps that a writer takes, whether consciously or not, fall into three major stages:

Stage I: Planning
- finding a subject and formulating questions about it
- limiting the subject
- determining audience and purpose
- gathering reliable data
- classifying and organizing the data
- outlining

Stage II: Writing
- writing the first draft
- integrating evidence
- commenting on significance of evidence

Stage III: Revising
- revising
- preparing the final draft
- editing and proofreading

Often several parts of the process will be going on at the same time; for example, there is often a good deal of interaction among the activities in the planning stage. Sometimes the order will be different; for example, you may not be clear about your purpose until you have finished gathering and then classifying and organizing data. And sometimes in the revising stage, you may want to go back and rethink your purpose, or dig up more material, or even further limit or expand your topic.

1a Finding and Limiting a Subject

1. For writing situations that are discipline-specific
Develop topics around researchable questions of current interest in the field and narrow them to fit the time allotted to the assignment and the length expected by your reader.

Consider some of the following when developing the proposal or statement of purpose often called for in such circumstances:

- a question of definition, a key term with a history of changing denotations over time [for a cultural geography course, "What is gendered space?"]
- a central debate in the scholarly writing produced in the discipline [for a Canadian studies course, "How do scholars of the 1970s and those of today differ on the evaluation of Pauline Johnson's poetry?"]
- a review of the scholarly literature surrounding a particular question in the field [for a children's literature course, "How can theories of ecocriticism be applied to the reading of Canadian children's literature set on the Prairies?"]
- a question or issue that crosses disciplinary boundaries (for example, a question preoccupying linguists and sociologists, or economists and geographers) [for a human geography course, "How will global climate change affect birth rates in Central and South America?"]
- an idea raised incidentally in lectures or seminars that deserves further investigation [for a film studies seminar course, "Do images of children in recent Canadian films provide clues to the way Canadian culture has constructed ideas of childhood?"]

Such possibilities should make it possible for you to produce a paper distinctive in its approach—something more and better than a cutting and pasting of the views of two or three major sources that may tend to exclude the perspective of the student writer.

In working out your research and preparing a plan for the paper, devise a reasonable timeline for research, planning, writing, revising, and editing. Consider the expectations of your reading audience and the availability of a variety of electronic and non-electronic sources both scholarly and current. Keep in mind that the use of Canadian sources may be important to your objectives and to your readers.

2. For writing situations that are not discipline-specific

If you are enrolled in a writing course that involves writing papers in a variety of forms and for a range of audiences, you may be working outside a particular discipline or area of study. In such circumstances, a specific subject area or discipline will not likely be attached to your writing assignments, and you will be seeking one for yourself. A few minutes of free-associating, jotting down and playing around with questions and any ideas that pop into your head, will usually lead you at least to a subject area if not a specific subject. Scanning the pages of a magazine, a newspaper, a scholarly website, or a journal is another way to stimulate a train of thought; editorial and letters pages are full of interesting subjects to write about, perhaps to argue about. Or think about the questions or problems you may have about the course for which you are writing the essay. Often the very thing that puzzles you provides a good topic. Possibilities are almost endless.

Try to find a subject that interests you, one that you will enjoy working with and living with for an extended period of time. Formulate a question or series of questions worth investigating and researching. If you are assigned a topic that doesn't particularly interest you, try to make it a learning experience: immerse yourself in it; you may be surprised at how interesting it can become.

Whether your assignment is discipline-specific or more general, consider producing in the initial stages a proposal or statement of purpose that you can discuss with your instructor or prospective readers. On the opposite page is a preliminary statement of purpose for a 1,000-word paper on nineteenth-century Canadian writers.

3. Limiting the subject

Once you have a subject, limit it: narrow it to a topic you can develop adequately within the length of the essay you are writing. More often than not, writers start with subjects too big to handle. To save both time and energy, to avoid frustration, and to guarantee a better essay, be disciplined at this stage. If anything, overdo the narrowing, for at a later stage it's easier to broaden than it is to cut.

Kevin Cheung   English 222/010
10 January 2011
Paper is due: 12 March 2011 (approximately
                      two months)
Target length: 1,000 words
Audience: fellow students and my instructor, all
                      with an interest in the subject
Subject: nineteenth-century Canadian writers
Topic: contrasting the responses of Catharine
                      Parr Traill and Susanna Moodie to their
                      first years in Canada
Questions: Why did these two individuals—sisters
                      close in age and living close to one
                      another in their first days in Upper
                      Canada—react so differently to their
                      new homeland?
                      How is it that Traill celebrates the land,
                      the people, even the winter weather?
                      How is it that Moodie is so critical of
                      the land, the people (especially her
                      neighbours), and the conditions
                      of life?

Major sources so far:
                      Charlotte Gray's *Sisters in the Wilderness*
                      Traill's *The Backwoods of Canada*
                      Moodie's *Roughing It in the Bush*
                      Atwood's *Journals of Susanna Moodie*

For example, let's say you wanted to write about "travelling"; that's obviously far too broad. "National travel" or "international travel" is narrower, but still too broad. "Travelling in Asia?" Better, but still too large, for where would you begin? How thorough could you be in a mere 500 or even 1,000 words? When you find yourself narrowing your subject to something like "How to survive on $20.00 a day in Tokyo" or "What to do if you have only

24 hours in Hong Kong," then you can confidently look forward to developing your topic with sufficient thoroughness and specificity.

1b Considering Audience and Purpose

1. Audience

The sharper the focus you can get on your audience, the better you can control your writing to make it effective for that audience. Try to define your audience for a given piece of writing as precisely as possible.

Some writing you do may have only one reader: the instructor. But some assignments may ask you to address some specific audience; sometimes an instructor will ask you to write "for an audience of your peers." In the absence of any other guideline, writing for your peers is not a bad idea. Your choice of the right tone and language to use and of what definitions and explanations to provide will often be appropriate if you keep an interested and serious but not fully informed audience in mind.

2. Purpose

All writing has the purpose of communicating ideas. In a course, you write for the special purpose of demonstrating your ability to communicate your knowledge to your audience. But you will write more effectively if you think of each essay as having one or more of the following purposes:

1. to inform
2. to convince or persuade
3. to enter into discussion or debate with others who have explored the topic

Usually one of the three purposes will dominate, but one or both of the others will often be present as well.

The clearer your idea of what you want to do in an essay, and why, and for whom, the better you will be able to make effective rhetorical choices. You may even want to begin by writing down, as a memo to yourself, a detailed description of your audience and as clear a statement of your purpose as you can formulate. Tape this memo to the wall over your desk. If your ideas become clearer as the work proceeds, you can refine these statements.

1c Gathering and Organizing Evidence

An essay can't be built solely on vague generalizations and unsupported statements and opinions; it must contain specifics: facts, details, data, examples. Whatever your subject, you must gather material by reading and researching, conducting formal interviews, talking to others, or by thinking about your personal experience. Collect as much information as you can within the time you have allotted for evidence gathering, even two or three times what you can use; you can then select the best and bank the rest for future use.

Gathering the Evidence

1. Brainstorming

If you are expected to generate material from your own knowledge and experience (instead of through formal research), sit down for a few minutes with a pencil and a sheet of paper, write your topic in the centre or at the top, and begin jotting down ideas. Put down everything that comes into your head about it. Let your mind run fast and free. Don't bother with sentences; don't worry about spelling; don't even pause to wonder whether the words and phrases are going to be of any use. Just keep scribbling. It shouldn't be long before you've filled the sheet with possible ideas, questions, facts, details, names, and examples. It may help if you also brainstorm your larger subject area, not just the narrowed topic, since some of the broader ideas could prove useful.

2. Using questions

Another way to generate material is to ask yourself questions about your subject or topic and write down the answers. Start with the reporter's standard questions: *Who? What? Where? When? Why? How?* and go on from there with more of your own: *What is it? Who is associated with it? In what way? Where and when is it, or was it, or will it be? How does it work? Why is it? What causes it? What does it cause? What are its parts? What is it a part of? Is it part of a process? What does it look like? What is it like or unlike? What is its opposite? What if it didn't exist?* Such questions and the answers you develop will make you think of more questions, and so on; soon you'll have more than enough material that is potentially useful. You may even find yourself writing consecutive sentences, since some questions prompt certain kinds of responses. For example, asking *What is it?* may lead you to begin defining your subject; *What is it like or unlike?* may lead you to begin comparing and contrasting it, classifying it, thinking of analogies and metaphors; *What causes it?* and *What does it cause?* may lead you to begin exploring cause-and-effect relations; *What are its parts?* or *What is it a part of?* could lead you to analyze your subject; *How does it work?* or *Is it part of a process?* may prompt you to analyze and explain a process.

Organizing the Evidence

1. Classifying

As you brainstorm a subject and jot down notes and answers, you'll begin to see connections between one idea and another and start putting them in groups or drawing circles around them and lines and arrows between them. Do this kind of classification when you have finished gathering material. You should end up with several groups of related items, which means that you will have classified your material according to some principle that arose naturally from it. During this part of the process you will find yourself discarding the weaker or less relevant details, keeping only those that best suit the topic; that is, you will have selected the best.

For a tightly limited topic and a short essay, you may have only one group of details, but for an essay of even moderate length, say 750 words or more, you will probably have several groups.

The map below was created by a student to classify and organize her ideas for an 800-word paper on the effects of war on the child characters in Joy Kogawa's novel *Obasan*.

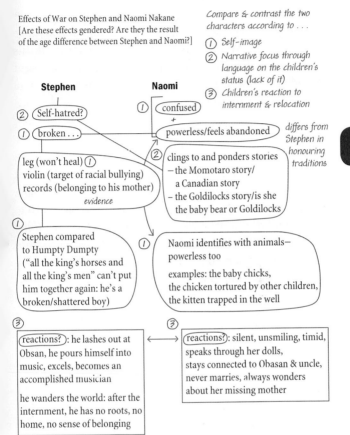

Effects of War on Stephen and Naomi Nakane
[Are these effects gendered? Are they the result
of the age difference between Stephen and Naomi?]

*Compare & contrast the two
characters according to . . .*

① *Self-image*

② *Narrative focus through
language on the children's
status (lack of it)*

③ *Children's reaction to
internment & relocation*

Stephen   **Naomi**

② Self-hatred?   ① confused
                              +
① broken . . .   powerless/feels abandoned   *differs from
Stephen in
honouring
traditions*

leg (won't heal) ①   ② clings to and ponders stories
violin (target of racial bullying)   – the Momotaro story/
records (belonging to his mother)   a Canadian story
evidence   – the Goldilocks story/is she
                              the baby bear or Goldilocks

①
Stephen compared   ① Naomi identifies with animals—
to Humpty Dumpty   powerless too
("all the king's horses and
all the king's men" can't put   examples: the baby chicks,
him together again: he's a   the chicken tortured by other children,
broken/shattered boy)   the kitten trapped in the well

③   ③
reactions? : he lashes out at ←→ reactions?: silent, unsmiling, timid,
Obsan, he pours himself into   speaks through her dolls,
music, excels, becomes an   stays connected to Obasan & uncle,
accomplished musician   never marries, always wonders
                                   about her missing mother
he wanders the world: after the
internment, he has no roots, no
home, no sense of belonging

2. Organizing after classifying

Once you have classified your material into groups, put the
groups into a meaningful order. Don't necessarily accept
the first arrangement that comes to mind; consider as
many different arrangements as the material will allow, and
then select the best one for your purpose and audience. The
order should be logical rather than accidental or arbitrary.

1d   Crafting a Thesis Statement

A crucial part of the planning or "pre-writing" stage is the
formulation of a **thesis statement**.

During the early stages, you gradually increase your
control over your proposed essay: you find and narrow a

subject, you think about audience and purpose, you gather evidence and generate ideas, and you classify and arrange your material. At some point while you are doing all this you will probably formulate a tentative thesis, a statement that identifies your topic and points the way to what you want to say about it.

1e   Crafting an Outline

A *thesis statement* leads off an **outline**; the ordered groups become *main headings*, and the details that make up each group, if they aren't simply absorbed by the main heading, become subdivisions of it in various levels of *subheadings*. And though tentative sketches of a possible beginning and ending aren't essential to an outline, it's usually worth trying to think of something of the sort at this stage; you can easily change later if you think of something better. On the opposite page is an example, a student's outline for a short essay. Note the layout of an outline: numerals and letters are followed by periods and a space or two; subheadings are indented at least two spaces past the beginning of the first word of a main heading. Few outlines will need to go beyond one or two levels of subheading, but if further subdivision is necessary, here is the way to indicate successive levels:

I.
II.
   A.
   B.
      1.
      2.
         a.
         b.
            (1.)
            (2.)
               (a.)
               (b.)

An outline drawn up before you write a major essay will save you time and effort at later stages. Writing the draft

THESIS STATEMENT: Students who have a social life are happier, smarter, and better prepared for the workforce than are students who concentrate only on their studies.

BEGINNING: All work and no play makes a dull student. Although many people, including my parents, believe that students should spend all their time studying, I believe students are better off socializing in moderation at university. Why?

I. They are happier.
   A. develop friendships
   B. develop maturity and a more balanced perspective towards life

II. They are smarter.
   A. receive academic support in study groups
   B. receive academic support from friends who are strong in certain disciplines

III. They are better prepared for the workforce.
   A. develop an effective network of contacts
   B. develop interpersonal skills
   C. develop communication skills

ENDING: So the next time my parents tell me to get off the phone because I should be studying, I will be ready with my answer. I will tell them I am leading a balanced life, improving academically, and getting ready for my future.

will be easier and smoother because it follows a plan: you know where you're going. You can avoid such pitfalls as unnecessary repetition, digression, and illogical or otherwise incoherent organization. In other words, a good outline can be like a map that keeps the writer from taking wrong turns, wandering in circles, or getting lost altogether.

Keep in mind, too, that an outline should not be binding. If as you write and revise you think of a better way to organize a part of your essay, or if some part of the outline proves clumsy when you try to set it down in paragraphs, or if you suddenly think of some new material that should be included, go with your instincts and revise accordingly. And as you proceed, you may also want to refine your thesis to reflect changes in your ideas.

1f   Writing a First Draft

Once you have a good outline to follow, drafting becomes smoother and more purposeful. With the shape of the whole essay laid out, you can concentrate on the main tasks of drafting: finding the right words, generating effective sentences, and constructing good transitions and strong paragraphs.

On going from your outline to your draft, keep the following in mind:

1. Sometimes a main heading and its subheading from the outline will become a single paragraph in the essay; sometimes each subheading will become a paragraph; and so on. The nature and density of your material will determine its treatment.

2. It may be possible to transfer the thesis statement from your outline to the essay unchanged, but more likely you will want to change it (perhaps several times) to fit the actual essay. The thesis is the statement of your purpose or of the position you intend to defend in the essay, so it should be as polished as possible. The kind of basic or mechanical statement suitable in an outline may be inappropriate in the essay itself.

1g   Beginnings

1. Postponing the beginning

Starting the actual writing can be a challenge: most writers have had the experience of staring at a computer screen or a blank sheet of paper while trying to think of a good way to begin. If you have no beginning in mind at this point, plunge right into the body of the essay and write it as rapidly as you can. Once you have finished writing the first draft, you'll have a better idea of what it is that needs to be introduced; you can then go back and do the beginning with relative ease.

2. Beginning directly

Just as it isn't always a good idea to begin a final paragraph with "In conclusion," so it's not always good practice to open routinely with something mechanical like "In this essay I will discuss" or "This essay is concerned with." On occasion, such as when your essay is unusually long or complicated or when you are presenting it as part of a research seminar, conference, or panel, it may be helpful to announce in advance what your essay is about, to provide readers with what amounts to a brief outline. But most essays don't require this kind of beginning and won't engage an audience with such a stiff introduction. Begin by talking about your topic. Rather than begin by informing readers of what you are going to say (and then at the end reminding them of what you have said), start with something substantial and, if possible, attention-getting. Try to end with something similarly sharp and definitive.

3. Determining subject and thesis

However you begin, it is necessary to identify your subject and to state your thesis somewhere near the beginning. For example, even if your title is something like "Imagery in Shakespeare's Sonnet 65," you should still, preferably in your first sentence, mention both the author and the title of the poem. The title of your essay is not a part of the essay's content; the essay should be able to stand on its own.

Special circumstances may, on occasion, call for you to delay the full statement of a thesis to near the end, for example as part of a strategy of building to a climax. Even then, you will probably provide at least some indication of your thesis near the beginning, perhaps in general terms.

4. Being direct, smooth, economical: some examples

Begin as directly, smoothly, and economically as you can. Here, for example, are three ways an essay with the title

"Imagery in Shakespeare's Sonnet 65" might begin; note how differences in order, punctuation, and wording make each succeeding one better and shorter than the one before:

(1) In Sonnet 65 by William Shakespeare, there is a great deal of imagery.

(2) William Shakespeare in his Sonnet 65 uses imagery to . . . .

(3) The imagery in Shakespeare's Sonnet 65 . . . .

Here is the beginning of an essay on Shakespeare's Sonnet 65. The writer can't seem to get going:

> William Shakespeare, famous English poet and writer of plays, has always been known for the way he uses imagery to convey the point he is making in a particular piece of work. Shakespeare's Sonnet 65 is no exception to this, and this is one of the better examples of his work that I have studied, for illustrating his use of imagery.
>
> The best example in the sonnet comes in lines five and six, where Shakespeare compares a "summer's honey breath" and a "wrackful siege of battering days."

Compare this with another student's beginning on the same topic:

> In Sonnet 65, Shakespeare appeals to a person's knowledge of visible properties in nature in an attempt to explain invisible properties of love and time.

The second writer has taken control of the material immediately. Even though no particular image has yet been mentioned, the second writer, in one crisp sentence, is far beyond where the first writer, well into a second paragraph, is.

 1h Revising, Editing, and Proofreading

The product of rapid composition is a first draft. Although some first drafts may come close to being acceptable finished products, don't gamble that your draft can pass for a polished essay. To polish your first draft, you will need to carefully revise, edit, and proofread what you have written.

1. Revising

Revision (re-vision, literally "scrutinizing again") is an extremely important stage of writing. Experienced writers revise a piece of writing at least two or three times before they consider it to be finished.

Revise carefully and slowly, looking for any way to improve what you've written. Don't aim just to correct errors made in haste, but also to remove clutter and improve diction, sentence structure, punctuation, coherence, paragraphing, organization, and so on. Some writers find that going through a draft for one thing at a time is effective—for example, going through it looking only at paragraphing, then going through it again looking only at the structure and variety of sentences, then at punctuation, and so on.

Adopt the role of an observant and alert reader looking for strengths and pinpointing weaknesses and errors. To do this effectively, try to allow yourself a cooling-off period; wait as long as possible between the drafting and the revising—at least two or three days—so that you can look at your own work with objectivity, as a dispassionate third-party reader would. If you're having trouble, you may find the Checklist for Use in Revising, Editing, and Proofreading (see the appendix) helpful during your revisions.

2. Editing and proofreading

Editing and proofreading take place during revision, of course, and also during drafting, but go over what you consider to be the final copy of your essay when you believe it is ready. This final proofreading will prove worthwhile; despite earlier careful scrutiny, you may discover not only typographical errors but also previously unnoticed slips in spelling, punctuation, and grammar.

Do your proofreading and editing with exaggerated care. Read each sentence, as a sentence, slowly (and aloud whenever possible); but also read each word as a word and check each punctuation mark. You might consider starting at the end of your work and reading backward, one word at a time, so that you won't get caught up in the flow of a sentence and overlook an error.

Do not put full trust in any of the spelling, grammar, and style checks that are part of word-processing programs. They can't possibly cover all the matters that require attention. Remember that spell checkers can't spot a misspelled word that happens to be the same as some other correctly spelled word—for example, *form* instead of *from*, or *through* instead of *though*; nor can they tell you that you've mistaken, say, *your* for *you're*, or *principal* for *principle*.

 Preparing the Final Draft

When you are through revising, editing, and proofreading a piece of writing, carefully prepare the final draft, the one that will be presented to your reader or readers. Once the work is out of your hands, it's too late to change anything; make sure it's in good shape when it leaves your hands. It should be neat, and it should be in the appropriate format for the kind of writing it is. For most of your academic writing, heed the requirements of your particular audience, and follow carefully the manuscript conventions listed and discussed in #26.

 PARAGRAPHS

To be effective, all paragraphs, but especially body paragraphs, require **unity**, **coherence**, and well-controlled **emphasis**. Writing a paragraph involves designing the best possible package to contain and convey your ideas. You have a sense of what point you wish to convey (your topic), and, usually early in the process, you have an array of items to include as well (your supporting ideas and evidence). You arrange your ideas, explanations, and evidence in the package by ordering them logically, linking them to one another using strategies for coherence. You may well spend some time rearranging to make the package look the way you want it to—to give each item the appropriate emphasis.

2a Unity

An effective body paragraph ordinarily deals with one main idea; its singleness of purpose engages its readers by focusing their attention on that main idea. If a paragraph is disrupted by irrelevant digressions or unnecessary shifts in point of view or focus, readers will lose the thread of the discourse and become confused. In other words, a paragraph has unity when every sentence in it contributes to its purpose and nothing in it is irrelevant to that purpose.

2b Organizational Coherence

Though a paragraph is unified because every sentence contributes to the development of its single theme or idea, it could still come apart if it doesn't have another essential quality: coherence. Coherence can be defined as the connection of ideas. Simply placing one sentence after another doesn't guarantee coherence. In fact, coherence is achieved only by carefully packing the contents of a paragraph and linking the ideas to one another. You can ensure coherence in your writing in two ways:

- by carefully organizing your material, and
- by using a variety of transitional devices that create structural coherence.

A body paragraph has a *beginning*, a *middle*, and an *ending*. Good organization means rational order. Typically, the beginning introduces the main idea; the middle clearly and logically follows from and develops the statement of that idea, and the ending is a natural conclusion that unobtrusively closes the discussion or provides a hook for the next paragraph.

1. The beginning: topic sentences
Body paragraphs typically open with a statement of the main idea, called a **topic sentence**.

FUNCTIONS OF TOPIC SENTENCES

A good topic sentence indicates what the paragraph will be about. It is a promise that the rest of the paragraph fulfills. If the paragraph is part of a larger context, such as an essay, the topic sentence will usually perform two other functions:

- It will refer to the subject of the essay and at least suggest the relation of the paragraph to that subject.
- It will provide a transition so that the new paragraph flows smoothly from the preceding paragraph.

It is sometimes possible to provide forward-looking material at the end of a paragraph. Don't struggle to get something transitional into the last sentence of a paragraph. The work of transition should be done by the first sentence of the next paragraph. In other words, tampering with a paragraph's final sentence merely for transitional purposes may diminish that paragraph's integrity and effectiveness.

EFFICIENCY OF TOPIC SENTENCES

Since it has so much to do, a good topic sentence, even more than other sentences, should be efficient. Here is one that is not:

> The poet uses a great deal of imagery throughout the poem.

The sentence indicates the topic—the poem's imagery—but promises nothing more than to show that the poem contains a lot of it. Further thought might lead to a revision like this—a topic sentence that not only has more substance in itself but also suggests the approach the paragraph will take:

> The poem's imagery, most of it drawn from nature, helps to create not only the poem's mood but its themes as well.

The same essay also contained the following inefficient topic sentence:

> In the second stanza, the poet continues to use images.

What is needed is something sharper, more specific, such as an assertion that provides a significant idea that can be usefully developed. For example,

> The imagery in the second stanza contrasts vividly with that in the first.

or

> In the second stanza, images of death begin the process that leads to the poem's ironic conclusion.

A good opening topic sentence should be more than just a table of contents; it should be a significant part of the contents of the paragraph. Pay close attention to the formulation of your topic sentences, for they can help you achieve both unity and coherence not only in individual paragraphs but also in an essay as a whole.

ON THE PLACEMENT OF TOPIC SENTENCES

In many paragraphs, the development fulfills the promise made in an opening topic sentence. Or, by conscious design, a topic sentence may be placed at the end or elsewhere in a paragraph. Sometimes delaying a topic sentence can increase readers' interest by creating a little mystery to get them to read on. And stating a topic at the end of a paragraph takes advantage of that most emphatic position.

A paragraph's topic, though single, may consist of more than one part. Similarly, it need not be stated all in one sentence. In this paragraph, for example, note that not until the end of the second sentence is the topic fully clear. It is not uncommon for a paragraph to have a second topic sentence, one that partly restates the topic and partly leads into the body of the paragraph.

And, rarely, a paragraph's topic may not be stated at all because the focal idea of a paragraph is clearly implied. This kind of paragraph occurs most often in narratives, where paragraphs begin in such a way that their relation to the preceding paragraph is sufficiently clear—perhaps indicated by no more than an opening *Then* or *When*.

See also #1g.

2. The middle

COHERENCE THROUGH ORDERLY DEVELOPMENT

A well-developed body paragraph fulfills the promise of its beginning. After considering the different possibilities, you should choose a way of presenting your material, and the order you choose to follow should be one that makes sense; one idea should lead logically to another until you reach your goal. Then your paragraph will be coherent.

PATTERNS OF DEVELOPMENT

Orderly development sometimes occurs automatically as one works through one's ideas in composing paragraphs and essays. But most writers must give some conscious thought to how a particular paragraph (or essay) can best be shaped. The most common *patterns of development* writers use to make paragraphs orderly and coherent are the following:

- *spatial* (moving through space, such as top to bottom or left to right; used in describing physical space)
- *chronological* (moving through time; used in narration and process analysis)
- *climactic* (moving from the least important to most important point; often used in academic writing)
- *inverse pyramid* (moving from the most important to least important point; used in reportage/print journalism)
- *inductive* (moving from data to assertions; often used in writing for sciences and social sciences)
- *deductive* (moving from assertions to supporting data or premises; often used in writing for the humanities)
- *block* (in a comparison of two items, a full discussion of the first item followed by a full discussion of the second item)
- *alternating* (in a comparison of two items, a back-and-forth discussion of the first and second items)

These patterns are not mutually exclusive within a paragraph or an essay.

3. The ending

As you compose and revise drafts, the endings of paragraphs will sometimes come naturally. But they are likely to do so only if, when you begin a paragraph, you know just where it is going. The final sentence of a paragraph, like all the others, should be a part of the whole: it will most often be a statement growing out of the substance of the paragraph, a sentence that rounds off its paragraph in a satisfying way.

SOME ADVICE FOR ENDING PARAGRAPHS

If a paragraph doesn't seem to be ending naturally, you may have to stop and think consciously about it. Here are a few pointers to help you do that:

- A good ending may point back to the beginning but not merely repeat it; if it repeats something, it will do so in order to put it in the new light made possible by the development of the paragraph.
- A good ending sentence doesn't usually begin with a stiff *In conclusion* or *To conclude*. Sometimes the best way to end a paragraph is simply to let it stop, once its point is made. A too-explicit conclusion might damage the effectiveness of an otherwise good paragraph that has a natural quality of closure at its end.
- A good ending might have a slight stylistic shift that marks a paragraph's closing, perhaps no more than an unusually short or long sentence. Or an ending might be marked by an allusion or brief quotation, as long as it is relevant and to the point and not there simply for its own sake.
- A good paragraph usually doesn't end with an indented ("block") quotation, or even a shorter full-sentence quotation that isn't set off. Even if you carefully introduce such a quotation, it will leave a feeling that you have abandoned your paragraph to someone else. Complete such a paragraph with at least a brief comment that explains the quotation, justifies it, or re-emphasizes its main thrust.

2c Structural Coherence

Careful organization and development go a long way toward achieving coherence. But you will sometimes need to use other techniques, providing links that ensure a smooth flow of thought from one sentence to another.

The main devices for structural coherence are parallelism, repetition, pronouns and demonstrative adjectives, and transitional words and phrases. Like the patterns of development, these devices are not mutually exclusive: two or more may work together in the same paragraph, sometimes even in the same words and phrases.

1. Parallelism (see #4d and #5h)

Parallel sentence structure is an effective way to bind successive sentences. Similar structural patterns in clauses and phrases work like a call and its echo. But don't try to maintain a series of parallel elements for too long. If the echoes remain obvious, they will be too noticeable and will diminish in power as they get farther from the original.

2. Repetition

Like parallelism, repetition of words and phrases effectively links successive sentences. But the caution against overdoing it is most applicable here. Repetition properly controlled for rhetorical effect can be powerful (as in Martin Luther King's famous "I have a dream" speech), but repetition, especially on paper, can also become evidence of a writer's limited vocabulary or ingenuity. Structure your repetitions carefully; don't put too many too close together. Generally use the device sparingly.

3. Pronouns and demonstrative adjectives

By referring to something mentioned earlier, a pronoun (see #7) or a demonstrative adjective (see #10) constructs a bridge within the paragraph between itself and its antecedent or referent.

It is also possible, of course, to use pronouns and demonstrative adjectives to create links between paragraphs, but avoid an ambiguous antecedent or referent, and avoid a distant antecedent.

Make it a point to use demonstrative adjectives rather than demonstrative pronouns. Demonstrative adjectives are clear and can add emphasis. Pronouns are not emphatic; rather they can be weak and ambiguous (see #7a, #7d, and #10a).

4. Transitional terms

Used strategically, transitional words and phrases can create a logical flow from one part or idea to another. The best transitional signal for a particular spot in a discourse creates coherence. Here are some of the more common and useful transitional terms:

- terms showing addition of one point to another

and	also	another	in addition
further	besides	moreover	

- terms showing similarity between ideas

again	equally	in other words
in the same way	likewise	similarly

- terms showing difference between ideas

but	although	conversely
despite	even though	however
yet	though	in contrast
whereas	nevertheless	in spite of
still	otherwise	on the contrary
on the other hand		

- terms showing cause and effect or other logical relations

as a result	because	consequently	for
hence	of course	since	then
therefore	thus		

- terms introducing examples or details

for example	in particular	namely	specifically
for instance	to illustrate	that is	

- terms expressing emphasis

chiefly	especially	more important
indeed	mainly	primarily

- terms showing relations in time and space

after	afterward	at the same time
before	earlier	in the meantime
later	meanwhile	simultaneously
then	while	subsequently
behind	beyond	farther away
here	nearby	in the distance
next	there	to the left

These and other such words and phrases, occurring usually at or near the beginnings of sentences, are the glue that helps hold paragraphs together. But if the paragraph isn't unified in its content, and if its parts haven't been arranged to fit with one another, even these explicit transitional terms won't give much structural coherence to your writing.

Note: Don't overuse transitional terms. If your paragraph already contains structural elements that make it coherent, it won't need any of these. Adding a transitional word or phrase to nearly every sentence will make writing stiff and mechanical sounding.

2d Emphasis and Variety

1. Emphasis

In a paragraph, as in a sentence, the most emphatic position is its ending, and the second most emphatic position is its beginning (see #4f). That is another reason the opening or topic sentence is so important a part of a paragraph.

Structure and diction are also important. Parallelism and repetition create emphasis. Independent clauses are more emphatic than subordinate clauses and phrases. Precise, concrete, and specific words are more emphatic than vague, abstract, and general ones. A long sentence will stand out among several shorter ones; a short sentence will stand out among longer ones. Keep these points in mind as you compose and revise your paragraphs; let emphasis contribute to the effectiveness of your writing.

2. Variety

Try to ensure that any extended piece of writing you produce contains a variety of paragraph lengths: long, short, medium. The reader may become unengaged if the essay has a constant similarity of paragraph lengths. (The same is true of sentences of similar length: see #4b). You should also try to provide a variety of patterns of development in your paragraphs. For example, parallelism, however admirable a device, would likely lose its effect if it were the basic pattern in several successive paragraphs.

Normally, then, the paragraphs that make up an extended piece of writing will vary in length. Ensure that each of your paragraphs is as long or as short as it needs to be to achieve its intended purpose. There is no optimum length for a paragraph. The length of a paragraph will be determined by the requirements of the particular job it is doing. In narration or dialogue, a single sentence or a single word may constitute a paragraph. In a complex exposition or argument essay, a paragraph may go on for a page or more—though such long paragraphs are rare in modern writing. Most body paragraphs consist of at least three or four sentences, and seldom more than nine or ten. Transitional paragraphs are usually short, sometimes only one sentence. Introductory and concluding paragraphs will be of various lengths, depending on the complexity of the material and on the techniques of beginning and ending that the writer is using.

ESSENTIALS OF GRAMMAR AND STYLE: SENTENCES

II

CONTENTS

INTRODUCTION

Part II introduces the basic elements and patterns of English sentences and defines and classifies different kinds of sentences. It also deals with the ways the various elements work together in sentences. When you have finished Part II, you will be able to understand how sentences work and how to avoid common problems when writing your own sentences.

3 SENTENCE ELEMENTS AND PATTERNS

All sentences have this purpose: to communicate ideas and/or feelings. We know how to interpret different kinds of utterances because we understand and accept the *conventions* of the way sentences communicate. Sentences are classified according to the kind of purpose each has. Consider the following examples:

Declarative: This seminar deals with the effects of globalization on education. (states a fact)

Interrogative: Is this computer virus affecting your e-mail? (asks a question)

Imperative: Please print the document. (gives a command, makes a request)

Exclamatory: That was an unforgettable trip! (exclaims, expresses strong feeling or emphasis)

A sentence may fall into more than one category:

"Should the voting age be raised?" the candidate asked. (interrogative and declarative)

Please contact me about your project: I have information that's relevant. (imperative and declarative)

Slow down! (imperative and exclamatory)

Your awareness of the *conventions* guides you in understanding the purposes of sentences you hear, read, speak, or write: you know almost instinctively how to frame a sentence to make it do what you want.

A more conscious grasp of the way sentences work will help you frame them even more effectively. It will help you when you're in doubt. And it will help you not only to avoid weaknesses and errors but also to revise and correct them when they do occur.

Since most sentences in written and academic discourse are *declarative*, their patterns are the ones you need to understand first. Most of the rest of this section, then, deals with the basic elements and patterns of declarative sentences. (See #4a for an expanded discussion of basic sentence elements and their modifiers.)

3a Subject and Predicate, Noun and Verb

A standard declarative sentence consists of two parts: a **subject**, whose essential element is a noun or a pronoun, and a **predicate**, whose essential element is a verb. The subject is what acts or is talked about; the predicate is what the subject does or what is said about it.

Subject	Predicate
Birds	fly.
I	disagree.

3b Articles and Other Modifiers

Frequently nouns are preceded by articles (*a, an, the*):

Subject	Predicate
The child	chattered.

And both subject and predicate often include **modifiers**, words that change or limit the meaning of nouns and verbs. Nouns are modified by **adjectives** (see #10):

Subject	Predicate
The young child	chattered.
A caged bird	will sing.

Verbs are modified by **adverbs** (see #11):

Subject	Predicate
The young child	chattered happily.
They	flew south.

3c   Structure Words

Subjects, verbs, modifiers, objects, and complements make up the substance of all sentences.

Many sentences also include words like *and, but, for, of, under,* and, *with*. Such words connect other elements in various ways, and they are sometimes called **structure** or **function words**. Most of them belong to two other classes of words, or "parts of speech": **conjunctions** (see #13b) and **prepositions** (see #13a). These parts of speech are discussed and illustrated at greater length in Part III.

3d–f   Phrases and Clauses

To master sentence structure and punctuation, you need to understand the differences between **phrases** and **clauses** and how they work in sentences. Phrases and clauses are groups of words that function as grammatical units or elements *within* sentences but that—except for **independent clauses**—cannot stand alone as sentences.

3d   Phrases

A **phrase** is a group of words lacking a subject and/or predicate but functioning as a grammatical unit within a sentence.

A **verb phrase** (see #8d) acts as the verb in this sentence:

> Most of the wedding guests <u>will be arriving</u> in the morning.

A **prepositional phrase** (see #13a) can be an adjectival modifier:

> Most <u>of the wedding guests</u> will be arriving in the morning.

or an adverbial modifier:

> Most of the wedding guests will be arriving <u>in the morning</u>.

The words *Most of the wedding guests* constitute a **noun phrase** functioning as the subject of the sentence. Any noun or pronoun along with its modifiers—so long as the group doesn't contain a subject–predicate combination—can be thought of as a noun phrase.

Similarly, a **gerund phrase** (see #12c) can function as a subject:

> Bungee jumping can be risky.

or as a direct object:

> She tried bungee jumping.

A **participial phrase**—always adjectival (see #12b)—can modify a subject:

> Trusting her instincts, Jane gave the candidate her support.

or a direct object:

> I am reading an article discussing human cloning.

An **infinitive phrase** (see #12a) can function as a direct object (noun):

> This organization wants to eradicate poverty.

or as a subject (noun):

> It may be impossible to eradicate poverty.

It can also function as an adjective, for example one modifying the subject:

> Their desire to eradicate poverty is idealistic.

or it can function as an adverb, for example one modifying the verb:

> They arranged the agenda to highlight the anti-poverty campaign.

Adverbial infinitive phrases can also act as **sentence modifiers** (see #11a and #11c), modifying not the verb or any other single word but rather all the rest of the sentence:

<u>To be honest,</u>

<u>To tell the truth,</u> ⎱ the meeting ended shortly after you left.

Two other kinds of phrases you should be familiar with are the **appositive** and the **absolute**.

An **appositive** is a word or group of words that renames or restates, in other terms, the meaning of a neighbouring word. For example, if you start with two simple sentences,

Marc is our lawyer. He looks after our business dealings.

you can turn the first into an appositive by reducing it and combining it with the second:

Marc, <u>our lawyer</u>, looks after our business dealings.

The noun phrase *our lawyer* is here said to be **in apposition to** *Marc*.

Most appositives are nouns or noun phrases that redefine, usually in more specific terms, the nouns they follow. Following are several other appositive patterns:

<u>A skilful lawyer</u>, Marc looks after our business dealings.
(appositive precedes the noun)

Searching frantically, <u>tossing books and papers everywhere</u>, they failed to find the missing passport.
(participial phrase functions as an appositive)

Document (<u>provide details of your sources for</u>) this argument. (verb phrase functions as an appositive)

Our lawyer, <u>Marc</u>, looks after our business dealings.
(a single word, a proper noun, functions as an appositive)

How she travelled—<u>whether she journeyed alone or not</u>—remains a mystery. (subordinate clause functions as an appositive)

(For the punctuation of appositives, see #15d and #25h.)

An **absolute phrase** has no direct grammatical link with what it modifies; it depends simply on juxtaposition, modifying the rest of the sentence by hovering over it like an umbrella. Most absolute phrases amount to a sentence with the verb changed to a participle (see #12b). Instead of using two sentences,

The intermission had ended. The last act finally began.

you can reduce the first to an absolute phrase modifying the second:

<u>The intermission having ended</u>, the last act finally began.

If the original verb is a form of *be,* the participle can sometimes be omitted:

<u>The thunderstorm (being) over</u>, the tennis match resumed.

Sometimes, especially with certain common expressions, the participle isn't preceded by a noun:

There were a few rough spots, but <u>generally speaking</u> the rehearsal was a success.

And sometimes infinitive phrases function as absolutes:

<u>To say the least</u>, the campaign was not a success.

You can also think of many absolutes as *with*-phrases from which the preposition has been dropped:

<u>(With) the thunderstorm over</u>, the tennis match resumed.

3

3e Independent (Main) Clauses

A clause is a group of words containing both a *subject* and a *predicate*. An **independent clause** can stand by itself as a sentence.

An independent clause can also function as only part of a sentence. For example, if you start with two separate independent clauses—that is, two simple sentences:

> The exam ended.

> The students submitted their papers.

you can combine them to form a **compound sentence** (see #3g):

> The exam ended; the students submitted their papers.

> The exam ended, and the students submitted their papers.

> The exam ended; therefore the students submitted their papers.

3f Subordinate (Dependent) Clauses

A **subordinate clause**, unlike an independent clause, usually cannot stand by itself. Even though, as a clause, it contains a subject and a predicate, it is by definition *subordinate*, *dependent* on another clause—an *independent* one—for its completion or meaning. In the following examples, the subordinate clauses are underlined; these sentences are called **complex sentences** (see #3g):

> <u>When the exam ended</u>, the students submitted their papers.

> The students submitted their papers <u>as the exam ended</u>.

> The students submitted the papers <u>that they had written during the exam</u>.

> The exam ended, <u>which meant that the students had to submit their papers</u>.

Subordinate clauses often begin with such words as *when*, *as*, *that*, and *which*, called **subordinators**, which clearly signal the presence of a subordinate clause (see #13b).

Like a phrase, a subordinate clause functions as a grammatical unit in its sentence. It can occupy several of the slots in the sentence patterns illustrated just above.

A **noun clause** can serve as the subject of a sentence:

> That free speech matters is evident.

as a direct object:

> Azin knows what she is doing.

or as a predicate noun:

> The question is what we should do next.

Adjectival clauses (also called **relative clauses**) modify nouns or pronouns, such as a direct object:

> The reporter questioned the police officer who had found the missing child.

or a subject:

> The project that I am working on is proceeding smoothly.

Adverbial clauses usually modify main verbs:

> We left because we were utterly bored.

3g   Kinds of Sentences: Grammatical Types

Sentences can be classified grammatically as **simple**, **compound**, **complex**, and **compound-complex**.

1. Simple sentences
A **simple** sentence has one subject and finite verb unit, and therefore contains only one clause, an independent clause:

>   S   V
> The boat leaks.

>   S   V
> The new museum opened on the weekend.

The subject or the verb, or both, can be compound—that is, consist of more than one part—but the sentence containing them will still be simple:

> <u>Claude and Kim</u> left early. (compound subject)

> She <u>watched and waited</u>. (compound verb)

> <u>The sergeant and his men</u> <u>moved</u> down the hill <u>and</u>
> <u>crossed</u> the river. (compound subject, compound verb)

2. Compound sentences

A **compound** sentence consists of two or more simple sentences—that is, independent clauses—linked by coordinating conjunctions (see #13b), by punctuation, or by both:

>   S   V   S   V
> The <u>conductor's baton</u> <u>fell</u>, and the <u>concert</u> <u>ended</u>.

>   S   V
> The <u>clouds</u> <u>massed</u> thickly against the hills; soon the
> S V
> <u>rain</u> <u>fell</u> in torrents.

> S   V   S   V
> <u>We</u> <u>wanted</u> to hear jazz, but <u>they</u> <u>played</u> bluegrass
> instead.

>   S   V   S
> <u>Gabriel's patience and persistence</u> <u>paid</u> off; <u>he</u> not only
> V   V
> <u>won</u> the prize but also <u>earned</u> his competitors' respect.

>   S V   S   V   S
> The <u>day</u> <u>was</u> mild, the <u>breeze</u> <u>was</u> warm, and <u>everyone</u>
> V
> <u>went</u> for a swim.

3. Complex sentences

A **complex** sentence consists of one independent clause and one or more subordinate clauses; in the following examples, the subordinate clauses are underlined:

We believe <u>that we have some original plans for the campaign</u>. (noun clause as direct object)

The strike was averted <u>before we reported for picket duty</u>. (adverbial clause modifying *was averted*)

This course is the one <u>that calls for the most field research</u>. (adjectival clause modifying *one*)

Marco Polo, <u>who left his native Venice as a teenager</u>, returned home after twenty-five years of adventure. (adjectival clause modifying *Marco Polo*)

<u>When the film ended</u>, the audience burst into applause <u>which lasted several minutes</u>. (adverbial clause modifying *burst*, adjectival clause modifying *applause*)

<u>Although it seems premature</u>, the government is proceeding with third reading of the legislation. (adverbial clause of concession, in effect modifying the rest of the sentence)

Note that when the meaning is clear, the conjunction *that* introducing a noun clause, or the relative pronouns *that* and *which* can be omitted:

He claimed <u>he was innocent</u>.

. . . the suitcase <u>he had brought with him</u>.

4. Compound-complex sentences

A **compound-complex** sentence consists of two or more independent clauses and one or more subordinate clauses:

Because the architect knows that the preservation of heritage buildings is vital, she is consulting widely, but as delays have developed, she has grown impatient, and therefore she is thinking of pulling out of a project that represents everything important to her.

We can analyze this example as follows:

> Because the architect knows (adverbial clause)
>
> that the preservation of heritage buildings is vital (noun clause)
>
> she is consulting widely (independent clause)
>
> but (coordinating conjunction)
>
> as delays have developed (adverbial clause)
>
> she has grown impatient (independent clause)
>
> and (coordinating conjunction)
>
> therefore (conjunctive adverb)
>
> she is thinking of pulling out of a project (independent clause)
>
> that represents everything important to her (adjective clause)

WORKING WITH SENTENCE ELEMENTS TO CREATE VARIETY AND EMPHASIS

Basic Sentence Elements and Their Modifiers

To achieve variety and emphasis in your writing, you will need to recognize and manipulate basic sentence elements and their modifiers.

1. Subject

The subject is what is talked about. It is the word or phrase answering the question *who?* or *what?* before the verb.

> <u>Osman</u> watched the performance. (*Who* watched? Osman. Osman is the source of the action of watching.)

The subject of a sentence will ordinarily be one of the following: a basic noun (see #6), a pronoun (see #7), a gerund or gerund phrase (see #12c), an infinitive or infinitive phrase (see #12a), or a noun clause:

> British Columbia joined Confederation on 20 July 1871.
> (noun)

> He is a Manitoba historian. (pronoun)

> Skydiving is a risky activity. (gerund)

> Visiting the website is part of our daily routine.
> (gerund phrase)

> To travel is to enjoy life. (infinitive)

> To order tofu is to make a healthy choice.
> (infinitive phrase)

> That British Columbia joined Canada because of the
> railway is common knowledge. (noun clause)

2. Finite verb

The **finite verb** is the focal point of the clause or the sentence. It indicates both the nature and the time of the action (see #8a):

> The prime minister will respond during Question Period.
> (action: responding; time: the future)

> Lewis Carroll invented the adventures of Alice for a child
> named Alice Liddell. (action: inventing; time: past)

> Cape Breton's fiddlers have a distinctive musical style.
> (action: having, possessing; time: present)

3. Object

If a verb is *transitive* (see #8a), it will have a **direct object**. Like the subject, the direct object may be a noun, a pronoun, a gerund or gerund phrase, an infinitive or infinitive phrase, or a noun clause:

> The CD features Bruce Cockburn. (noun)

> The increase in gasoline taxes worried us. (pronoun)

Our economy needs <u>farming</u>. (gerund)

He enjoys <u>writing reports</u>. (gerund phrase)

We wanted <u>to participate</u>. (infinitive)

You need <u>to define your terms</u>. (infinitive phrase)

The reporter revealed <u>that his source feared retaliation</u>. (noun clause)

Along with a direct object, there may also be an **indirect object** or an **objective complement**:

We gave <u>you</u> a blank cheque. (*you*: indirect object; *cheque*: direct object)

She judged the situation <u>untenable</u>. (*situation*: direct object; *untenable*: objective complement)

4. Subjective complement

Similarly, a *linking verb* (see #8a) typically requires a **subjective complement**. This complement will usually be either a *predicate noun* or a *predicate adjective*. A predicate noun may be a noun or a pronoun, or (especially after *be*) a gerund or gerund phrase, an infinitive or infinitive phrase, or a noun clause:

We are <u>friends</u>. (noun)

Was he the <u>one</u>? (pronoun)

His passion is <u>travelling</u>. (gerund)

His passion is <u>travelling the back country</u>. (gerund phrase)

My first impulse was <u>to run</u>. (infinitive)

Our next challenge will be <u>to take action</u>. (infinitive phrase)

She remains <u>what she has long been</u>: a loyal friend. (noun clause)

A predicate adjective will ordinarily be a descriptive adjective, a participle, or an idiomatic prepositional phrase:

His music has become <u>joyful</u>. (descriptive adjective)

The novel's plot is <u>intriguing</u>. (present participle)

They seem <u>dedicated</u>. (past participle)

The government is <u>out of ideas</u>. (prepositional phrase)

The linking verb *be* (and sometimes others) can also be followed by an adverbial word or phrase (I am *here*; he is *in his office*).

4

These elements—**subject, finite verb**, and **object** or **complement**—are the core elements of major sentences. They are closely linked in the ways indicated above, with the verb as the focal and uniting element.

5. Modifiers
Modifiers add to the core grammatical elements. They limit or describe other elements so as to modify—that is, to change—a listener's or reader's idea of them. The two principal kinds of modifiers are *adjectives* (see #10) and *adverbs* (see #11). Also useful, but less frequent, are *appositives* and *absolute phrases* (see #3d). An adjectival or adverbial modifier may even be part of the core of a sentence if it completes the predicate after a linking verb (Recycling is *vital*; Peter is *home*). An adverb may also be essential if it modifies an intransitive verb that would otherwise seem incomplete (Peter lives *in a condominium*). But generally modifiers do their work by adding to—enriching—a central core of thought.

ADJECTIVAL MODIFIERS (see #10a–b)
Adjectival modifiers modify nouns, pronouns, and phrases or clauses functioning as nouns. They commonly answer the questions *which? what kind of? how many?* and *how much?* An adjectival modifier may be a single-word adjective, a series of adjectives, a participle or participial

phrase, an infinitive or infinitive phrase, a prepositional phrase, or a relative clause:

<u>Early</u> settlers of <u>western</u> Canada encountered <u>sudden</u> floods, <u>prolonged</u> droughts, and <u>early</u> frosts. (single words modifying nouns immediately following)

We are <u>skeptical</u>. (predicate adjective modifying the pronoun *We*)

That the author opposes globalization is <u>evident</u> in his first paragraph. (predicate adjective modifying the noun clause *That the author opposes globalization*)

<u>Four ambitious young</u> reporters are competing to work on this front-page story. (series modifying *reporters*)

The <u>train</u> station is filled with commuters and tourists. (noun functioning as adjective, modifying *station*)

<u>Grinning</u>, he replied to her e-mail message. (present participle modifying *he*)

<u>Brimming with confidence</u>, they began their performance. (present participial phrase modifying *they*)

They continued the climb toward the summit, <u>undaunted</u>. (past participle modifying *they*)

Gisele applied for the position, <u>having been encouraged to do so by her adviser</u>. (participial phrase, perfect tense, passive voice, modifying *Gisele*)

They prepared a meal <u>to remember</u>. (infinitive modifying *meal*)

Our tendency <u>to favour jazz</u> is evident in our CD collection. (infinitive phrase modifying *tendency*)

The report <u>on the evening news</u> focused on forest fires in northern British Columbia. (prepositional phrase modifying *report*)

The soccer team, <u>which was travelling to a tournament in Mexico</u>, filed slowly through airport security. (relative clause modifying *team*)

ADVERBIAL MODIFIERS (see #11a–b)

Adverbial modifiers modify verbs, adjectives, other adverbs, and whole clauses or sentences. They commonly answer the questions *how? when? where?* and *to what degree?* An adverbial modifier may be a single word, a series, an infinitive or infinitive phrase, a prepositional phrase, or an adverbial clause:

Mix the chemicals <u>thoroughly</u>. (single word modifying the verb *mix*)

As new parents, we are <u>completely</u> happy. (single word modifying the adjective *happy*)

They planned their future together <u>quite</u> enthusiastically. (single word modifying the adverb *enthusiastically*)

<u>Apparently</u>, the stem cell experiment is being delayed. (single word modifying the rest of the sentence)

He loves her <u>truly</u>, <u>madly</u>, <u>deeply</u>. (series modifying the verb *loves*)

<u>To succeed</u>, you must work well with others. (infinitive modifying the verb *must work*)

She was lucky <u>to have been selected</u> for the exchange program. (infinitive phrase modifying the predicate adjective *lucky*)

The passenger ship arrived <u>at the port</u>. (prepositional phrase modifying the verb *arrived*)

We disagreed <u>because we were taking different theoretical approaches to the text</u>. (clause modifying the verb *disagreed*)

The election results trickled in slowly <u>because the ballots were being counted by hand</u>. (clause modifying the adverb *slowly* or the whole preceding clause, *The election results trickled in slowly.*)

Shut off your computer <u>when you leave on vacation</u>. (clause modifying the preceding independent clause)

4b-i Length, Variety, and Emphasis

To create emphasis and to avoid monotony, vary the lengths and kinds of your sentences. This is a process to practise when revising a draft to strengthen its style. Examine some pieces of prose that you particularly enjoy or that you find unusually clear and especially readable: you will likely discover that they contain both a pleasing mixture of short, medium, and long sentences and a similar variety of kinds and structures.

4b Variety in Lengths

4

A sentence may, in rare cases, consist of one word, or it may go on for a hundred words or more. There are no strict guidelines to tell you how long to make your sentences. If you're curious, do some research to determine the average sentence length in several pieces of writing you have handy. You'll probably find that the average is somewhere between 15 and 25 words per sentence, that longer sentences are more common in formal and specialized writing, and that shorter sentences are more frequent in informal and popular writing, in e-mail, and in narrative and dialogue.

A string of short sentences will sound choppy and fragmented; avoid the staccato effect by interweaving some longer ones. On the other hand, a succession of long sentences may make your ideas hard to follow; give your readers a break—and your prose some sparkle—by using a few short, emphatic sentences to change your pace occasionally. Even a string of medium-length sentences can bore readers into inattention. Impart some rhythm, some shape, to your paragraphs by varying sentence length.

1. Short sentences

If you receive feedback that you're writing too many short sentences, try

- building them up by elaborating their elements with modifiers, including various kinds of phrases and clauses;

- combining some of them to form compound sub-jects, predicates, and objects or complements; or
- combining two or more of them—especially if they are simple sentences—into a compound, complex, or compound-complex sentence.

2. Long sentences

If you find yourself writing too many long sentences, check them for three possible problems:

1. You may be rambling or trying to pack too much into a single sentence, possibly destroying its unity and making it difficult to read. Try breaking it up into more unified or more easily manageable parts.
2. You may be using too many words to make your point. Try cutting out any deadwood (see #14f).
3. You may have slipped into what is called "excessive subordination"—too many loosely related details obscuring the main idea, or confusing strings of sub-ordinate clauses modifying each other. Try removing some of the clutter, reducing clauses to phrases and phrases to single words.

4c Variety in Kinds

A string of simple and compound sentences risks coming across to a reader as simplistic. In some narratives and in certain technical and business documents, successive simple and compound sentences may be appropriate for recounting a sequence of events, but in academic writing, let the complexity of your ideas be reflected in complex and compound-complex sentences. On the other hand, a string of complex and compound-complex sentences may become oppressive. Give your readers a breather now and then by changing pace.

4d Variety in Structures

Avoid an unduly long string of sentences using the same syntactical structure. For example, though the standard order of elements in declarative sentences is subject–verb–object or subject–verb–complement, consider varying that order occasionally for emphasis. Use an occasional interrogative sentence, whether a rhetorical question (a question that doesn't expect an answer) or a question that you proceed to answer as you develop a paragraph.

In particular, try not to begin a string of sentences with the same kind of word or phrase or clause—unless you are purposely setting up a controlled succession of parallel structures for emphasis or coherence (see #2c). Imagine the effect of several sentences beginning with such words as *Similarly, Especially, Consequently,* and *Nevertheless.* Whatever else the sentences contained, the sameness would be distracting. Or imagine a series of sentences all starting with a subject-noun, or with a present-participial phrase. To avoid such undesirable sameness, take advantage of the way modifiers of various kinds can be moved around in sentences.

4e Emphasizing a Whole Sentence

To make sure your readers perceive the relative importance of your ideas the same way you do, learn to control emphasis.

You can emphasize whole sentences in several ways:

- Set a sentence off by itself, as a short paragraph. (Use this strategy judiciously.)
- Put an important sentence at the beginning or, even better, at the end of a paragraph.
- Put an important point in a short sentence among several long ones, or in a long sentence among several short ones.
- Shift the style or structure of a sentence to make it stand out from those around it (see #2d). In particular, a stylistically enhanced sentence—for example, a periodic sentence, a sentence with parallel or balanced structure, or a richly metaphorical or allusive sentence—stands out beside plainer sentences.

4f-i Emphasis Within a Sentence

You can also emphasize important parts of individual sentences. The principal devices for achieving emphasis *within* sentences are position and word order, repetition, stylistic contrast, and syntax. In addition, you can add emphasis by effective use of punctuation (see Part IV).

4f Emphasis by Position and Word Order

The most emphatic position in a sentence is its ending; the second most emphatic position is its beginning. The longer the sentence, the stronger the effect of emphasis by position. Consider the following:

a.   The best teacher I've ever had was my high-school chemistry teacher, a brilliant woman in her early fifties.

b.   A brilliant woman in her early fifties, my high-school chemistry teacher was the best teacher I've ever had.

c.   My high-school chemistry teacher, a brilliant woman in her early fifties, was the best teacher I've ever had.

d.   The best teacher I've ever had was a brilliant woman in her early fifties who taught me chemistry in high school.

Each sentence contains the same three ideas, but each distributes the emphasis differently. In each the last part is the most emphatic, the first part next, and the middle part least.

Loose sentences and periodic sentences
A *loose, cumulative,* or "*right-branching*" sentence makes its main point in an early independent clause and then adds modifying subordinate elements:

> The concert began modestly, with the performers sitting casually onstage and taking up their instruments to play their first song.

In contrast to the loose is the *periodic* (or "*left-branching*") sentence, which wholly or partly delays its main point, the independent clause, until the end:

> With the performers sitting casually onstage and taking up their instruments to play their first song, the concert began modestly.

Full periodic sentences are usually the result of careful thought and planning. However, they can sometimes sound contrived, less natural, and therefore should not be used without forethought.

4

Using the expletive and the passive voice for emphasis

Two basic sentence patterns, the *expletive* and the *passive voice*, can be weak and unemphatic in some contexts. Used strategically, however, they can enable you to achieve a desired emphasis. For example:

> Passive voice can be used to move a certain word or phrase to an emphatic place in a sentence.

Here, putting the verb in the passive voice (*can be used*) makes *Passive voice* the subject of the sentence and enables this important element to come at the beginning; otherwise, the sentence would have to begin less strongly (for example, with *You can use passive voice*). This next example makes strategic use of the expletive pattern:

> There are advantages to using the expletive pattern for a deliberate change of pace in your writing.

In this case, opening the sentence with *There* is preferable to opening with long and unwieldy alternatives.

Use expletives and passive voice when you need to delete or delay mention of the agent or otherwise shift the subject of a sentence.

4g Emphasis by Repetition

Repeat an important word or idea to emphasize it, to make it stay in your readers' minds. Unintentional repetition can be wordy and tedious; but intentional, controlled repetition—used sparingly—can be very effective, especially in sentences with balanced or parallel structures:

> If you have the courage to face adventure, the adventure can sometimes give you courage.

> If it's a challenge they seek, it's a challenge they'll find.

4h Emphasis by Contrast

A word or phrase that differs in style or tone from those that surround it may stand out in contrast:

> The chef—conservative as her behaviour sometimes appears—dazzles the kitchen staff with her gutsy culinary experiments.

> My grandmother may be almost ninety years old, but she approaches each day with a child's *joie de vivre*.

4i Emphasis by Syntax

Put your most important claims in independent clauses; put lesser claims in subordinate clauses and phrases. Sometimes you have more than one option, depending on what you want to emphasize:

> Reading the menu, she frowned at the high prices.

> Frowning at the high prices, she read the menu.

But more often the choice is determined by the content. Consider the way subordination affects emphasis in the following pairs of sentences:

> *original:* I strolled into the laboratory, when my attention was attracted by the pitter-pattering of a little white rat in a cage at the back.

> *revised:* When I strolled into the laboratory, my attention was attracted by the pitter-pattering of a little white rat in a cage at the back.

5 COMMON SENTENCE PROBLEMS

Here we define some common problems that can affect the clarity of sentences, and we suggest ways to avoid or correct them.

The three sentence errors that can most impede clear communication in your writing are the *fragment*, the *comma splice*, and the *run-on sentence*. Edit closely for them.

5a Sentence Fragments

A **fragment** is a group of words that is not an acceptable sentence, either major or minor, but that is punctuated as if it were a sentence.

> *frag:* We looked for three sources. For example, statistics, case studies, and government reports.
>
> *revised:* We looked for three sources: statistics, case studies, and government reports.

5b Comma Splices

A **comma splice** occurs when two independent clauses are joined with only a comma, rather than with a semicolon. The error usually stems from a misunderstanding of sentence structure.

> *cs:* The team lost the series, the coach lost her job.
>
> *revised:* The team lost the series; the coach lost her job.

5c Run-on (Fused) Sentences

A **run-on sentence**, sometimes called a **fused sentence**, is in fact not a single sentence but two sentences run together. An error most likely to occur when a writer is rushed, it can sometimes, like the comma splice, result from a problem in understanding how sentences work.

> ***fs:*** We left the museum they entered as we exited.
>
> ***revised:*** We left the museum; they entered as we exited.

5d Misplaced Modifiers

1. Movability and poor placement

Part of the meaning in English sentences is conveyed by the position of words in relation to each other. And though there are certain standard or conventional arrangements, a good deal of flexibility is possible. Adverbial modifiers are especially movable. Because of this flexibility, writers sometimes put a modifier where it conveys an unintended or ambiguous meaning, or where it is linked by juxtaposition to a word it can't logically modify. To say precisely what you mean, you have to be careful in placing your modifiers—especially adverbs. The following sentence demonstrates how misplacement can produce absurdity:

> ***mm:*** While testifying before the Transport Committee, the minister denied allegations heatedly concerning inadequate passenger screening reported in a recent CBC documentary at Pearson airport.

The adverb *heatedly* belongs before *denied*, the verb it modifies. The adjective phrase *reported in a recent CBC documentary* belongs after *allegations*, the noun it modifies. And the adverbial phrase *at Pearson airport* belongs after the phrase *concerning inadequate passenger screening*.

Usually it is best to keep modifiers and the words they modify as close together as possible:

> ***mm:*** Love is a <u>difficult</u> emotion to express in words.
>
> ***clear:*** Love is an emotion (that is) difficult to express in words.

2. *Only, almost,* etc.

Pay particular attention to such adverbs as *only*, *almost*, *just*, *merely*, and *even*. In speech, we often place these words casually, but in writing we should put them where they clearly mean what we want them to:

> *mm:* Hardy <u>only</u> wrote novels as a sideline; his main interest was poetry.
>
> *clear:* Hardy wrote novels <u>only</u> as a sideline; his main interest was poetry.

> *mm:* The students <u>almost</u> washed fifty cars last Saturday.
>
> *clear:* The students washed <u>almost</u> fifty cars last Saturday.

3. Squinting modifiers

A **squinting modifier** is a word or phrase put between two elements either of which it could modify:

> *squint:* It was so warm <u>for a week</u> we did hardly any skiing at all.

Which clause does the adverbial phrase modify? It is ambiguous. A speaking voice could impart clarifying emphasis to such a sentence, but a writer must substitute words or structures for the missing vocal emphasis. Here, adding *that* removes the ambiguity:

> *clear:* It was so warm that for a week we did hardly any skiing at all.
>
> *clear:* It was so warm for a week that we did hardly any skiing at all.

5e Dangling Modifiers

Like a pronoun without an antecedent (see #7), a **dangling modifier** has no word in the rest of the sentence to attach to; instead it is left dangling, grammatically unattached, and so it often tries to attach itself, illogically, to some other word. Most dangling modifiers are *verbal phrases*; be watchful for them in editing drafts of your work.

1. Dangling participial phrases

> *dm:* <u>Strolling casually beside the lagoon</u>, my eyes fell upon two children chasing a pair of geese.

Since the adjectival phrase wants to modify a noun, it tries to link with the subject of the adjacent clause, *eyes*. Eyes can scarcely be said to "stroll." To avoid the unintentionally humorous dangler, simply change the participial phrase to a subordinate clause:

> *revised:* As I strolled casually beside the lagoon, my eyes fell upon two children chasing a pair of geese.

Or, if you want to keep the effect of the opening participial phrase, rework the clause so that its subject is the logical word to be modified:

> *revised:* Strolling casually beside the lagoon, I let my gaze fall upon two children chasing a pair of geese.

2. Dangling gerund phrases

When a gerund phrase is the object of a preposition, it can dangle much like a participial phrase:

> *dm:* After being informed of the correct procedure, our attention was directed to the next steps.

It isn't "our attention" that was "informed." The passive voice contributes to the confusion here.

> *revised:* After informing us of the correct procedure, the instructor directed our attention to the next steps.

3. Dangling infinitive phrases

> *dm:* To follow Freud's procedure, the speaker's thoughts must be fully explored.

Ineffective passive voice is the issue, depriving the infinitive phrase of a logical word to modify.

> *revised:* To follow Freud's procedure, one must explore the speaker's thoughts fully.

4. Dangling elliptical clauses

An **elliptical clause** is an adverbial clause abridged so that its subject and verb are implied rather than stated;

the subject of the independent clause then automatically serves also as the implied subject of the elliptical clause. If the implied subject is different from the subject of the independent clause, the subordinate element will dangle, sometimes illogically.

> *dm:* Once in disguise, the hero's conflict emerges.

It isn't "the hero's *conflict*" that is in disguise, but the *hero*. Either supply a logical subject and verb for the elliptical clause, or retain the elliptical clause and make the other subject logically agree with it:

> *revised:* Once the hero is in disguise, his conflict emerges.

> *revised:* Once in disguise, the hero begins to reveal his conflict.

5. Dangling prepositional phrases and appositives

A prepositional phrase can also dangle. In this example, an indefinite *it* (see #7d) is the issue:

> *dm:* Like a child in a toy shop, it is all she can bear not to touch everything.

> *revised:* Like a child in a toy shop, she can hardly bear not to touch everything.

And so can an appositive prove to be problematic:

> *dm:* A superb racing car, a Ferrari's engine is a masterpiece of engineering.

The phrase seems to be in apposition with the noun *engine*, but it is illogical to equate an engine with an entire car (the possessive *Ferrari's* is adjectival). Revise it:

> *revised:* A superb racing car, a Ferrari has an engine that is a masterpiece of engineering.

5f Mixed Constructions

(EAL) Avoiding mixed constructions can be a particular challenge for anyone whose first language has a different sentence structure than English has. To begin a sentence with one construction and then inadvertently shift to another can create confusion.

> *mix:* Eagle Creek is a small BC community is located near Wells Gray Provincial Park.

The writer here sets up two clauses beginning with *is* but then omits a subject for the second occurrence of *is*. Either drop the first *is* and add commas around the resulting appositive phrase (*a small BC community*), or add *that* or *which* before the second *is*.

> *mix:* Since the hockey rink is in use all day, therefore we have to rent it for use at midnight.

Here the writer begins with a subordinating *Since* but then uses *therefore* to introduce the second clause, which would be correct only if the first clause were independent. Fix this by dropping either the *Since* or the *therefore*.

5g Shifts in Perspective: Inconsistent Point of View

Be consistent in your point of view within a sentence and, except in special cases, from one sentence to the next. Avoid illogical shifts in the *tense*, *mood*, and *voice* of verbs, and in the *person* and *number* of pronouns.

1. Shifts in tense

> *shift:* The professor explained what she expected of us and then she sits in her chair and tells us to begin.

All of the events described in this sentence occurred at a particular time in the past. So, change *sits* and *tells* to the past tense to coincide with *explained*.

2. Shifts in mood

> *shift:* If it <u>were</u> Sunday and I <u>was</u> through with my work, I would go skiing with you.

This sentence begins and ends in the subjunctive, but *was* is indicative. Correct this by changing indicative *was* to subjunctive *were*.

3. Shifts in voice

> *shift:* Readers should not ordinarily have to read instructions a second time before some sense <u>can be made</u> of the details.

In this case, stay with active voice (and the same subject):

> *revised:* Readers should not ordinarily have to read instructions a second time before they can make sense of the details.

4. Shifts in person of pronoun

Shifts in person from words such as *one*, *a person*, *somebody*, or *someone* to the second-person *you*, while common in informal conversation, are likely to be questioned in print, and particularly in more formal academic writing. Edit to produce consistency in person.

> *shift:* If <u>one</u> wants to be a cautious investor, <u>you</u> should not invest in the stock market.

> *revised:* If <u>you</u> want to be a cautious investor, <u>you</u> should not invest in the stock market.

> *revised:* If <u>one</u> wants to be a cautious investor, <u>he or she</u> should not invest in the stock market.

5. Shifts in number of pronoun

> *shift:* If the committee wants <u>its</u> recommendations followed, <u>they</u> should have written <u>their</u> report more carefully.

The committee changed from a collective unit (*it*) to a collection of individuals (*they*, *their*); the committee should be either singular or plural throughout.

5h   Faulty Parallelism

Parallelism, the balanced and deliberate repetition of identical grammatical structures (words, phrases, clauses), can be a strong stylistic technique. It makes for vigorous, balanced, and rhythmical sentences. Like any other device, parallelism can be overdone, but more commonly writers underuse it. In most writing, some parallel structure is appropriate. Build parallel elements into your sentences, and now and then try making two or three successive sentences parallel with each other. Here is a sentence from a paper on computer crime. Note how parallelism (along with alliteration) strengthens the first part, thereby helping to set up the second part:

> Although one can distinguish <u>the malicious from the mischievous</u> or <u>the harmless hacker from the more dangerous computer criminal</u>, security officials take a dim view of anyone who romps through company files.

Be careful as you experiment, for it is easy to set up a parallel structure and then lose track of it. Study the following examples of **faulty parallelism**.

1. With coordinate elements
Coordinate elements in a sentence should have the same grammatical form. If they don't, the sentence will lack parallelism and therefore be ineffective.

> *fp:* Reading should be <u>engrossing</u>, <u>active</u>, and <u>a challenge</u>.

The first two complements are predicate adjectives, the third a predicate noun. Change *a challenge* to the adjective *challenging* so that it will be parallel.

The coordinate parts of compound subjects, verbs, objects, and modifiers should be parallel in form.

> *fp:* <u>Eating huge meals</u>, <u>too many sweets</u>, and <u>snacking between meals</u> can lead to obesity.

This sentence can be corrected either by making all three parts of the subject into gerunds:

> *revised:* Eating huge meals, eating too many sweets, and snacking between meals can lead to obesity.

or by using only the first gerund and following it with three parallel objects:

> *revised:* Eating huge meals, too many sweets, and between-meal snacks can lead to obesity.

Another example:

> *fp:* He talks about his computer in terms suggesting a deep affection for it and that also demonstrate a thorough knowledge of it.

Simply change the participial phrase (*suggesting . . .*) to a relative clause (*that suggest . . .*) so that it will be parallel with the second part.

It is particularly easy for a writer to produce faulty parallelism by omitting a second *that*:

> *fp:* Marvin was convinced that the argument was unsound and he could profitably spend some time analyzing it.

A second *that*, before *he*, corrects the error and clarifies the meaning.

2. With correlative conjunctions

Check for parallel structure when using correlative conjunctions:

> *fp:* Whether for teaching a young child the alphabet or in educating an adult about the latest political controversy, television is probably the best device we have.

The constructions following the *whether* and the *or* should be parallel: change *in* to *for*.

The correlative pair *not only . . . but also* can be particularly troublesome:

> *fp:* She not only <u>corrected my grammar</u> but also <u>my spelling</u>.

The error can be corrected either by repeating the verb *corrected* (or using some other appropriate verb, such as *criticized* or *repaired*) after *but also*:

> *revised:* She not only <u>corrected my grammar</u> but also <u>corrected my spelling</u>.

or by moving *corrected* so that it occurs before *not only* rather than after it:

> *revised:* She corrected not only <u>my grammar</u> but also <u>my spelling</u>.

3. In a series

In any series of three or more parallel elements, make sure that little beginning words like prepositions, pronouns, and the *to* of infinitives precede either the first element alone or each of the elements. And don't omit needed articles:

> *fp:* The new library is noted for <u>a large auditorium</u>, <u>state-of-the-art computer lab</u>, <u>an impressive collection of journals</u>, and <u>brilliant, hard-working staff</u>.

The article *a* is missing before the second and fourth items and should be added to make the items parallel. Another way to fix this would be to remove the articles and insert the possessive pronoun *its* before the first item.

> *fp:* She urged her teammates <u>to obey the rules</u>, <u>to think positively</u>, and <u>ignore criticism</u>.

Check your work by jotting down the items in such a series in a vertical list after the word that introduces them: any slips in parallelism should then be clearer to you.

> *correction:* She urged her teammates to obey the rules,
> to think positively,
> **and** to ignore criticism.

PART III

ESSENTIALS OF GRAMMAR AND STYLE: PARTS OF SPEECH; DICTION

CONTENTS

INTRODUCTION

English words fall traditionally into eight categories called **parts of speech**. Five of these can be inflected (changed in their form) in one or more ways:

- noun
- pronoun
- verb
- adjective
- adverb

The other three are not inflected (that is, they do not change form):

- preposition
- conjunction
- interjection

Note that the term *inflection* applies only to the change of a word's form within its part of speech. That is, when the noun *boy* is inflected to make it plural, the new form, *boys*, is still a noun; when the pronoun *they* is inflected to *them* or *theirs*, the new forms are still pronouns.

Many words can be changed so that they function as different parts of speech. For example the noun *centre* can be made into the adjective *central*, or the noun *meaning* into the adjective *meaningful*, or the verb *vacate* into the noun *vacation*. Such changes are not inflections but **derivations**; a word can be *derived* from a word of a different part of speech, often by the addition of one or more suffixes: *trust, trustful, trustfully, trustfulness*. And many words, even without being changed, can serve as more than one part of speech; for example:

> She is <u>cool</u> under pressure. (adjective)
>
> Relations between the two leaders may <u>cool</u> after the meeting. (verb)
>
> Keep your <u>cool</u> in a crisis. (noun)

Part III first discusses the eight parts of speech—their inflections (if any) and other grammatical properties; their subcategories; how they work with other words in sentences; and some of their important derivatives (verbals)—and calls attention to some of their potential trouble spots, such as **agreement** and a verb's **tenses**. Part III ends with a section on diction, the choice of words in the writing we all do.

 **NOUNS**

A **noun** is a word that names or stands for a person, place, thing, class, concept, quality, or action: *woman, character, city, country, citizen, ship, garden, machine, silence, vegetable, road, freedom, beauty, river, spring.* **Proper nouns** are names of specific persons, places, or things and begin with a capital letter: *Dorothy, Rumpelstiltskin, Saskatoon, Canada,* the *Titanic.* All the others, called **common nouns**, are capitalized only if they begin a sentence:

> <u>Freedom</u> is a precious commodity.

or form part of a proper noun:

> <u>Spring</u> <u>Garden</u> <u>Road</u>
>
> the <u>Peace</u> <u>Arch</u>

or are personified or otherwise emphasized, for example in poetry:

> Our noisy years seem moments in the being
> Of the eternal <u>Silence</u>. . . .

> (Wordsworth)

One can also classify nouns as either **concrete**, for names of tangible items (*doctor, elephant, utensil, book, barn*), or **abstract**, for names of intangible things or ideas (*freedom, honour, happiness, history*).

Collective nouns are names of collections or groups often considered as units: *army, committee, family, herd, flock*.

 Inflection of Nouns:
Number; Possessive Case

 Nouns can be inflected in two ways: for **number** and for **possessive case**.

1. For number

Most common concrete nouns that stand for **countable** things are either **singular** or **plural**. Most singular nouns are inflected to indicate the plural by the addition of *s* or *es*: *girl, girls*; *box, boxes*. But some are made plural in other irregular ways: *child, children*; *stimulus, stimuli*.

Some concrete nouns, however, called **mass** nouns, name materials that are measured, weighed, or divided, rather than counted—for example *gold, oxygen, rice, sand,* and *pasta*. As **uncountable** or **noncountable** nouns, these are not inflected for the plural. Also uncountable are **abstract** nouns and nouns that stand for ideas, activities, and states of mind or being; for example, *honour, journalism, skiing, happiness*.

Some nouns, however, can be either countable or uncountable, depending on the context in which they are used. For example:

The butcher sells <u>meat</u>. (uncountable)

The delicatessen offers several delicious smoked <u>meats</u>. (countable, equivalent to *kinds of smoked meat*)

They insisted on telling the truth as a matter of <u>honour</u>. (uncountable)

Many <u>honours</u> were heaped upon the returning hero. (countable)

For detailed information on countable and uncountable nouns, consult a learner's dictionary such as the *Oxford Advanced Learner's Dictionary (OALD)*.

2. For possessive case

Whether a noun is a *subject* (**subjective** case) or an *object* (**objective** case) is shown by word order rather than inflection. But nouns are inflected for **possessive** case. By adding an apostrophe and an *s*, or sometimes only an apostrophe, you inflect a noun so that it shows possession or ownership: *my mother's job, the children's toys, the students' grades.*

6b Grammatical Functions of Nouns

Nouns function in sentences in the following ways:

- as the subject of a verb:

  <u>Students</u> work hard.

- as the direct object of a verb:

  Our team won the <u>championship</u>.

- as the indirect object of a verb:

  We awarded <u>Yoko</u> the prize.

- as the object of a preposition:

  We gave the prize to <u>Yoko</u>.

- as a predicate noun after a linking verb:

  Genevieve is an <u>accountant</u>.

- as an objective complement:

  The judges declared Yoko the <u>winner</u>.

- as an appositive to any other noun:

  Andre, the <u>chef</u>, stopped Roger, the <u>dishwasher</u>.

Nouns in the *possessive case* function as adjectives:

> <u>Maria's</u> coat is expensive. (Which coat? Maria's.)

> I did a <u>day's</u> work. (How much work? A day's.)

or as predicate nouns, after a linking verb:

> The expensive-looking coat is <u>Maria's</u>.

Even without being inflected for possessive case, many nouns can also function as adjectives within noun phrases: the *school* paper, an *evening* gown, the *automobile* industry, the *dessert* course, and so on.

A noun (or pronoun) referring to someone being directly addressed, as in dialogue or in a letter, is called a *noun of address*. Such nouns, usually proper names, are not directly related to the syntax of the rest of the sentence and are set off with punctuation:

> Soon, <u>Steve</u>, you'll see what I mean.

6c   Nouns and Articles: *a, an,* and *the*

Articles modify nouns. They are also sometimes called *markers* or *determiners* because an article indicates that a noun will soon follow.

The definite article *the* and the indefinite articles *a* or *an* are used idiomatically, and therefore, they often challenge people whose first language doesn't include articles. An advanced learner's dictionary can be invaluable in helping you decide which article, if any, to use. If you are having difficulty proofreading for articles, keep your dictionary handy.

Here are some guiding principles for the use of articles.

1. Using the indefinite article

The form *a* of the indefinite article is used before words beginning with a consonant (*a dog, a building, a computer, a yellow orchid*), including words beginning with a pronounced *h* (*a horse, a historical event, a hotel, a hypothesis*) and words beginning with a *u* or *o* whose initial sound is that of *y* or *w* (*a useful book, a one-sided contest*).

The form *an* is used before words beginning with a vowel sound (*an opinion, an underdog, an ugly duckling*). If the *h* is not pronounced, we use *an* as in *an honour*.

Generally a person or thing designated by the indefinite article is not specific:

> He wants to buy <u>a</u> racehorse.

The indefinite article *a* is like *one*: it is often used before singular countable nouns.

2. Using the definite article

Generally, the definite article designates one or more particular persons or things whose identity is established by context (familiarity) or a modifier (clauses, phrases, superlative adjectives, ordinal numbers). In the following examples, the definite article is used because **context** is understood or the reader is familiar with the noun being modified:

> Go to <u>the</u> bookstore (the one we both know about)
> and get the required textbook (the one that is unique
> to the course).

> <u>The</u> black racehorse is in <u>the</u> barn.

If the noun is followed by a **modifying clause** or **phrase**, the definite article is often used:

> My parents gave me <u>the</u> scooter I wanted. (*scooter* is
> particularized by the modifying clause *I wanted*)

The definite article can also be used to indicate exclusiveness; *the* is then equivalent to *the only* or *the best*. In fact, we often use *the* in front of **superlative adjectives**:

> He is <u>the</u> happiest person I know.

We also can indicate exclusiveness with the use of **ordinals**. Ordinals are numerical adjectives such as *first, second, third*, and so on:

6

The first act of the play takes place in Vienna.

The third sequel appealed to adolescent tastes.

3. Using the definite article with proper nouns

Definite articles go with some **proper nouns** but not with others. Strangely, *the* often goes with place names that are plural or have modifying phrases that begin with "of."

We Say	But also
Canada	the Dominion of Canada
Great Britain	the United Kingdom
Gabriola Island	the Thousand Islands
Mount Baker	the Rockies
Western University	the University of Saskatchewan

4. Using articles with uncountable nouns or plural nouns

Uncountable nouns, whether mass or abstract, take no article if the mass or abstract sense governs:

> *art:* The poem features a direct simple praise of nature.

Here *a* must be removed because *praise* in this context is uncountable. But notice the difference if the concrete noun *hymn* is inserted:

> *revised:* The poem features a direct, simple hymn of praise to nature.

Also avoid using *a* or *an* with plural countable nouns:

> *art:* She wanted a writing notebooks.

> *revised:* She wanted writing notebooks.

However, you can use *the* with plural nouns if they are particularized by a modifier.

> *revised:* She wanted the writing notebooks that are made in Italy. (Here *notebooks* is particularized by *that are made in Italy*.)

5. Using articles with abstract nouns

If a usually abstract noun is used in a countable but not particularized sense, the indefinite article precedes it; if in a particularized way, the definite article:

> This is <u>an</u> honour. (countable)

> He did me <u>the</u> honour of inviting me. (uncountable, specific)

6. Using the definite article in front of nouns that represent groups

The definite article usually precedes an adjective functioning as a noun that represents a group:

> <u>The</u> young should heed the advice of <u>the</u> elderly.

This rule can also be applied to species of animals or inventions when emphasizing the class.

> <u>The</u> computer is a prominent feature of our lives.

7. Using the definite article with titles of artistic works

Titles of artistic works are not usually preceded by articles, but usage is inconsistent, and some idiomatically take the definite article. It would be incorrect to say:

> ***art:*** Donne's poetic power is evident in the Sonnet X.

Either omit *the* or change it to *his*. It would be natural to refer to "the *Adventures of Huckleberry Finn*."

8. Using articles with names of academic fields and courses

With names of academic fields and courses, whether proper nouns or abstract common nouns, no article is used:

> She is enrolled in Psychology 301.

> He reads books on psychology.

7 PRONOUNS

A pronoun is a word that *stands for* or *in place of* a noun, or functions like a noun in a sentence. Most pronouns refer to nouns that come earlier, their **antecedents**:

> Joshua offered an opinion, but he didn't feel confident about it.

 Pronoun Types

There are eight different pronoun types:

- personal
- impersonal
- interrogative
- relative
- demonstrative
- indefinite
- reflexive (or intensive)
- reciprocal

Like nouns, pronouns can function as subjects of verbs, direct and indirect objects, and objects of prepositions; some can also function as appositives and predicate nouns. Some pronouns are inflected much more than nouns, and some require close proofreading for case, reference, and agreement.

1. Personal pronouns
Personal pronouns refer to specific persons or things. They are inflected in four ways:

FOR PERSON
- **First-person** pronouns (*I*, *we*, etc.) refer to the person or persons doing the speaking or writing.
- **Second-person** pronouns (*you*, *yours*) refer to the person or persons being spoken or written to.
- **Third-person** pronouns (*he*, *she*, *it*, *they*, etc.) refer to the person(s) or thing(s) being spoken or written about.

FOR NUMBER
- **Singular** pronouns (*I*, *she*, etc.) refer to individuals.

> I am writing. She is writing.

- **Plural** pronouns (*we*, *they*, etc.) refer to groups.

  <u>We</u> are writing. <u>They</u> are writing.

FOR GENDER (SECOND- AND THIRD-PERSON PRONOUNS)

- **Masculine** pronouns (*he*, *him*, *his*) refer to males.
- **Feminine** pronouns (*she*, *her*, *hers*) refer to females.
- The **neuter** pronoun (*it*) refers to ideas or things, and sometimes to animals.

  (In the plural forms—*we*, *you*, *they*, etc.—there is no indication of gender.)

FOR CASE

- Pronouns that function as **subjects** must be in the **subjective** case:

  <u>I</u> paint. <u>She</u> paints. <u>They</u> are painting.

- Pronouns that function as **objects**—whether direct or indirect—must be in the **objective** case:

  The idea hit <u>them</u>. Give <u>her</u> the book. Give <u>it</u> to <u>me</u>.

- Pronouns that indicate possession or ownership must be in the **possessive** case:

  That turtle is <u>his</u>. This turtle is <u>mine</u>. Where is <u>yours</u>?

  (Note that pronouns in the possessive case—*yours*, *theirs*, *its*, *hers*, etc.—do not take an apostrophe before the *s* to indicate possession.)

The following chart shows all the inflections of personal pronouns:

	Subject	Object	Possessive Pronoun	Possessive Adjective
singular				
1st person	I	me	mine	my
2nd person	you	you	yours	your
3rd person	he	him	his	his
	she	her	hers	her
	it	it		its

	Subject	Object	Possessive Pronoun	Possessive Adjective
plural				
1st person	we	us	ours	our
2nd person	you	you	yours	your
3rd person	they	them	theirs	their

Possessive (or **pronominal**) **adjectives** always precede nouns (*My* car is in the shop); **possessive pronouns** may function as subjects, objects, and predicate nouns (Let's take *yours*).

2. Impersonal pronouns

In formal contexts, the **impersonal pronoun** *one*, meaning essentially "a person," serves in place of a first-, second-, or third-person pronoun:

> One must keep one's priorities straight.

The pronoun *it* is also used as an impersonal pronoun, usually as the subject of some form of *be* and usually referring to time, weather, distance, and the like:

> It is getting late. It's almost four o'clock.

> It's warm. It feels warmer than it did yesterday.

> It is a mile and a half from here to the station.

3. Interrogative pronouns

Interrogative pronouns are *question words* used usually at or near the beginning of *interrogative sentences*. *Who* is inflected for objective and possessive case, *which* for possessive case only:

Subjective	Objective	Possessive
who	whom	whose
which	which	whose
what	what	

Who refers to persons, *which* and *what* to things; *which* sometimes also refers to persons, as in *Which of you is going?* The compound forms *whoever* and *whatever*, and sometimes even *whichever* and *whomever*, can also function as interrogative pronouns. Here are some examples showing interrogative pronouns functioning in different ways:

- as a subject:

  <u>Who</u> said that?

  <u>Which</u> of these experts are you citing?

- as the direct object of a verb:

  <u>Whom</u> do you suggest for the position?

- as the object of a preposition:

  To <u>whom</u> did you recommend the restaurant?

  To <u>what</u> do I owe this honour?

- as an objective complement:

  <u>What</u> did you call me?

In front of a noun, an interrogative word functions as an **interrogative adjective**:

  <u>Whose</u> book is this?

4. Relative pronouns

A **relative pronoun** usually introduces an *adjective clause*—called a **relative clause**—in which it functions as subject, object, or object of a preposition. The pronoun links, or *relates*, the clause to an antecedent in the same sentence, a noun or pronoun that the whole clause modifies.

The principal relative pronouns are *who*, *which*, and *that*. *Who* and *which* are inflected for case:

Subjective	Objective	Possessive
who	whom	whose
which	which	whose
that	that	

Who refers to persons (and sometimes to animals thought of as persons), *which* to things, and *that* to either persons or things. Consider some examples of how relative pronouns function:

> Margaret, who is leaving in the morning, will call us later tonight. (*who* as subject of verb *is*; clause modifies *Margaret*)

> Joel contacted the reporter whom he had met at the crime scene. (*whom* as direct object; clause modifies *reporter*)

> At midnight Sula began to revise her essay, which was due in the morning. (*which* as subject of verb *was*; clause modifies *essay*)

> She avoided working on the annual report that she was having trouble with. (*that* as object of preposition *with*; clause modifies *report*)

A relative clause is either **restrictive** and unpunctuated, or **nonrestrictive** and set off with punctuation. It is **restrictive** if it gives us information that is essential to identifying the antecedent (e.g. *whom he had met at the crime scene*); it is **nonrestrictive** if the information it gives us is not essential to identifying the antecedent and could be left out of the sentence (e.g. *which was due in the morning*). Any of the three relative pronouns (*who, which, that*) can be used to introduce a restrictive relative clause, but only *which* and *who* can introduce a nonrestrictive relative clause. If the relative pronoun in a restrictive clause is the object of a verb or a preposition, it can usually be omitted:

> She avoided working on the annual report [that or which] she was having trouble with.

But if the preposition is placed before the pronoun (e.g. *with which*), the pronoun cannot be omitted:

> She was working on the annual report with which she was having trouble.

And don't omit the relative pronoun when it is necessary to prevent misreading:

> *incorrect:* Different varieties of tea shops sell are medicinal.

A *that* or a *which* after *tea* prevents misreading the subject of the verb as "different varieties of tea shops."

When *whose* precedes and modifies a noun in a relative clause, it functions as what is called a **relative adjective**:

> Jana was the one <u>whose</u> advice he most valued.

And sometimes a **relative adverb**, often *when* or *where*, introduces a relative clause:

> Here's an aerial photo of the town <u>where</u> I live. (The clause *where I live* modifies the noun *town*.)

> My parents told me about the time <u>when</u> I learned to walk. (The *when*-clause modifies the noun *time*.)

Sometimes *what* and the *ever*-compounds (*whatever, whoever, whomever, whichever*) are also considered relative pronouns, even though they introduce noun clauses (e.g. "Remember *what I said*." "Take *whichever one you want*."). *Who, whom,* and *which* may also introduce such noun clauses.

5. Demonstrative pronouns
Demonstrative pronouns, which can be thought of as pointing to the nouns they refer to, are inflected for *number*:

Singular	**Plural**
this	these
that	those

This and *these* usually refer to something nearby or something just said or about to be said; *that* and *those* usually refer to something farther away or more remote in time or longer in duration:

> The clerk was helpful; <u>this</u> was what pleased her the most.

These are the main points I will cover in today's lecture.

That was the story he told us the next morning.

Those were his exact words.

These pronouns also often occur in prepositional phrases with *like* and *such as*:

Someone who wears a shirt like that has no fashion sense.

I need more close friends like those.

A cute house such as this will sell immediately.

Note: Useful as demonstrative pronouns can be, employ them sparingly in writing, for they are often vague in their reference. If you think a demonstrative pronoun is too vague, follow it with a noun to turn it into a *demonstrative adjective*: *this* belief, *that* statement, *these* buildings, *those* arguments.

6. Indefinite pronouns

(EAL) **Indefinite pronouns** refer to indefinite or unknown persons or things, or to indefinite or unknown quantities of persons or things. The major issue with these words is whether they are *singular* or *plural*. Think of indefinite pronouns as falling into four groups:

- Group 1: compounds ending with *body*, *one*, and *thing*. These words function like nouns—that is, they need no antecedents—and they are almost always considered *singular*:

anybody	everybody	nobody	somebody
anyone	everyone	no one	someone
anything	everything	nothing	something

- Group 2: a few other indefinite pronouns that are almost always *singular*:

another	each	either	much
neither	one	other	

- Group 3: a few that are always *plural*:

  | both | few | many | several |

- Group 4: a few that can be either *singular* or *plural*, depending on context and intended meaning:

  | all | any | more | most |
  | none | some | | |

Only *one* and *other* can be inflected for number, by adding *s* to make them plural: *ones*, *others*. Several indefinite pronouns can be inflected for possessive case; unlike personal pronouns, they take *'s*, just as nouns do (or, with *others'*, just an apostrophe):

anybody's	anyone's	everybody's	everyone's
nobody's	no one's	somebody's	someone's
one's	other's	another's	others'

The remaining indefinite pronouns must use *of* to show possession; for example:

That was the belief <u>of many</u> who were present.

When in the possessive case, indefinite pronouns function as adjectives. In addition, all the words in groups 2, 3, and 4, except *none,* can also function as adjectives:

| <u>any</u> boat | <u>some</u> people | <u>few</u> people |
| <u>more</u> money | <u>each</u> day | <u>either</u> direction |

The adjective expressing the meaning of *none* is *no*:

Send <u>no</u> attachments.

Sometimes the cardinal numbers (*one, two, three,* etc.) and the ordinal numbers (*first, second, third,* etc.) are also classed as indefinite pronouns:

How many ducks are on the pond? I see <u>several</u>. I see <u>seven</u>.

Do you like these stories? I like <u>some</u>, but not <u>others</u>.
I like the <u>first</u> and the <u>third</u>.

7. Reflexive and intensive pronouns

Reflexive and intensive pronouns are formed by adding *self* or *selves* to the possessive form of the first- and second-person personal pronouns, to the objective form of third-person personal pronouns, and to the impersonal pronoun *one*.

Singular	Plural
myself	ourselves
yourself	yourselves
himself	themselves
herself	
itself	
oneself	

A **reflexive pronoun** is used as an object when that object is the same person or thing as the subject:

He treated <u>himself</u> to bubble tea. (direct object)

She gave <u>herself</u> a treat. (indirect object)

We kept the idea to <u>ourselves</u>. (object of preposition)

These pronouns are also used as **intensive pronouns** to emphasize a subject or object. An intensive pronoun comes either right after the noun it emphasizes or at the end of the sentence:

Although he let the others choose their positions, Angelo <u>himself</u> is going to pitch.

The professor told us to count up our scores <u>ourselves</u>.

They are also used in prepositional phrases with *by* to mean "alone" or "without help":

I can do this job by <u>myself</u>.

Note: Do not use this form of pronoun as a substitute for a personal pronoun:

> The team and I [not *myself*] played a great game tonight.

8. Reciprocal pronouns

(EAL) Like a reflexive pronoun, a **reciprocal pronoun** refers to the subject of a sentence, but this time the subject is always plural. The two reciprocal pronouns themselves are singular and consist of two words each:

> each other (referring to a subject involving two)

> one another (referring to a subject involving three or more)

They can be inflected for possessive case by adding *'s*:

> each other's   one another's

These pronouns express mutual interaction between or among the parts of a plural subject:

> The president and the prime minister praised each other's policies.

> The computers in this office speak to one another, even though the employees never do.

7b   Case

Determining the correct case of personal, interrogative, and relative pronouns is sometimes challenging. If you know how a pronoun is functioning grammatically, you will know which form to use. Here are some guidelines to help you with the kinds of sentences that sometimes cause problems:

1. A pronoun functioning as the *subject* should be in the *subjective* case. Whenever you use a pronoun as part of a *compound subject*, make sure it is in the *subjective* case. Someone who wouldn't say "*Me* am

going to the store" could slip and say something like "Susan and *me* studied hard for the examination" instead of the correct

Susan and I studied hard for the examination.

If you're not sure, remove the other part of the subject; then you'll know which pronoun sounds right:

[Susan and] I studied hard for the examination.

2. A pronoun functioning as a direct or indirect *object* should be in the *objective* case. When you use a pronoun as part of a compound object, make sure it's in the *objective* case. Again, test by removing the other part:

They asked [Ingrid and] me to take part in the play.

3. A pronoun functioning as the *object* of a preposition should be in the *objective* case:

ca: This information is between you and I.

revised: This information is between you and me.

The objective *me* is correct in this instance, for it is the object of the preposition *between*.

4. A pronoun functioning as a *predicate noun* after a linking verb should be in the *subjective* case. In other words, if the pronoun follows the verb *be*, it takes the subjective form:

It is they who must decide, not we.

If such usages sound stuffy and artificial to you—as they do to many people—find another way to phrase your sentences; for example:

They, not we, must decide.

Again, watch out for compound structures:

ca: The nominees are Yashmin and me.

revised: The nominees are Yashmin and I.

5. Pronouns following the conjunctions *as* and *than* in comparisons should be in the *subjective* case if they are functioning as subjects, even if their verbs are not expressed but left "understood":

   Roberta is as bright as <u>they</u> [are].

   Aaron has learned less than <u>I</u> [have].

   If, however, the pronouns are functioning as objects, they should be in the *objective case*:

   I trust <u>her</u> more than [I trust] <u>him</u>.

6. Use the appropriate case of the interrogative and relative pronouns *who* and *whom, whoever* and *whomever.* Although *who* is often used instead of *whom* in speech and informal writing, you should know how to use the two correctly when you want to write or speak more formally.

   a. Use the *subjective* case for the *subject* of a verb in a question or a relative clause:

      <u>Who</u> is going?

      Dickens was a novelist <u>who</u> was extremely popular in his own time.

   b. Use the *objective* case for the *object* of a verb or preposition:

      <u>Whom</u> do you prefer in that role?

      He is the candidate <u>whom</u> I most admire.

      She is the manager for <u>whom</u> the employees have the most respect.

      If such usages with *whom* seem to you unnatural and stuffy, avoid them by rephrasing:

      She is the manager that the employees respect most.

   c. In noun clauses, the case of the pronoun is determined by its function in its clause, not by other words:

How can you tell <u>who won</u>? (subjective case)

I'll give the prize to <u>whomever the judges declare
the winner</u>. (objective case, object
of preposition)

7c Agreement of Pronouns with Their Antecedents

Any pronoun that refers to or stands for an *antecedent* must
agree with—i.e. be the same as—that antecedent in **person**
(first, second, or third), **number** (singular or plural), and
gender (masculine, feminine, or neuter). For example:

<u>Joanne</u> wants to go to university so that <u>she</u> will be
prepared to take <u>her</u> place in the world. (Pronouns are
third person, feminine, and singular to agree
with *Joanne*.)

The following sections point out the most common
sources of trouble with pronoun agreement. Note that
these errors all have to do with *number*—whether a pronoun should be *singular* or *plural*. Mistakes in gender and
person also occur, but not as frequently.

1. Antecedents joined by *and*
When two or more singular antecedents are joined by *and*,
use a *plural* pronoun:

Both Jennifer and Chinmoy contributed <u>their</u> know-how.

If such a compound is preceded by *each* or *every*, however,
the pronoun should be *singular*:

Each book and periodical in the library has <u>its</u> own
catalogue number.

2. Antecedents joined by *or* or *nor*
When two or more antecedents are joined by *or* or *nor*, use
a *singular* pronoun if the antecedents are singular:

Either David or Jonathan will bring <u>his</u> car.

Neither Maylin nor her mother gave <u>her</u> consent.

If one antecedent is masculine and the other feminine, rephrase the sentence.

Use a *plural* pronoun if the antecedents are plural:

> Neither the players nor the coaches did their jobs properly.

If the antecedents are mixed singular and plural, a pronoun should agree with the nearest one. But if you move from a plural to a singular antecedent, the sentence will almost inevitably sound awkward; try to construct such sentences so that the last antecedent is plural:

> *awk:* Neither the actors nor the director could control his temper.

> *revised:* Neither the director nor the actors could control their tempers.

For more information on agreement of verbs with compound subjects joined by *or* or *nor*, see #9b.

3. Indefinite pronoun as antecedent

If the antecedent is an *indefinite pronoun*, you'll usually use a *singular* pronoun to refer to it. The indefinite pronouns in Group 1 (the compounds with *body*, *one*, and *thing*) are singular, as are those in Group 2 (*another*, *each*, *either*, *much*, *neither*, *one*, *other*):

> Each of the boys worked on his own project.

> Either of these women is likely to buy that sports car for herself.

> Everything has its proper place.

Indefinite pronouns from Group 3 (*both*, *few*, *many*, *several*) are always plural:

> Only a few returned their ballots.

The indefinite pronouns in Group 4 (*all*, *any*, *more*, *most*, *none*, *some*) can be either singular or plural; the intended meaning is usually clearly either singular or plural:

Some of the food on the menu could be criticized for its lack of nutrients.

Some of the ships in the fleet had been restored to their original beauty.

Confusion sometimes arises with the indefinite pronoun *none*. Although *none* began by meaning *no one* or *not one*, it now commonly has the plural sense:

None of the boy scouts knew how to fix their bicycles.

With a mass noun, or if your intended meaning is *not a single one*, treat *none* as singular:

None of the food could be praised for its quality.

None of the boy scouts knew how to fix his bicycle.
(Here, you could perhaps even change *None* to *Not one*.)

When any of these words function as *adjectives*, the same principles apply:

Each boy worked on his own project.

Either woman is likely to buy that car for herself.

Only a few people returned their ballots.

Some food can be praised for its nutritional value.

Some ships had been restored to their original beauty.

Note: The word *every* used as an adjective requires a *singular* pronoun:

Every boy has his own project.

4. Collective noun as antecedent

If the antecedent is a *collective noun*, use either a singular or a plural pronoun to refer to it, depending on context and desired meaning. If the collective noun stands for the group seen as a unit, use a *singular* pronoun:

The team worked on its power play during the practice.

If the collective noun stands for the members of the group seen as individuals, use a *plural* pronoun:

> The <u>team</u> took up <u>their</u> starting positions.

5. Agreement with demonstrative adjectives
Demonstrative adjectives agree in number with the nouns they modify (usually *kind* or *kinds* or similar words):

> *agr:* <u>These kind</u> of doctors work especially hard.
>
> *revised:* <u>This kind</u> of doctor works especially hard.
>
> *revised:* <u>These kinds</u> of doctors work especially hard.

7d   Pronoun Reference

A pronoun's **reference** to an antecedent must be clear. The pronoun or the sentence will be unclear if the antecedent is remote, ambiguous, vague, or missing.

1. Remote antecedent
An antecedent should be close enough to its pronoun to be unmistakable; your reader shouldn't have to pause and search for it. An antecedent should seldom appear more than one sentence before its pronoun within a paragraph.

> *ref:* People who expect to find happiness in material things may discover that the life of the mind is more important than the life filled with possessions. Material prosperity may seem fine at a given moment, but in the long run its delights fade into inconsequential boredom and emptiness. <u>They</u> then realize, too late, where true happiness lies.

The word *People* is too far back to be a clear antecedent for the pronoun *They*. If the second sentence had also begun with *They*, the connection would be clearer. Or the third sentence might begin with a more particularizing phrase, like "Such people . . ."

2. Ambiguous reference

A pronoun should refer clearly to only one antecedent:

> *ref:* When Donna's mother told her that <u>she</u> had won an award, <u>she</u> was obviously delighted.

Each *she* could refer either to Donna (*her*) or to Donna's mother. When revising, rephrase the sentence:

> *weak:* When Donna's mother told her that she (her mother) had won an award, she (Donna) was obviously delighted.

> *clear:* Donna was obviously delighted when her mother told her about winning an award.

> *clear:* Donna's mother had won an award, and she was obviously delighted when she told Donna about it.

> *clear:* Donna was obviously delighted when her mother said, "I won an award!"

Another example:

> *ref:* His second film was far different from his first. It was a war story set in Belgium.

Combine two sentences, reducing the second to a subordinate element:

> *clear:* His second film, a war story set in Belgium, was far different from his first.

> *clear:* His second film was far different from his first, which was a war story set in Belgium.

3. Vague reference

Vague reference is usually caused by the demonstrative pronouns *this* and *that* and the relative pronoun *which*:

> *ref:* The doctors are overworked, and there are no beds available. <u>This</u> is an intolerable situation for the hospital.

> *clear:* The overworked doctors and the lack of available beds make for an intolerable situation for the hospital.

> *ref:* The doctors are overworked, and there are
> no beds available, which is an intolerable
> situation for the hospital.

> *clear:* The doctors are overworked, and there are no
> beds available. These two circumstances make
> for an intolerable situation for the hospital.

Don't catch the "this" virus; sufferers from it are driven to begin a large proportion of their sentences and other independent clauses with a *this*. Whenever you catch yourself beginning with a *this*, look carefully to see

- if the reference to the preceding clause, sentence, or paragraph is as clear on paper as it may be in your mind;
- if the *this* could be replaced by a specific noun or noun phrase, or otherwise avoided (for example by rephrasing or subordinating);
- whether, if you decide to keep *this*, it is an ambiguous demonstrative pronoun; if so, try to make it a *demonstrative adjective*, giving it a noun to modify— even if no more specific than "This *idea*," "This *fact*," or "This *argument*."

4. Missing antecedent
Sometimes a writer may have an antecedent in mind but fail to write it down:

> *ref:* In the early seventeenth century, the
> Renaissance attitude was concentrated
> mainly on the arts rather than on developing
> the scientific part of <u>their</u> minds.

The writer was probably thinking of "the people of the Renaissance." Simply changing *their* to *people's* would clear up the difficulty.

> *ref:* Whenever a student assembly is called, <u>they</u>
> are required to attend.

> *revised:* Whenever an assembly is called, students are
> required to attend.

5. Indefinite *you*, *they*, and *it*

In formal writing, avoid the pronouns *you*, *they*, and *it* when they are indefinite:

> *informal:* In order to graduate, you must have at least 120 course credits.
>
> *formal:* In order to graduate, a student must have at least 120 course credits.
>
> *informal:* In some cities they do not have enough recycling facilities.
>
> *formal:* Some cities do not have enough recycling facilities.

Although it is correct to use the expletive or impersonal *it* and say "*It* is raining," "*It* is seven o'clock," and so on, avoid such indefinite uses of *it* as the following:

> *informal:* It states in our textbook that we should be careful how we use the pronoun *it*.
>
> *formal:* Our textbook states that we should be careful how we use the pronoun *it*.

7e   Pronouns and Inclusive Language

Several indefinite pronouns, as well as indefinite nouns like *person* and many other nouns used in a generalizing way, present an additional challenge: avoiding gender bias.

In centuries past, if a *singular antecedent* had no grammatical gender but could refer to either male or female, it was conventional to use the masculine pronoun *he* (*him*, *his*, *himself*) in a generic sense, meaning any person, male or female:

> *biased:* Everyone in the room raised his hand.
>
> *biased:* A writer should be careful about his diction.

Today this practice is regarded as inappropriate and inaccurate.

All of us should avoid biased language. Colloquially and informally, many writers simply do so by using a plural pronoun:

> ***agr:*** <u>Anyone</u> who doesn't pay <u>their</u> taxes is asking for trouble.

Here are five solutions you can use when writing in a formal context:

1. If you are referring to a group or class consisting entirely of either men or women, use the appropriate pronoun, whether masculine or feminine:

   > <u>Everyone</u> in the room raised <u>his</u> hand.

   > <u>Everyone</u> in the room raised <u>her</u> hand.

   If the group is mixed, try to avoid the problem, for example by using the indefinite article:

   > <u>Everyone</u> in the room raised <u>a</u> hand.

2. Make the antecedent itself plural: then the plural pronoun referring to it is grammatically appropriate, and no problem of gender arises:

   > <u>All those</u> in the room raised <u>their</u> hands.

   > <u>Writers</u> should be careful about <u>their</u> diction.

3. If your purpose and the formality of the context permit, you can use the impersonal pronoun *one* or the second person *you*:

   > If <u>one</u> is considerate of others' feelings, <u>one</u> will get along better.

   > If <u>you</u> are considerate of others' feelings, <u>you</u> will get along better.

4. Revise so that no gendered pronoun is necessary:

   > Everyone's hand went up.

5. If a sentence doesn't lend itself to such changes, or if you want to keep its original structure for some other reason, you can still manage. Don't resort to strings

of unsightly devices such as *he/she, him/her, her/his, him/herself*, or *s/he*. But an occasional *he or she* or *she or he* and the like is acceptable:

> If anyone protests, <u>he or she</u> will be asked to leave.

> A writer should be careful about <u>her or his</u> diction.

But don't do this too often, as such repetitions can become tedious and cluttering.

 # 8 VERBS

Verbs are core parts of speech. A verb is the focal point of a clause or a sentence. Standard sentences consist of subjects and predicates: every subject has a predicate, and the heart of every predicate is its **verb**.

Verbs express not only *action* but also *occurrence, process,* and *condition* or *state of being*. All verbs *assert* or *ask* something about their subjects, sometimes by *linking* a subject with a complement. Some verbs are single words; others are phrases consisting of two or more words. Here are some sentences with the verbs underlined:

> He <u>throws</u> curves.

> Karen <u>is</u> a lawyer.

> By midnight, I <u>will have driven</u> two hundred kilometres.

> <u>Are</u> you <u>listening</u>?

> The two columns of figures <u>came out</u> even.

8a Transitive, Intransitive, and Linking Verbs

Verbs are classified according to the way they function in sentences.

A verb taking a *direct object* is considered **transitive**. A transitive verb makes a transition, conveys a movement, from its subject to its object:

> He <u>introduced</u> me to his uncle.

> She <u>expresses</u> her ideas eloquently.

A direct object answers the question consisting of the verb and *what* or *whom*: Introduced *whom*? Me. Expresses *what*? Ideas.

A verb without a direct object is considered **intransitive**:

> What <u>has happened</u> to the aquarium's whale?

> The earthquake <u>occurred</u> during the night.

Many verbs can be either transitive or intransitive, depending on how they function in particular sentences:

> I <u>ran</u> the business effectively. (transitive)

> I <u>ran</u> to the store. (intransitive)

A third kind of verb is called **linking** or copulative. The main one is *be* in its various forms. Some other common linking verbs are *become, seem, remain, act, get, feel, look, appear, smell, sound,* and *taste.* Linking verbs don't have objects, but are yet incomplete; they need a **subjective complement**. A linking verb is like an equal sign in an equation: something at the right-hand (predicate) end is needed to balance what is at the left-hand (subject) end. The complement will be either a *predicate noun* or a *predicate adjective.*

> Angela <u>is</u> a lawyer. (predicate noun: *lawyer*)

> Angela <u>is</u> not well. (predicate adjective: *well*)

> Mikhail <u>became</u> a pilot. (predicate noun: *pilot*)

> Mikhail <u>became</u> uneasy. (predicate adjective: *uneasy*)

Verbs such as *act, sound, taste, smell,* and *feel* can also function as transitive verbs: She *acted* the part. He *sounded* his horn. He *smelled* the hydrogen sulphide. I *tasted* the soup. He *felt* the bump on his head.

Similarly, many of these verbs can also function as regular intransitive verbs, sometimes accompanied by *adverbial* modifiers: We *looked* at the painting. Santa *is* on the roof. Teresa *is* at home. We *are* here. But whenever one of these verbs is accompanied by a predicate noun or a predicate adjective, it is functioning as a linking verb.

8

8b   Inflection of Verbs: Principal Parts

Verbs are the most complex, the most highly inflected, of the eight parts of speech. Verbs are inflected

- for **person** and **number**, in order to agree with a subject;
- for **tense**, in order to show an action's time—present, past, or future—and aspect—simple, perfect, or progressive;
- for **mood**, in order to show the kind of sentence—indicative, imperative, or subjunctive; and
- for **voice**, in order to show whether a subject is active (performing an action) or passive (being acted upon).

Every verb (except some auxiliaries) has what are called its **principal parts**:

1. its **basic** form (the form listed in a dictionary),
2. its **past-tense** form,
3. its **past participle**, and
4. its **present participle**.

Verbs regularly form both the *past tense* and the *past participle* simply by adding *ed* to the basic form. If the basic form already ends in *e*, only *d* is added:

Basic Form	Past-tense Form	Past Participle
push	pushed	pushed
move	moved	moved

Present participles are regularly formed by adding *ing* to the basic form. Verbs ending in an unpronounced *e* usually drop it before adding *ing*:

Basic Form	Present Participle
push	pushing
move	moving

In addition, some verbs double a final consonant before adding *ed* or *ing*:

grin   grinned   grinning

Good dictionaries list any irregular principal parts, ones not formed by simply adding *ed* or *ing*.

Note: The basic form of a verb is sometimes called the **infinitive** form, meaning that it can be preceded by *to* to form an infinitive: *to be, to push, to agree.* Infinitives, participles, and gerunds are called **non-finite verbs**, or **verbals**; they function not as verbs but as other parts of speech. **Finite verbs**, unlike non-finite forms, are restricted or limited by person, number, tense, mood, and voice; they function as the main verbs in sentences.

8c Irregular Verbs

(EAL) Some of the most common English verbs are **irregular** in the way they make their past-tense forms and their past participles. Whenever you aren't certain about the principal parts of a verb, check your dictionary. If you're looking for a verb that is a compound or that has a suffix, look for the main verb: for *misread, proofread,* or *reread,* look under *read* instead.

8d Auxiliary Verbs

(EAL) Auxiliary or helping verbs go with other verbs to form verb phrases indicating tense, voice, and mood. The auxiliary *do* helps in forming questions, forming negative sentences, and expressing emphasis:

<u>Did</u> you arrive on time?

I <u>did not</u> arrive on time.

I <u>did</u> wash my face!

Modal auxiliaries
There are also what are called **modal auxiliaries**. The principal ones are *can, could, may, might, must, should,* and

would. They combine with main verbs and other auxiliaries to express such meanings as ability, possibility, obligation, and necessity.

The following chart illustrates the principal modal verbs currently in use in North American English:

The Modal	Used to Express . . .
can	ability
could	
may	permission
might	possibility
ought to	obligation
should	
must	
shall	probability, prediction
will	
should	condition
would	

Consider the following examples:

I can understand that.

There could be thunderstorms tomorrow.

I would tell you the answer if I could.

The instructor may decide to cancel the quiz.

The equivalent phrases *able to* (*can*), *ought to* (*should*), and *have to* (*must*) also function as modal auxiliaries.

COULD, MIGHT

Could and *might* also serve as the past-tense forms of *can* and *may*, for example if demanded by the sequence of tenses after a verb in the past tense:

He was sure that I could handle the project.

She said that I might watch the rehearsal if I was quiet.

MIGHT, MAY

Might and *may* are sometimes interchangeable when expressing possibility:

> She <u>may</u> (<u>might</u>) challenge the committee's decision.

> He <u>may</u> (<u>might</u>) have finished the job by now.

But usually there is a difference, with *may* indicating a stronger possibility, *might* a somewhat less likely one.

To express a condition contrary to fact, *might* is the right word:

> If you had edited your essay, you <u>might</u> [not *may*] have received a higher grade.

That is, you *didn't* edit carefully, and you *didn't* get a higher grade. *Might* is necessary for clear expression of a hypothetical as opposed to a factual circumstance.

8

8e   Verb Tenses and Their Functions

(EAL)   Verbs not only indicate action but also control time. The verb by its inflection indicates the *time* of an action, event, or condition. Through its **tense** a verb shows *when* an action occurs:

> ***past tense:*** Yesterday, I <u>practised</u>.

> ***present tense:*** Today, I <u>practise</u>.

> ***future tense:*** Tomorrow, I <u>will practise</u>.

Following are brief descriptions and illustrations of the main functions of each tense. Although these points are sometimes oversimplifications of very complex matters, and although there are other exceptions and variations than those listed, these guidelines should help you to use the tenses and to take advantage of the possibilities they offer for clear expression.

Tense		Verb Form
1. Simple Present	I/you	dance
	he/she/it	dances
	we/you/they	dance
2. Simple Past	I/you/he/she/ it/we/you/they	danced
3. Simple Future	I/you/he/she/ it/we/you/they	will dance
4. Present Perfect	he/she/it	has danced
	I/you/we/ you/they	have danced
5. Past Perfect	I/you/he/she/ it/we/you/they	had danced
6. Future Perfect	I/you/he/she/ it/we/you/they	will have danced
7. Present Progressive	I	am dancing
	you	are dancing
	he/she/it	is dancing
	we/you/they	are dancing
8. Past Progressive	I	was dancing
	you	were dancing
	he/she/it	was dancing
	we/you/they	were dancing
9. Future Progressive	I/you/he/she/ it/we/you/they	will be dancing
10. Present Perfect Progressive	I/you	have been dancing
	he/she/it	has been dancing
	we/you/they	have been dancing
11. Past Perfect Progressive	I/you/he/she/ it/we/you/they	had been dancing
12. Future Perfect Progressive	I/you/he/she/ it/we/you/they	will have been dancing

8

1. Simple present

Generally, use this tense to describe an action or condition that is happening now, at the time of the utterance:

> The pitcher <u>throws</u>. The batter <u>swings</u>. It <u>is</u> a high fly ball . . .

It can also indicate a general truth or belief:

> Ottawa <u>is</u> one of the coldest capitals in the world.

or describe a customary or habitual or repeated action or condition:

> I <u>paint</u> pictures for a living.

or describe the characters or events in a literary or other work, or what an author does in such a work:

> While he <u>is</u> away from Denmark, Hamlet <u>arranges</u> to have Rosencrantz and Guildenstern put to death. After he returns he <u>holds</u> Yorick's skull and <u>watches</u> Ophelia being buried. He <u>duels</u> with Laertes and <u>dies</u>. Without a doubt, death <u>is</u> one of the principal themes in the play.

> In *Pride and Prejudice*, Jane Austen <u>shows</u> the consequences of making hasty judgments of others.

2. Simple past

Use this tense for a single or repeated action or condition that began and ended in the past:

> She <u>earned</u> a lot of money last summer.

> I <u>was</u> happy when I received my paycheque.

3. Simple future

The most common and straightforward way to indicate future time is to use the simple future, putting *will* or *shall* before the basic form of the verb:

> She <u>will arrive</u> tomorrow morning.

4. Present perfect

Use this tense for an action or condition that began in the past and that continues to the present; though commonly considered "completed" as of the moment, some actions or conditions referred to in this tense could continue after the present:

> I have earned a lot of money this summer.

> James Bond has just entered the casino.

You can use this tense for something that occurred entirely in the past, if you intend to imply the sense of "before now" or "so far" or "already":

> I have painted a picture; take a look at it.

> I have visited Greece three times.

5. Past perfect

Use this tense for an action completed in the past before a specific past time or event. Notice that there are at least two actions taking place in the past:

> Though I had seen the film twice before, I went again last week.

6. Future perfect

Use this tense for an action or condition that will be completed before a specific future time or event:

> I will already have eaten when you arrive.

7. Present progressive

Use this tense for an action or condition that began at some past time and is continuing now, in the present:

> Global warming is causing a significant rise in sea levels around the world.

Sometimes the simple and the progressive forms of a verb say much the same thing:

> We hope for snow. We are hoping for snow.

But usually the progressive form emphasizes an activity, or the singleness or continuing nature of an action, rather than a larger condition or general truth:

> A tax hike <u>hurts</u> many people.
> The tax hike <u>is hurting</u> many people.

Stative verbs, verbs that express sense, cognitive, or emotional states, don't often appear in the progressive form. Unless the stative verb is expressing an action, do not use it in the progressive tense.

> *incorrect:* After being sprayed by the skunk, the dog is smelling bad now. (condition)
>
> *correct:* After having its nose injured, the dog is smelling poorly. (activity)

Here is a short list of some common stative verbs:

appear	appreciate	be	believe	dislike
feel	hear	imagine	know	like
look	love	remember	resemble	seem
smell	understand	want	wish	

8. Past progressive
Use this tense for an action in progress during some past time, especially if you want to emphasize the continuing nature of the action:

> I remember that I <u>was painting</u> a picture that day.

Sometimes the past progressive tense describes an interrupted action or an action during which something else happens:

> When the telephone rang I <u>was making</u> tempura.

9. Future progressive
Use this tense for a continuing action in the future or for an action that will be occurring at some specific time in the future:

> I <u>will be painting</u> pictures as long as I can hold a brush.

10. Present perfect progressive

Use this tense to emphasize the continuing nature of a single or repeated action that began in the past and that has continued at least up to the present. This tense is suitable for showing trends in the sense of showing changes over time.

> I <u>have been working</u> on this sketch for an hour.

> The profits <u>have been increasing</u> in the last quarter.

11. Past perfect progressive

Use this tense to emphasize the continuing nature of a single or repeated past action that was completed before or interrupted by some other past action:

> We <u>had all been expecting</u> something quite different.

> I <u>had been pondering</u> the problem for an hour when suddenly the solution popped into my head.

12. Future perfect progressive

This tense is seldom used in academic writing. Use it to emphasize the continuing nature of a future action before a specific time in the future or before a second future action:

> If she continues to dance, by the year 2023 she <u>will have been dancing</u> for over half her life.

8f   Tense Sequence

(EAL) When two or more verbs occur in the same sentence, they will sometimes be of the same tense, but often they will be of different tenses.

1. Compound sentences

In a compound sentence, the verbs can be equally independent; use whatever tenses the sense requires:

> I <u>am leaving</u> [present progressive] now, but she <u>will leave</u> [future] in the morning.

> The polls <u>have closed</u> [present perfect]; the clerks <u>will</u> soon <u>be counting</u> [future progressive] the ballots.

2. Past tense in independent clauses

In complex or compound-complex sentences, if the verb in an independent clause is in any of the past tenses, the verbs in any clauses subordinate to it will usually also be in one of the past tenses. For example:

> I <u>told</u> her that I <u>was</u> sorry.

> They <u>agreed</u> that this time the newly elected treasurer <u>would</u> not <u>be</u> a gambler.

Refer to a time *earlier* than that of the verb in the simple past tense by using the *past perfect* tense:

> We <u>had left</u> the party before they arrived.

But there are exceptions. When the verb in the subordinate clause states a general or timeless truth or belief, or something characteristic or habitual, it stays in the present tense:

> Einstein <u>showed</u> that space, time, and light <u>are</u> linked.

And the context of the sentence sometimes dictates that other kinds of verbs in subordinate clauses should not be changed to a past tense. If you feel that a tense other than the past would be clearer or more accurate, use it; for example:

> I <u>learned</u> yesterday that I <u>will be</u> able to get into the new program in the fall.

The rule calls for *would*, but *will* is logical and clear. Notice that the adverbial marker "in the fall" tells us the action will occur in the future.

Here is another example of a sentence in which the "sequence of tenses" rule is best ignored:

> The secretary <u>told</u> me this morning that Professor Barnes <u>is</u> ill and <u>will not be teaching</u> class this afternoon.

8

8g Mood

English verbs are usually considered to have three moods. The most common mood is the **indicative**, which is used for statements of fact or opinion and for questions:

> The weather forecast for tomorrow <u>sounds</u> promising.

The **imperative** mood is used for most commands and instructions:

> <u>Put</u> the picnic hamper in the trunk.

The **subjunctive** mood in English is less common, and it presents some challenges. It is fading from contemporary English. You need consider only two kinds of instances where the subjunctive still functions.

1. Use the subjunctive in a *that*-clause after verbs expressing demands, obligations, requirements, recommendations, suggestions, wishes, and the like:

   > The doctor recommended that she <u>take</u> a voyage.

   > I wish [that] I <u>were</u> in Paris.

2. Use the subjunctive to express conditions that are hypothetical or impossible—often in *if*-clauses or their equivalents:

   > He looked as if he <u>were</u> going to explode. (But he didn't explode.)

   > If Lise <u>were</u> here she <u>would</u> back me up. (But she isn't here.)

   An *as if* or *as though* clause almost always expresses a condition contrary to fact, but not all *if*-clauses do; don't be misled into using a subjunctive where it's not appropriate:

   > ***wrong:*** He said that if there <u>were</u> another complaint he would resign.

The verb should be *was*, for the condition could turn out to be true: there may be another complaint.

Since only a few subjunctive forms differ from those of the indicative, they are easy to learn and remember. The third-person-singular subjunctive form loses its *s*:

> *indicative:* I like the way she <u>paints</u>.
>
> *subjunctive:* I suggested that she <u>paint</u> my portrait.

The subjunctive forms of the verb *be* are *be* and *were:*

> *indicative:* He <u>is</u> friendly. (I <u>am</u>, you/we/ they <u>are</u>)
>
> *subjunctive:* The judge asked that she <u>be</u> excused. (that I/you/we/ they <u>be</u>)

> *indicative:* I know that I <u>am</u> in Edmonton.
>
> *subjunctive:* I wish that I <u>were</u> in Florence.

Note that both *be* and *were* function with either singular or plural subjects. Note also that the past-tense form *were* functions in present-tense expressions of wishes and contrary-to-fact conditions. Other verbs also use their past tense as a subjunctive after a present-tense wish:

> I wish that I <u>shopped</u> less.

After a past-tense wish, use the standard past-perfect form:

> He wished that he <u>had been</u> more attentive.

> She wished that she <u>had played</u> better.

 8h   Voice

There are two voices, *active* and *passive.* The active voice is direct: *I made this toy boat.* The passive voice is less direct, reversing the normal subject–verb–object pattern: *This toy boat was made by me.* The passive-voice verb uses some form of *be* followed by a past participle: *was made.* What in active voice would be a direct object (*boat*) in passive voice becomes the subject of the verb. And passive constructions often leave unmentioned the agent of the action or state they describe: *The toy boat was made* (by whom isn't specified).

The passive voice

Using the passive voice, some people can promise action without committing themselves to perform it, and they can admit error without accepting responsibility:

> *passive:* Be assured [by whom?] that action will be taken [by whom?].
>
> *active:* I assure you that I will act.
>
> *passive:* It is to be regretted [by whom?] that an error has been made [by whom?].
>
> *active:* I am sorry we made an error.

When possible, use the direct and more vigorous active voice.

> *passive:* Mixing the chemicals, hydrogen sulphide <u>was formed</u>.

In this example, describing an experiment, the passive not only is ineffective but also leads to a *dangling modifier*; there is no subject in the sentence to explain who is doing the mixing. The frequency of such errors is itself a good reason to be sparing with passive voice. The active voice eliminates the grammatical error:

> *active:* By mixing the chemicals, the chemist produced hydrogen sulphide.

WHEN TO USE THE PASSIVE VOICE
Use the passive voice when the active voice is impossible or when the passive is for some other reason clearly preferable or demanded by the context. Generally, use passive voice

- when the agent, or doer of the act, is indefinite or not known;
- when the agent is less important than the act itself; or
- when you want to emphasize either the agent or the act by putting it at the beginning or end of the sentence.

Note: Don't confuse passive constructions with the past tense just because the past participle is used. Passive constructions can appear in any of the tenses.

9 AGREEMENT BETWEEN SUBJECT AND VERB

A verb should agree with its subject in number and person. Here are the main circumstances to pay attention to in your own writing.

9a Words Intervening Between Subject and Verb

When something plural comes between a singular subject and its verb, the verb must still agree with the subject:

> Far below, a <u>landscape</u> of rolling brown hills and small trees <u>lies</u> among the small cottages.

> <u>Each</u> of the poems <u>has</u> certain striking qualities.

> <u>Neither</u> of the parties <u>was</u> willing to compromise.

Similarly, don't let an intervening singular noun affect the agreement between a plural subject and its verb.

9b Compound Subjects

1. A compound subject made up of two or more singular nouns joined by *and* is usually plural:

   > Careful thought and attention to detail <u>are</u> essential.

   Occasional exceptions occur. If two nouns identify the same person or thing, or if two nouns taken together are thought of as a unit, the verb is singular:

   > Macaroni and cheese <u>is</u> a student favourite.

   Note: Phrases such as *in addition to, as well as, along with,* and *together with* are prepositions, not conjunctions like *and*. A singular subject followed by one of them still takes a singular verb:

   > The cat as well as the dog <u>comes</u> when I whistle.

   > Ms. Hondiak, along with her daughters, <u>is</u> attending law school this year.

   Compound subjects preceded by *each* or *every* take a singular verb:

   > Each dog and cat <u>has</u> its own supper dish.

2. When the parts of a subject are joined by the coordinating conjunction *or* or by the correlative conjunctions *either . . . or, neither . . . nor, not . . . but, not only . . . but also,* or *whether . . . or,* the part nearest the verb determines whether the verb is singular or plural:

   > One or the other of you <u>has</u> the winning ticket. (both parts singular: verb singular; note that the subject is *one or the other,* not *you*)

   > Neither my parents nor I <u>was</u> to blame. (first part plural, second part singular: verb singular)

9c Agreement with Indefinite Pronouns

Most indefinite pronouns are singular: *another, anybody, anyone, anything, each, either, everybody, everyone, everything, much, neither, nobody, no one, nothing, one, other, somebody, someone, something.* A few (namely *all, any, more, most, none, some*) can be either singular or plural, depending on whether they refer to a single quantity or to a number of individual units within a group:

> <u>Some</u> of the pasta <u>is</u> eaten. (a single amount; *pasta* is singular, a mass noun)
> <u>Some</u> of the cookies <u>are</u> missing. (a number of cookies; *cookies* is plural)

> <u>All</u> of this novel <u>is</u> good. (a whole novel; *novel* is singular)
> <u>All</u> of his novels <u>are</u> well written. (a number of novels; *novels* is plural)

> <u>Most</u> of the champagne <u>was</u> drunk. (a single mass; *champagne* is singular)
> <u>Most</u> of the cases of champagne <u>have</u> been exported. (a number of cases; *cases* is plural)

> <u>None</u> of the work <u>is</u> finished. (a single unit; *work* is singular)
> <u>None</u> of the reports <u>are</u> ready. (a number of reports; *reports* is plural)

9d Subject Following Verb

When the normal subject–verb order is reversed, the verb still must agree with the real subject, not some word that happens to precede it:

> There <u>is</u> only one <u>answer</u> to this question.
> There <u>are</u> several possible <u>solutions</u> to the problem.

> Here <u>comes</u> the judge.
> Here <u>come</u> the clowns.

When compounded singular nouns follow an opening *there* or *here*, most writers make the verb agree with the first noun:

> There <u>was</u> <u>a computer</u> and <u>a copier</u> in the next room.

But others find this kind of syntax awkward sounding. By rephrasing the sentence you can easily avoid the issue and save a few words as well:

> A computer and a copier were in the next room.

9e Agreement with Relative Pronouns

Whether a relative pronoun is singular or plural depends on its antecedent. Therefore when a relative clause has *who*, *which*, or *that* as its subject, the verb must agree in number with the pronoun's antecedent:

> Her success is due to her intelligence and perseverance, which <u>have</u> overcome all obstacles. (The antecedent of *which* is *intelligence and perseverance*.)

Questions about agreement most often occur with the phrases *one of those . . . who* and *one of the . . . who*:

> He is one of those people who <u>have</u> difficulty presenting.

Have is correct, since the antecedent of *who* is the plural *people*, not the singular *one*.

10 ADJECTIVES

An **adjective** modifies—limits, qualifies, particularizes—a noun or pronoun. Adjectives generally answer the questions *Which? What kind of? How many? How much?*

> <u>The</u> <u>black</u> cat was <u>hungry</u>; he ate <u>five</u> sardines and drank <u>some</u> milk.

10a Kinds of Adjectives

Adjectives fall into two major classes: **non-descriptive** and **descriptive.**

1. Non-descriptive adjectives

The several kinds of **non-descriptive** adjectives include some that are basically *structure words*:

- **articles**: *a*, *an*, *the*
- **demonstrative adjectives**:

  <u>this</u> hat   <u>that</u> problem

  <u>these</u> women   <u>those</u> books

- **interrogative and relative adjectives**:

  <u>Which</u> book is best?   <u>What</u> time is it?

  <u>Whose</u> opinion do you trust?

  She is the one <u>whose</u> opinion I trust.

- **possessive adjectives**—the possessive forms of personal and impersonal pronouns and of nouns):

  <u>my</u> book   <u>her</u> car   <u>its</u> colour

  <u>their</u> heritage   <u>one's</u> beliefs   a <u>man's</u> coat

  the <u>river's</u> mouth <u>Hamlet's</u> ego   <u>Shirley's</u> job

  the <u>car's</u> engine

- **indefinite and numerical adjectives**:

  <u>some</u> money   <u>any</u> time   <u>more</u> fuel

  <u>several</u> keys   <u>three</u> ducks   <u>thirty</u> ships

  the <u>fourth</u> act   <u>much</u> sushi

2. Descriptive adjectives

Descriptive adjectives give information about such matters as the size, shape, colour, nature, and quality of whatever a noun or pronoun names:

  a <u>tempting</u> dessert   a <u>well-done</u> steak

  a <u>once-in-a-lifetime</u> chance   <u>Canadian</u> literature

  an <u>experimental</u> play   <u>composted</u> leaves

  a <u>fascinating</u> place <u>to visit</u>   a <u>dictionary</u> definition

  <u>looking refreshed</u>, he . . .   the man <u>of the hour</u>

the festival <u>to exceed all others</u>

the rabbits <u>who caused all the trouble</u>

a <u>large</u>, <u>impressive</u>, <u>three-storey</u>, <u>grey</u>, <u>Victorian</u> house

As these examples illustrate, adjectival modifiers can be single, in groups or series, or in compounds; they can be proper adjectives, formed from proper nouns; they can be words that are adjectives only or words that can also function as other parts of speech, including nouns functioning as adjectives; they can be present participles, past participles, or infinitives; they can be participial phrases, infinitive phrases, or prepositional phrases; or they can be relative clauses.

10b Comparison of Descriptive Adjectives

Most descriptive adjectives can be inflected or supplemented for *degree* in order to make *comparisons*. The basic or dictionary form of an adjective is called its **positive** form: *high*, *difficult*, *calm*. Use it to compare two things that are equal or similar, or with qualifiers such as *not* and *almost* that are dissimilar:

This assignment is <u>as difficult as</u> last week's.

It is <u>not nearly so difficult as</u> I expected.

To make the **comparative** form, add *er* or put *more* (or *less*) in front of the positive form: *higher*, *calmer*, *more difficult*, *less difficult*. Use it to compare two unequal things:

My grades are <u>higher</u> now than they were last year.

Your part is <u>more difficult</u> than mine.

For the **superlative** form, add *est* or put *most* (or *least*) in front of the positive form: *highest*, *calmest*, *most difficult*, *least difficult*. Generally, use it to compare three or more unequal things:

Whose talent is the <u>greatest</u>?

He is the <u>calmest</u> and <u>least pretentious</u> person I know.

10

You can usually follow these guidelines:

- For adjectives of one syllable, usually add *er* and *est*:

Positive	**Comparative**	**Superlative**
short	shorter	shortest

- For adjectives of *three or more* syllables, usually use *more* and *most* (or *less* and *least*):

beautiful	more beautiful	most beautiful
tiresome	more tiresome	most tiresome

- For most adjectives of two syllables ending in *al, ect, ed, ent, ful, ic, id, ing, ish, ive, less,* and *ous* (and any others where an added *er* or *est* would sound wrong), generally use *more* and *most* (or *less* and *least*):

formal	more formal	most formal
direct	more direct	most direct
polished	more polished	most polished
potent	more potent	most potent
tactful	more tactful	most tactful

- For other adjectives of two syllables, you usually have a choice; for example:

gentle	gentler, more gentle	gentlest, most gentle
lively	livelier, more lively	liveliest, most lively

When there is a choice, the forms with *more* and *most* will usually sound more formal and more emphatic than those with *er* and *est*.

However, adjectives of three or more syllables, and even shorter ones ending in *ous* and *ful* and so on, almost always require *more* and *most*.

Note: A few commonly used adjectives form their comparative and superlative degrees irregularly:

good	better	best
bad	worse	worst
far	farther; further	farthest; furthest

| little | littler; less, lesser | littlest; least |
| much, many | more | most |

Good dictionaries list all irregular forms after the basic entry, including those in which a spelling change occurs.

 10c Placement and Ordering of Adjectives

1. Placement of adjectives

Adjectival modifiers usually come just before or just after what they modify. Articles always, and other determiners almost always, precede the nouns they modify, usually with either no intervening words or only one or two other adjectives:

> Trying to save <u>some</u> money, <u>the</u> manager decided to close <u>his</u> store early.

> <u>The wise</u> manager decided not to hire <u>his scatterbrained</u> nephew.

Predicate adjectives almost always follow the subject and linking verb:

> The forest is <u>cool</u> and <u>green</u> and <u>full of mushrooms</u>.

> Shortly after his operation he again became <u>healthy</u>.

Adjectives serving as *objective complements* usually follow the subject–verb–direct object:

> I thought the suggestion <u>preposterous</u>.

Most other single-word adjectives, and many compound adjectives, precede the nouns they modify:

> The <u>tall</u>, <u>dark</u>, and <u>handsome</u> hero lives on only in <u>romantic</u> fiction.

Compound adjectives and adjectives in phrases are often comfortable after a noun:

> Elfrida, <u>radiant and delighted</u>, left the room, <u>secure</u> in her victory.

10

Relative clauses and various kinds of phrases customarily follow the nouns they modify:

> He is one detective <u>who believes in being thorough</u>.

> The president <u>of the company</u> will retire next month.

The only adjectival modifier not generally restricted in its position is the participial phrase:

> <u>Having had abundant experience</u>, Kenneth applied for the job.

> Kenneth, <u>having had abundant experience</u>, applied for the job.

> Kenneth applied for the job, <u>having had abundant experience</u>.

2. Ordering of adjectives

(EAL) Adjectives usually follow an idiomatic order: a determiner (an article, possessive, or demonstrative) comes first, then numbers, then adjectives that express a general description, followed by physical-state adjectives (including age, size, shape, colour, and temperature), proper adjectives, and then noun adjuncts (including adjectives ending in "ic(al)" or "al") before the main noun. The following examples illustrate this order:

> the one brilliant young Canadian movie star

> their third expensive white impractical chesterfield

> a sophisticated small Indian restaurant

> your four new square sushi dishes

> Sue's two funny daring Swedish theatrical friends

11 ADVERBS

Adverbs are often thought of as especially tricky. This part of speech is sometimes called the "catch-all" category, since any word that doesn't seem to fit elsewhere is usually assumed to be an adverb. Adverbs, therefore, are a little more complicated than adjectives.

11a Kinds and Functions of Adverbs

Whereas adjectives can modify only nouns and pronouns, adverbs can modify *verbs*, *adjectives*, other *adverbs*, and *independent clauses* or whole *sentences*. Adverbial modifiers generally answer such questions as *How? When? Where? Why?* and *To what degree?* That is, they indicate such things as *manner* (How?); *time* (When? How often? How long?); *place* and *direction* (Where? In what direction?); *cause*, *result*, and *purpose* (Why? To what effect?); and *degree* (To what degree? To what extent?). They also express affirmation and negation, conditions, concessions, and comparisons. Here are some examples:

> Fully expecting to fail, he slumped disconsolately in his seat and began the examination.

To what degree? *Fully*: the adverb of degree modifies the participial (verbal) phrase *expecting to fail*. How? *Disconsolately*: the adverb of manner modifies the verb *slumped*. Where? *In his seat*: the prepositional phrase functions as an adverb of place modifying the verb *slumped*.

> Because their budget was tight, they eventually decided not to buy a car.

Why? *Because their budget was tight*: the adverbial clause of cause modifies the verb *decided* or, in a way, all the rest of the sentence. When? *Eventually*: the adverb of time modifies the verb *decided*. The negating *not* modifies the infinitive (verbal) *to buy*.

> If you're tired, I will walk the dog.

The conditional clause modifies the verb (*will walk*).

> Although she dislikes the city *intensely*, she agreed to go *there* in order to keep peace *in the family*.

Intensely (degree) modifies the verb *dislikes*. *There* (place) modifies the infinitive *to go*. *Although she dislikes the city intensely* is an adverbial clause of concession. The prepositional phrase *in order to keep peace in the family* is an adverb of purpose modifying the verb *agreed*. The smaller adverbial prepositional phrase *in the family* modifies the infinitive phrase *to keep peace*, answering the question *Where?*

> Meredith was <u>better</u> prepared <u>than I was</u>.

The adverb *better* modifies the adjective *prepared*; it and the clause *than I was* express comparison or contrast.

Adverbs as condensed clauses
Some single-word adverbs and adverbial phrases, especially sentence modifiers, can be thought of as reduced clauses:

> <u>Fortunately</u> [It is fortunate that], the cut was not deep.

> <u>When possible</u> [When it is possible], let your writing sit <u>before proofreading it</u> [before you proofread it].

Other kinds of adverbs: relative, interrogative, conjunctive

1. The **relative adverbs** *where* and *when* are used to introduce relative (adjective) clauses:

   > She returned to the town <u>where she had grown up</u>.

   > Adam looked forward to the moment <u>when it would be his turn</u>.

2. The **interrogative adverbs** (*where*, *when*, *why*, and *how*) are used in questions:

   > <u>Where</u> are you going? <u>Why</u>? <u>How</u> soon? <u>How</u> will you get there? <u>When</u> will you return?

3. **Conjunctive adverbs** usually join whole clauses or sentences to each other and indicate the nature of the connection:

Only fifteen people showed up. <u>Nevertheless</u>, the promoter didn't let his disappointment show.

The tornado almost flattened the town; <u>however</u>, only Dorothy and her dog were reported missing.

Note: Since conjunctive adverbs can easily be shifted around within a clause, you may find it helpful to apply this test if you aren't sure whether a particular word is a conjunctive adverb or a conjunction. Just remember that adverbs can move around in the sentence; conjunctions cannot.

Only Dorothy and her dog, however, were reported missing.

11b   Comparison of Adverbs

Like descriptive adjectives, most adverbs that are similarly descriptive can be inflected or supplemented for degree. The following are some guidelines on how adverbs are inflected:

- Some short adverbs without *ly* form their comparative and superlative degrees with *er* and *est*; for example:

Positive	Comparative	Superlative
fast	faster	fastest
hard	harder	hardest
high	higher	highest

- *Less* and *least* also sometimes go with these; for example:

Students work <u>least hard</u> on the days following an exam.

They still ran fast, but <u>less fast</u> than they had the day before.

- Adverbs of three or more syllables ending in *ly* use *more* and *most*, *less* and *least*; for example:

happily	more happily	most happily
stridently	less stridently	least stridently

- Most two-syllable adverbs, whether or not they end in *ly*, also use *more* and *most*, *less* and *least*, though a few can also be inflected with *er* and *est*; for example:

slowly	more slowly	most slowly
grimly	less grimly	least grimly
alone	more alone	most alone
kindly	more kindly	most kindly

- Some adverbs form their comparative and superlative degrees irregularly:

badly	worse	worst
well	better	best
much	more	most
little	less	least
far	farther, further	farthest, furthest

- A few adverbs of place use *farther* and *farthest*; for example:

down	farther down	farthest down
north	farther north	farthest north

- As with adjectives, the adverbs *much*, *far*, and *by far* serve as intensifiers in comparisons:

  Bob and Louise live <u>much</u> more comfortably than they used to.

  They flew <u>far</u> lower than they should have.

  He practises harder <u>by far</u> than anyone else in the orchestra.

11c Placement of Adverbs

1. Adverbs modifying adjectives or other adverbs

An intensifying or qualifying adverb almost always goes just before the adjective or adverb it modifies:

<u>almost</u> always   <u>strongly</u> confident   <u>very</u> hot

<u>only</u> two   <u>most</u> surely

2. Modifiers of verbs

Whether single words, phrases, or clauses, most modifiers of verbs are more flexible in their position than are any other part of speech. Often they can go almost anywhere in a sentence and still function clearly:

<u>Proudly</u>, he pointed to his photo in the paper.

He <u>proudly</u> pointed to his photo in the paper.

He pointed <u>proudly</u> to his photo in the paper.

He pointed to his photo in the paper <u>proudly</u>.

3. Sentence modifiers

Sentence modifiers usually come at the beginning, but they, too, can be placed elsewhere for purposes of emphasis or rhythm:

<u>Fortunately</u>, the groom was able to stand.

The groom, <u>fortunately</u>, was able to stand.

The groom was, <u>fortunately</u>, able to stand.

The groom was able to stand, <u>fortunately</u>.

With longer or more involved sentences, however, a sentence modifier at the end loses much of its force and point, obviously; obviously it works better if placed earlier, as this sentence demonstrates. (See also #16b, on the placement and punctuation of conjunctive adverbs, and #5d, on misplaced modifiers.)

12 VERBALS

Infinitives, participles, and gerunds are called **verbals**, forms that are derived from verbs but that cannot function as main or finite verbs. Verbals are **non-finite** forms, not restricted by person and number as finite verbs are. They function as other parts of speech yet retain some characteristics of verbs: they can have objects, they can be modified by adverbs, and they can express tense and voice. Verbals often introduce *verbal phrases*, groups of words that themselves function as other parts of speech. Verbals enable you to inject much of the strength and liveliness of verbs into your writing even though the words are functioning as adjectives, adverbs, and nouns.

12a Infinitives

An infinitive usually consists of the word *to* (often called "the sign of the infinitive") followed by the basic form: *to be, to live*. Infinitives can function as *nouns*, *adjectives*, and *adverbs*.

1. Infinitives as nouns

> To save the wolves was Farley Mowat's primary intention.

The infinitive phrase *To save the wolves* is the subject of the verb *was*. The noun *wolves* is the direct object of the infinitive *To save*.

> She wanted to end the game quickly.

The infinitive phrase *to end the game quickly* is the direct object of the verb *wanted*.

2. Infinitives as adjectives

> His strong desire to be a doctor made him studious.

The infinitive phrase *to be a doctor* modifies the noun *desire*. Since *be* is a linking verb, the infinitive is here followed by the predicate noun *doctor*.

> The cappuccino coupons are the ones <u>to save</u>.

The infinitive *to save* modifies the pronoun *ones*.

3. Infinitives as adverbs

> She was lucky <u>to have</u> such a friend.

The infinitive phrase *to have such a friend* modifies the predicate adjective *lucky*. The noun phrase *such a friend* is the direct object of the infinitive *to have*.

> He went to Niagara-on-the-Lake <u>to experience</u> the Shaw Festival.

The infinitive phrase *to experience the Shaw Festival* is an adverb of purpose modifying the verb *went; the Shaw Festival* is the direct object of the infinitive *to experience*.

 Participles

The **past participle** and **present participle** work with various auxiliaries to form a finite verb's *perfect* and *progressive* tenses. But without the auxiliaries to indicate *person* and *number*, the participles are non-finite and cannot function as verbs. Instead they function as *adjectives*, modifying nouns and pronouns:

> <u>Beaming</u> happily, Josef received his well-deserved diploma.

Present participles always end in *ing*, regular past participles in *ed* or *d*. Irregular past participles end variously: *made*, *mown*, *broken*, etc. A regular past participle is identical to the past-tense form of a verb, but you can easily check a given word's function in a sentence. In the example above, the past-tense form *received* clearly has *Josef* as its subject; the past participle *deserved*, with no subject, is an adjective modifying *diploma*. More examples:

> <u>Painted</u> houses require more care than brick ones.

The past participle *painted* modifies the noun *houses*.

> <u>Impressed</u>, she recounted the film's more <u>thrilling</u> episodes.

The past participle *impressed* modifies the subject, *she*; the present participle *thrilling* modifies the noun *episodes* and is itself modified by the adverb *more*.

> The subject <u>discussed</u> most often was the message behind the song.

The past participle *discussed* modifies the noun *subject* and is itself modified by the adverbial *most often*.

> Suddenly <u>finding</u> himself alone, he became very <u>flustered</u>.

The present participle *finding* introduces the participial phrase *finding himself alone*, which modifies the subject, *he*; *finding*, as a verbal, has *himself* as a direct object and is modified by the adverb *suddenly*. The past participle *flustered* functions as a predicate adjective after the linking verb *became*; it modifies *he* and is itself modified by the adverb *very*.

12

12c Gerunds

When the *ing* form of a verb functions as a noun, it is called a **gerund**:

> André gave himself a good <u>talking</u> to.

> <u>Moving</u> offices can be hard work.

> Sylvester has a profound fear of <u>flying</u>.

> Careful preparation—<u>brainstorming</u>, <u>organizing</u>, and <u>outlining</u>—helps produce good essays.

The gerund *talking* is a direct object and is itself modified by the adjective *good*. The gerund *Moving* is the subject of the sentence, and has *offices* as a direct object. The gerund *flying* is the object of the preposition *of*. In the final example, the three gerunds constitute an appositive or definition of the subject noun, *preparation*.

Note: In formal usage, a noun or a personal pronoun preceding a gerund will usually be in the possessive case:

His cooking left much to be desired.

She approved of Bob's cleaning the house.

 # 13 CONNECTING WORDS; INTERJECTIONS

This section on the parts of speech will conclude with a look at connecting words (prepositions and conjunctions) and emotive words (interjections).

13a Prepositions

Prepositions are structure words or function words; they do not change their form. A preposition is part of a prepositional phrase, and it usually precedes the rest of the phrase, which includes a noun or pronoun as the object of the preposition:

> She sent an e-mail to her spouse.

Make a question of the preposition and ask *what* or *whom* and the answer will always be the object: *To* whom? Her spouse.

1. Functions of prepositions and prepositional phrases
A preposition *links* its object to some other word in the sentence; the prepositional phrase then functions as either an *adjectival* or an *adverbial* modifier:

> He laid the camera on the table.

Here, *on* links *table* to the verb *laid*; the phrase *on the table* therefore functions as an adverb describing *where* the camera was laid.

> It was a time for celebration.

Here, *for* links *celebration* to the noun *time*; the phrase therefore functions as an adjective indicating *what kind of* time.

2. Placement of prepositions

Usually, like articles, prepositions signal that a noun or pronoun soon follows. But prepositions can also come at the ends of clauses or sentences, for example in a question, for emphasis, or to avoid stiffness:

> Which backpack do you want to look <u>at</u>?

> They had several issues to contend <u>with</u>.

It isn't wrong to end a sentence or clause with a preposition, in spite of what many people have been taught; just don't do it so often that it calls attention to itself.

3. Common prepositions

Most prepositions indicate a spatial or temporal relation, or such things as purpose, concession, comparison, manner, and agency. Here is a list of common prepositions; note that several consist of more than one word:

13

about	beneath	in front of	past
above	beside	in order to	regarding
according to	besides	in place of	regardless of
across	between	in relation to	round
across from	beyond	inside	since
after	but	in spite of	such as
against	by	into	through
ahead of	by way of	like	throughout
along	concerning	near	till
alongside	considering	next to	to
among	contrary to	notwithstanding	toward(s)
apart from	despite	of	under
around	down	off	underneath
as	during	on	unlike
as for	except	on account of	until
at	except for	onto	up

away from	excepting	on top of	upon
because of	for	opposite	with
before	from	out	within
behind	in	outside	without
below	in addition to	over	

A learner's dictionary will be extremely helpful in guiding you in the use of prepositions.

13b Conjunctions: Coordinate, Correlative, Subordinate

Conjunctions are another kind of structure word or function word. As their name indicates, conjunctions are words that "join together." There are three kinds of conjunctions: *coordinating, correlative,* and *subordinating.*

1. Coordinating conjunctions
There are only seven **coordinating conjunctions,** so they are easy to remember:

and   but   for   nor   or   so   yet

When you use a coordinating conjunction, choose the appropriate one. *And* indicates addition, *nor* indicates negative addition (equivalent to *also not*), *but* and *yet* indicate contrast or opposition, *or* indicates choice, *for* indicates cause or reason, and *so* indicates effect or result.

Coordinating conjunctions have three main functions, which are discussed below.

JOINING WORDS, PHRASES, AND SUBORDINATE CLAUSES
And, but, or, and *yet* join coordinate elements within sentences. The elements joined are usually of equal importance and of similar grammatical structure and function. When joined, they are sometimes called compounds. Here are examples of how various kinds of sentence elements may be compounded:

I saw <u>Jean</u> and <u>Ralph</u>. (two direct objects)

<u>Jean</u> and <u>Ralph</u> saw me. (two subjects)

> They <u>whooped</u> and <u>hollered</u>. (two verbs)
>
> The gnome was <u>short</u>, <u>fat</u>, and <u>melancholic</u>. (three predicate adjectives)
>
> He ate <u>fast</u> and <u>noisily</u>. (two adverbs)
>
> The bird flew <u>in the door</u> and <u>out the window</u>. (two adverbial prepositional phrases)
>
> <u>Tired</u> but <u>determined</u>, the hiker plodded on. (two past participles)
>
> People <u>who invest wisely</u> and <u>who spend carefully</u> often have boring lives. (two adjective clauses)

Obviously the elements being joined won't always have identical structures, but don't disappoint readers' natural expectations that compound elements will be parallel.

When three or more elements are compounded, the conjunction usually appears only between the last two, though *and* and *or* can appear throughout for purposes of rhythm or emphasis:

> There was a tug-of-war <u>and</u> a sack race <u>and</u> an egg race <u>and</u> a three-legged race <u>and</u> . . . well, there was just about any kind of game anyone could want at a picnic.

JOINING INDEPENDENT CLAUSES

All seven coordinating conjunctions can join independent clauses to make compound (or compound-complex) sentences. The clauses will be grammatically equivalent, since they are independent; but they needn't be grammatically parallel or even of similar length, though they often are both, for parallelism is a strong stylistic force. Here are some examples:

> The players fought, the umpires shouted, <u>and</u> the fans booed.
>
> Jean saw me, <u>but</u> Ralph didn't.

> I won't do it, <u>nor</u> will she. (With *nor* there must be some sort of negative in the first clause. Note that after *nor* the normal subject–verb order is reversed.)

> There was no way to avoid it, <u>so</u> I decided to get as much out of the experience as I could.

JOINING SENTENCES

In spite of what many of us have been taught, it isn't wrong to begin a sentence with *And* or *But*, or for that matter any of the other coordinating conjunctions. Be advised, however, that *For*, since it is so similar in meaning to *because*, often sounds strange at the start of a sentence, as if introducing a fragmentary subordinate clause. *And* and *But* make good openers—as long as you don't overuse them. An opening *But* or *Yet* can nicely emphasize a contrast or other turn of thought. An opening *And* can also be emphatic:

> He told the employees of the company he was sorry. <u>And</u> he meant it.

For punctuation with coordinating conjunctions, see Part IV.

2. Correlative conjunctions

 Correlative conjunctions come in pairs. They *correlate* ("relate together") two parallel parts of a sentence. The following are the principal ones:

either . . . or	neither . . . nor
whether . . . or	both . . . and
not . . . but	not only . . . but also

Correlative conjunctions enable you to write sentences containing forcefully balanced elements, but don't overdo them. They are also more at home in formal than in informal writing. Some examples:

> <u>Either</u> Rodney <u>or</u> Elliott is going to drive.

> She accepted <u>neither</u> the first <u>nor</u> the second job offer.

<u>Whether</u> by accident <u>or</u> by design, the number turned out to be exactly right.

<u>Both</u> the administration <u>and</u> the student body are pleased with the new plan.

She <u>not only</u> plays well <u>but also</u> sings well.

<u>Not only</u> does she play well, <u>but</u> she <u>also</u> sings well.

Notice, in the last two examples, how *also* (or its equivalent) can be moved away from the *but*. And in the last example, note how *does* is needed as an auxiliary because the clause is in the present tense. Except for these variations, make what follows one term exactly parallel to what follows the other: *the first || the second*; *by accident || by design*; *plays well || sings well*.

Further, with the *not only . . . but also* pair, you should usually make the *also* (or some equivalent) explicit. Its omission results in a feeling of incompleteness:

incomplete: He was not only smart, but charming.

complete: He was not only smart, but also charming.

complete: He was not only smart, but charming as well.

To ensure that you use this correlative pairing effectively, keep in mind the following:

a. For clauses containing *compound verbs* (one or more auxiliary verbs attached to a main verb), place *not only* at the beginning of the clause and then place the first auxiliary verb *before* the subject. Then, place *but* before the subject of the second clause and *also* after the auxiliary verb.

He has been a great star and he has served his fans well.

<u>Not only</u> has he been a great star, <u>but</u> he has <u>also</u> served his fans well.

b. For sentences in the *simple present* or *simple past* tenses (other than those in which the main verb is *to be*), you must add the appropriate form of *do/does/*

did before the subject of the *not only* clause when *not only* appears at the beginning of the clause.

> She looks rested and she looks happy.
> Not only *does* she look rested, <u>but</u> she <u>also</u> looks happy.

> She looked rested and she looked happy.
> Not only *did* she look rested, <u>but</u> she <u>also</u> looked happy.

> She is rested and she is happy.
> Not only *is* she rested, <u>but</u> she is <u>also</u> happy.

c. When *not only* appears inside the clause, you do not have to reverse the order of the auxiliary verb and subject, nor do you have to add *do/does/did*.

> She has worked hard at her job and at her hobbies.

> She has worked hard <u>not only</u> at her job <u>but also</u> at her hobbies.

3. Subordinating conjunctions

A **subordinating conjunction** introduces a *subordinate* (or *dependent*) clause and links it to the *independent* (or *main* or *principal*) clause to which it is grammatically related:

> She writes <u>because</u> she has something to say.

The subordinating conjunction *because* introduces the adverbial clause *because she has something to say* and links it to the independent clause whose verb it modifies. The *because*-clause is *subordinate* because it cannot stand by itself: by itself it would be a *fragment*. Note that a subordinate clause can also come first:

> <u>Because</u> she has something to say, she writes articles for magazines.

> <u>That</u> Raj will win the prize is a foregone conclusion.

Here *That* introduces the noun clause *That Raj will win the prize*, which functions as the subject of the sentence.

Note that whereas a coordinating conjunction is like a spot of glue between two structures and not a part of either, a subordinating conjunction is an integral part of its clause. In the following sentence, for example, the subordinating conjunction *whenever* is a part of the adverbial clause that modifies the imperative verb *Leave*:

> Leave <u>whenever you feel tired</u>.

Here is a list of the principal subordinating conjunctions:

after	if	that	where(ever)
although	if only	though	whereas
as	in case	till	whether
as though	lest	unless	which
because	once	until	while
before	rather than	what	who
even though	since	whatever	why
ever since	than	when(ever)	

There are also many terms consisting of two or more words ending in *as*, *if*, and *that* that serve as subordinating conjunctions, including *inasmuch as, insofar as, as long as, as soon as, as far as, as if, even if, only if, but that, except that, now that, in that, provided that*, and *in order that*.

13c Interjections

An **interjection** is a word or group of words *interjected* or dropped into a sentence in order to express emotion. Strictly speaking, interjections have no grammatical function; they are simply thrust into sentences and play no part in their syntax, though sometimes they act like sentence modifiers. They are often used in dialogue and are not that common in academic writing.

> But—<u>good heavens!</u>—what did you expect?

> <u>Gosh</u>, what fun!

> It was, <u>well</u>, a bit of a disappointment.

A mild interjection is usually set off with commas. A strong interjection is sometimes set off with dashes and is often accompanied by an exclamation point. An interjection may also be a minor sentence by itself:

Ouch! That hurt!

The style of a piece of writing is largely determined by diction: by choice of words, figurative language, and sounds. Diction, then, is near the heart of effective writing and style. This section isolates the principal challenges writers encounter in choosing and using words and offers some suggestions for meeting them.

14a Level

14

In any piece of writing, use words that are appropriate to you, to your topic, and to the circumstances in which you are writing. Consider the *occasion*, the *purpose*, and the *audience*. Avoid words and phrases that call attention to themselves rather than to the meaning you want to convey. In writing a formal academic essay, adopt diction appropriate to the discipline *in which* and the audience *for which* you are writing. In other writing for your courses or for the workplace, avoid slang and colloquial or informal terms at one extreme, and pretentious language at the other. It is usually preferable to adopt a straightforward, moderate style, a level of diction that respects the intelligence of the reader and strives to communicate with the reader as effectively as possible.

1. Slang

Since **slang** is diction opposite to **formal diction**, it is seldom appropriate in a formal context.

If you are considering using slang in your writing, consult not only one or more good dictionaries but also members of your audience: trust your ear, your common sense, and your good taste. If you do use a slang term, do not use quotation marks to call attention to it.

2. Informal, colloquial

Even dictionaries can't agree on what constitutes slang versus **informal** or **colloquial** usage. There are many words and phrases that may be labelled *inf* or *colloq* in a dictionary, and although not slang, they do not ordinarily belong in formal writing. For example, unless you are aiming for a somewhat informal level, you should avoid such abbreviations as *esp.*, *etc.*, *no.*, *orig.*, and *OK*; and you may wish to avoid contractions (*can't*, *don't*, etc.), though they are common in our own discourse in this book and in everyday speech.

3. "Fine writing"

Unnecessarily formal or pretentious diction is called "fine writing"—here, an ironic term of disapproval. Efforts to impress with such writing often backfire. Imagine yourself trying to take seriously someone who wrote "It was felicitous that the canine in question was demonstrably more exuberant in emitting threatening sounds than in attempting to implement said threats by engaging in actual physical assault," instead of simply saying "Luckily, the dog's bark was worse than its bite." This is an exaggerated example; but it illustrates how important it is to be straightforward.

14b Concrete and Abstract Diction

1. Concreteness and specificity

Concrete words denote tangible things, capable of being apprehended by our physical senses (*children*, *skyscraper*, *flowers*). **Abstract** words denote intangibles, like ideas or qualities (*postmodernism*, *agriculture*, *nature*). Much of the writing you do is a blend of the abstract and the concrete. The more concrete your writing, the more readily your readers will grasp it, for the concreteness will provide images for their imaginations to respond to. If you write

Transportation is becoming a major problem in our city.

and leave it at that, readers will understand you. But if you write, or add,

> In the downtown core of this city, far too many cars and far too few buses travel the streets.

you know that your readers will see exactly what you mean: in their minds they will see the traffic jams and the over-loaded buses.

As your writing moves from generalizations to specifics, it will move from the abstract to the concrete. *General* and *specific* are relative terms: a general word designates a *class* (e.g. *modes of transportation*); a more specific word desig-nates members of that class (*vehicles, ships, airplanes*); a still more specific word designates members of a still smaller class (*cars, trucks, bicycles, buses*); and so on, getting nar-rower, the classes and sub-classes getting smaller, until—if one needs to go that far—one arrives at a single, unique item, a class of one, such as the particular car sitting in your own parking spot.

Of course it is appropriate to write about "plant life," and then to narrow it, say, to "flowers"; and if you can write about "marigolds," "roses," "daffodils," and so on, you'll be more specific. Don't vaguely write "We experienced a warm day" when you could write more clearly, "We stayed outdoors all afternoon in the 25-degree weather," or "We basked in the warm spring sunshine all afternoon."

Of course, abstract and general terms are legitimate and often necessary, for one can scarcely present all ideas con-cretely. Try, though, to be as concrete and specific as your subject and the context will allow.

2. Weak generalizations

A common weakness of student writing is an overdepend-ence on unsupported generalizations. Consider: "Children today are reluctant readers." Few readers would or should accept such a general assertion, for the statement calls for considerably more illustration, evidence, and qualification. It evokes all kinds of questions: All children? Of all ages? In all countries? What are they reluctant to read? What is the connotation of *reluctant* here? Is such reluctance really

14

something new? Merely stating a generalization or assumption is not enough; to be clear and effective it must be illustrated and supported by specifics.

14c Euphemisms

Euphemisms are substitutes for words whose meanings are felt to be unpleasant and therefore, in certain circumstances, undesirable. In social settings we tend to ask for the location not of the toilet, which is what we want, but of the restroom, the bathroom, the washroom, or the powder room.

But the euphemism is sometimes abused. Euphemisms used to gloss over some supposed unpleasantness may deceive. Innocent civilians killed in bombing raids are referred to as "collateral damage," and assassination squads are termed "special forces." What was once an economic depression is now, in an attempt to mitigate its negative implications, termed a "recession," or an "economic downturn," or even a mere "growth cycle slowdown." Government officials who have patently lied admit only that they "misspoke" themselves.

Such euphemisms commonly imply a degree of dignity and virtue not justified by the facts. Calling genocide "ethnic cleansing" seriously distorts the meanings of both "ethnic" and "cleansing." Some euphemisms cloud or attempt to hide the facts in other ways. Workers are "laid off" or "declared redundant" or even "downsized" rather than "fired." An escalation in warfare is described as a "troop surge"; a civil war is referred to as "factional unrest" or "an insurgency." George Orwell, in his 1946 essay "Politics and the English Language," referred to such usages as linguistic dishonesty.

Other euphemisms help people avoid the unpleasant reality of death, which is often called "passing away" or "loss"; the lifeless body, the cadaver or corpse, is deemed "the remains." Such usages may be acceptable, even desirable, in certain circumstances, since they may enable one to avoid aggravating the pain and grief of the bereaved. But in other circumstances, direct, more precise diction is preferable.

14d Wrong Words

Any error in diction is a "wrong word," but a particular kind of incorrect word choice is customarily marked **wrong word**. The use of *infer* where the correct word is *imply* is an example. Don't write *effect* when you mean *affect*. Other kinds of wrong word choices occur as well; here are a few examples:

ww: Late in the summer I met my best friend, <u>which</u> I hadn't seen since graduation.

ww: Many miles of beach on the west coast of Vancouver Island are <u>absent</u> of rocks.

Whom, not *which*, is the correct pronoun for a person. The wrong phrase came to the second writer's mind; *devoid of* was the one wanted.

14

14e Idiom

(EAL) A particular kind of word choice has to do with **idiom**. An idiom is an expression peculiar to a given language, one that may not make logical or grammatical sense but that is understood because it is customary. Here are some peculiarly English turns of phrase: *to have a go at, to be at loose ends.* These idioms have a colloquial flavour about them, and may even sound like clichés or euphemisms; but other similar idioms are a part of our everyday language and occur in formal writing as well; for example: to "do justice to" something, to "take after" someone, to "get along with" someone.

Most mistakes in idiom result from using a wrong preposition in combination with certain other words. For example, we get *in* or *into* a car, but *on* or *onto* a bus; one is usually angry *with* a person, but *at* a thing. Here are some examples of errors in idiom:

incorrect: Her feelings <u>toward</u> her new job are mixed.
(*correct*: feelings about)

> *incorrect:* She took the liberty <u>to introduce</u> herself to the group. (*correct:* liberty of introducing)

> *incorrect:* He plans to get married <u>with</u> my youngest sister. (*correct:* get married to)

Idiomatic expressions sometimes involve choosing between an infinitive and a prepositional gerund phrase. After some expressions either is acceptable; for example:

> He is afraid <u>to lose</u>. He is afraid <u>of losing</u>.

> They are hesitant <u>to attend</u>. They are hesitant <u>about attending</u>.

But some terms call for one or the other:

> They propose <u>to go</u>. They are prepared <u>to go</u>.

> They insist <u>on going</u>. They are insistent <u>on going</u>.

Idiom is a matter of usage. But a good learner's dictionary such as the *Oxford Advanced Learner's Dictionary (OALD)* can often help. Other references that help with idiom (and with other matters) are *Fowler's Modern English Usage*, the *Canadian Oxford Dictionary*, and the *Guide to Canadian English Usage*. Students for whom English is an additional language will benefit from using specialized learner's dictionaries, which offer a wealth of information about idiomatic uses of articles and prepositions and examples of idioms used in complete sentences.

14f Wordiness, Clichés, Jargon, and Associated Problems

Avoid diction that decreases precision and clarity. Using too many words, or tired words, or fuzzy words weakens communication. Jargonauts are fond of wordy and pretentious phrases like "make a determination" (instead of simply *determine*), or "at this point in time" (instead of *now*), or "due to the fact that" (instead of *because*), or "be of assistance to" (instead of *help*).

1. Wordiness

Generally, the fewer words you use to make a point, the better. Useless words clutter up a sentence; they dissipate its force, cloud its meaning, blunt its effectiveness.

> *w:* What a person should try to do when communicating by writing is to make sure the meaning of what he is trying to say is clear.

> *revised:* A writer should strive to be clear.

EXPLETIVES

When used to excess, expletive constructions can be a source of weakness and wordiness. There is nothing inherently wrong with them, and they are invaluable in enabling us to form certain kinds of sentences the way we want to. If you can get rid of an expletive without creating awkwardness or losing desired emphasis, do it. Don't write

> *w:* There are several reasons why it is important to revise carefully.

when you can so easily get rid of the excess caused by the *there are* and *it is* structure:

> *revised:* Careful revision is important for several reasons.

> *revised:* For several reasons, careful revision is important.

2. Repetition

Repetition can be useful for coherence and emphasis. But unnecessary repetition usually produces wordiness, and often awkwardness as well. Consider this example:

> *rep:* Looking at the general appearance of the buildings, you can see that special consideration was given to the choice of colours for these buildings.

> *revised:* Looking at the buildings, you can see that special consideration was given to the choice of colours.

3. Redundancy

Redundancy, another cause of wordiness, is repetition of an idea rather than a word. Something is redundant if it has already been expressed earlier in a sentence. To begin a sentence, "In my opinion, I think . . . " is redundant. To speak of a "new innovation" is to be redundant. Here are some other phrases that are redundant:

advance planning	erode away
added bonus	general consensus
basic fundamentals	low ebb
but nevertheless	mental attitude
character trait	more preferable
climb up	necessary prerequisite
close scrutiny	new record
completely eliminate	past history
consensus of opinion	reduce down
continue on	refer back
enter into	revert back

One common kind of redundancy is called "doubling"—adding an unnecessary second word (usually an adjective) as if to make sure the meaning of the first is clear:

> ***red:*** The report was brief and concise.

Either *brief* or *concise* alone would convey the meaning.

4. Ready-made phrases

Prefabricated or formulaic phrases that leap to our minds whole are almost always wordy. They are a kind of cliché, and many also sound like jargon. You can often edit them out of a draft altogether, or at least use shorter equivalents:

> at that time, at that point in time (use *then*)
>
> at the present time, at this time, at this point in time (use *now*)

at the same time (use *while*)

by means of (use *by*)

due to the fact that, because of the fact that, on account of the fact that, in view of the fact that, owing to the fact that (use *because*)

during the course of, in the course of (use *during*)

for the purpose of (use *for, to*)

for the reason that, for the simple reason that (use *because*)

in all likelihood, in all probability (use *probably*)

in height (use *high*)

in length (use *long*)

in order to (use *to*)

in spite of the fact that (use *although*)

in the event that (use *if*)

in this day and age (use *now, today*)

period of time (use *period, time*)

previous to, prior to (use *before*)

5. Triteness, clichés

Trite or hackneyed expressions, clichés, are another form of wordiness: they are tired, worn out, all too familiar, and therefore contribute little to a sentence. Since they are, by definition, prefabricated phrases, they are another kind of deadwood that can be edited out of a draft.

Here are a few examples to suggest the kinds of expressions to edit from your work:

a bolt from the blue	last but not least
a heart as big as all outdoors	lock, stock, and barrel
a matter of course	love at first sight
all things being equal	many and diverse
as a last resort	moment of truth
as a matter of fact	needless to say

as the crow flies

beat a hasty retreat

busy as a bee

by leaps and bounds

by no manner of means

by no means

clear as crystal (or mud)

conspicuous by its absence

cool as a cucumber

corridors of power

doomed to disappointment

easier said than done

from dawn till dusk

gentle as a lamb

good as gold

if and when

in a manner of speaking

in one ear and out the other

in the long run

it goes without saying

it stands to reason

nipped in the bud

no way, shape, or form

off the beaten path (or track)

on the right track

one and the same

par for the course

pride and joy

raining cats and dogs

rears its ugly head

rude awakening

sadder but wiser

seeing is believing

sharp as a tack

slowly but surely

smart as a whip

strike while the iron is hot

strong as an ox

talk turkey

the wrong side of the tracks

when all is said and done

Edit for the almost automatic couplings that occur between some adjectives and nouns:

acid test

ardent admirers

budding genius

bulging biceps

blushing bride

consummate artistry

devastating effect

drastic action

festive occasion

hearty breakfast

heated opposition

knee-jerk reaction

proud possessor

sacred duty

severe stress

tangible proof

vital role

14

6. Jargon

The word **jargon**, in a narrow sense, refers to terms peculiar to a specific discipline, such as psychology, chemistry, literary theory, or computer science, terms unlikely to be fully understood by an outsider. Here we use it in a different sense, to refer to all the incoherent, unintelligible phraseology that clutters contemporary expression. The private languages of particular disciplines or special groups are quite legitimately used in writing for members of those communities. Much less legitimate are the gobbledygook and bafflegab that so easily find their way into the speech and writing of most of us.

The following list is a sampling of words and phrases that are virtually guaranteed to decrease the quality of expression, whether spoken or written:

along the lines of, along that line, in the line of

angle

aspect

background (as a verb)

basis, on the basis of, on a . . . basis

bottom line

case

concept, conception

concerning, concerned

connection, in connection with, in this (that) connection

considering, consideration, in consideration of

definitely

dialogue (especially as a verb)

escalate

eventuate

evidenced by

expertise

facet

14

factor

implemented, implementation

importantly

indicated to (for *told*)

input, output

in regard to, with regard to, regarding, as regards

in relation to

in respect to, with respect to, respecting

in terms of

in the final analysis

meaningful

mega-

motivation

ongoing

parameters

phase

picture, in the picture

posture

realm

relate to

relevant

replicate

scenario, worst-case scenario

sector

self-identity

situation

standpoint, vantage point, viewpoint

type, -type

viable

-wise

worthwhile

14

Writers addicted to wordiness and jargon will prefer long words to short ones, and pretentious-sounding words to relatively simple ones. Generally, choose the shorter and simpler form. For example, the shorter word in each of the following pairs is preferable:

analysis, analyzation	(re)orient, (re)orientate
connote, connotate	preventive, preventative
courage, courageousness	remedy (vb.), remediate
disoriented, disorientated	symbolic, symbolical
existential, existentialistic	use (n. & vb.), utilize, utilization

 Usage: A Checklist of Troublesome Words and Phrases

This section features words and phrases that have a history of being especially confusing or otherwise troublesome. This list is selective rather than exhaustive; we have tried to keep it short enough to be manageable.

advice, advise
Advice is a noun, usually used in uncountable form. *Advise* is the transitive verb form.

> My faculty advise has given me good <u>advice</u> in planning my major. [noun]

> He <u>advised</u> his brother to consider studying abroad for a year. [transitive verb in past-tense form; its direct object is *his brother*.]

affect, effect
Affect is a transitive verb meaning "to act upon" or "to influence"; *effect* is a noun meaning "result, consequence":

> He tried to <u>affect</u> the outcome, but his efforts had no <u>effect</u>.

amount, number
Use *number* only with countable things (i.e. with nouns that have both singular and plural forms), *amount* only

with mass, uncountable nouns: a *number* of coins, an *amount* of change; a large *number* of cars, a large *amount* of traffic. *Number* usually takes a singular verb after the definite article and a plural verb after the indefinite article.

> The number of students taking the workshop is encouraging.

> A number of students are planning to take the workshop.

between, among
Generally, use *between* when there are two persons or things, and *among* when there are more than two:

> There is ill feeling between the two national leaders.

> They divided the cost equally among the three of them.

complementary, complimentary
Complementary is the adjective describing something that adds to or completes something else. *Complimentary* is the adjective describing something free (*complimentary* tickets or passes) or comments intended to praise or flatter someone.

> Complementary exercises reinforcing the principles covered in this module are available on the course website. (the exercises will complete the module)

> We won complimentary passes to the Toronto Film Festival. (the passes are free)

comprise, compose
Distinguish carefully between these words. Strictly, *comprise* means "consist of, contain, take in, include":

> The municipal region comprises several cities and towns.

Compose means "constitute, form, make up":

> The seven cities and towns compose the municipal region.

continual, continuous
These words are sometimes considered interchangeable, but *continual* more often refers to something that happens

14

frequently or even regularly but with interruptions, and *continuous* to something that occurs constantly, without interruptions:

> The speaker's voice went on in a continuous drone, in spite of the heckler's continual attempts to interrupt.

farther, further
Use *farther* and *farthest* to refer to physical distance and *further* and *furthest* everywhere else, such as when referring to time and degree or when the meaning is something like "more" or "in addition":

> To go any farther down the road is the furthest thing from my mind.

> Rather than delay any further, he began his research, beginning with the book farthest from him.

> Without further delay, she began her speech.

14

feel(s)
Don't loosely use the word *feel* when what you really mean is *think* or *believe*. *Feel* is more appropriate to emotional or physical attitudes and responses, *think* and *believe* to those dependent on reasoning:

> The defendant felt cheated by the decision; she believed that her case had not been judged impartially.

good, bad, badly, well
To avoid confusion and error with these words, remember that *good* and *bad* are adjectives, *badly* and *well* adverbs (except when *well* is an adjective meaning "healthy").

> The model looks good in that business suit. (He is attractive.)

> That suit looks bad on you because it fits badly.

> Nathan acted bad. (He was naughty.)

> Nathan acted badly. (His performance as Hamlet was terrible.)

happen, occur

These verbs sometimes pose a problem for students with English as an additional language. Both verbs are intransitive and cannot take the passive-voice form in any tense.

> *wrong:* The revolution <u>was happened</u> in 1917.
> *right:* The revolution <u>happened</u> in 1917.

> *wrong:* My parents' wedding <u>was occurred</u> in September 1970.
> *right:* My parents' wedding <u>occurred</u> in September 1970.

infer, imply

Use *imply* to mean "suggest, hint at, indicate indirectly" and *infer* to mean "conclude by reasoning, deduce." A listener or reader can *infer* from a statement something that its speaker or writer *implies* in it:

> Her speech strongly <u>implied</u> that we could trust her.

> I <u>inferred</u> from her speech that she was trustworthy.

its, it's

Its—without the apostrophe—is the possessive form of *it*; *it's*—with the apostrophe—is the contracted form of *it is*, or occasionally of *it has* (as in "*It's* been a long day").

lack, lack of, lacking, lacking in

Lack in its various forms and parts of speech can sometimes pose problems for students with English as an additional language. Note the following standard usages:

> This paper <u>lacks</u> a clear argument. (*lack* as a transitive verb)

> A major weakness of his argument was its <u>lack</u> of evidence. (*lack* as a noun followed by the preposition *of*)

> <u>Lacking</u> confidence, she gave up on her research. (*lacking* as a present participle followed by a direct object)

<u>Lacking</u> in experience, they had difficulty in job interviews.
(*lacking* as a present participle in combination with the preposition *in*)

less, fewer

Fewer refers to things that are countable (i.e. that appear as plural nouns); *less* is sometimes used the same way (e.g. on the signs at the express checkout lanes in supermarkets—"9 items or less"), but usually it is preferable to use it for things that are measured rather than counted or considered as units (i.e. with uncountable nouns):

<u>fewer</u> dollars, <u>less</u> money

<u>fewer</u> hours, <u>less</u> time

<u>fewer</u> cars, <u>less</u> traffic

let, make

The verbs *let* and *make* are parts of an idiom that causes problems, especially for those with English as an additional language. When *let* or *make* is followed by a direct object and an infinitive, the infinitive does not include the customary *to*:

id: They <u>let</u> me <u>to borrow</u> their new car.
revised: They <u>let</u> me <u>borrow</u> their new car.

id: Our professor <u>made</u> us <u>to participate</u> in the experiment.
revised: Our professor <u>made</u> us <u>participate</u> in the experiment.

lie, lay

Since *lay* is both the past tense of *lie* and the present tense of the verb *lay*, some writers habitually confuse these two verbs. If necessary, memorize their principal parts: *lie, lay, lain; lay, laid, laid.* The verb *lie* means "recline" or "be situated"; *lay* means "put" or "place." *Lie* is intransitive; *lay* is transitive:

I <u>lie</u> down now; I <u>lay</u> down yesterday; I <u>have lain</u> down several times today.

> I lay the book on the desk now; I laid the book on the desk yesterday; I have laid the book on the desk every morning for a week.

like, as, as if, as though

Like is a preposition:

> Roger is dressed exactly like Ray.

But if Ray is given a verb, then he becomes the subject of a clause, forcing *like* to serve incorrectly as a conjunction; use the conjunction *as* when a clause follows:

> ***us:*** Roger is dressed exactly like Ray is.
> ***revised:*** Roger is dressed exactly as Ray is.

In slightly different constructions, use *as if* or *as though* to introduce clauses:

> It looks like rain.

> It looks as if [or *as though*] it will rain.

loan, lend

Although some people restrict *loan* to being a noun, it is generally acceptable as a verb equivalent to *lend*—except in such figurative uses as "Metaphors *lend* colour to one's style" and "*lend* a hand."

may, might

Don't confuse your reader by using *may* where *might* is required:

(a) after another verb in the past tense:

> ***us:*** She thought she may get a raise. (use *might*)

In the present tense, either *may* or *might* would be possible:

> She thinks she may get a raise. (It's quite likely that she will.)

> She thinks she might get a raise. (It's less likely, but possible.)

(b) for something hypothetical rather than factual:

> ***us:*** This imaginative software program <u>may</u> have helped Beethoven, but it wouldn't have changed the way Mozart composed.

of

Avoid incorrect use of *of* as a result of mispronunciation:

> We would <u>of</u> stayed for dinner if not for the weather.
> (have)

> The prime minister should <u>of</u> apologized for his remarks.
> (have)

Because of the way we sometimes speak, such verb phrases as "would have," "could have," "should have," and "might have" are mispronounced (*would've, could've, should've, might've*). Because of the way we hear these words, the *'ve* mistakenly becomes *of.*

14

presently

Since some people think that *presently* should mean only "in a short while, soon," and others think that it instead, or also, means "at present, currently, now," resulting in at least occasional ambiguity, many writers try to avoid the word. Use alternative terms and your meaning will be clear.

raise, rise

The verb *raise* is transitive, requiring an object: "I *raised* my hand; he *raises* horses." *Rise* is intransitive: "The temperature *rose* sharply; I *rise* each morning at dawn." If necessary, memorize their principal parts: *raise, raised, raised*; *rise, rose, risen.*

recommend

When this transitive verb appears in a clause with an indirect object, that object must be expressed as a prepositional phrase with *to* or *for,* and it must follow the direct object:

> ***id:*** She recommended <u>me</u> this restaurant.
> ***id:*** She recommended <u>to me</u> this restaurant.
> ***revised:*** She recommended this restaurant <u>to me</u>.

A number of other verbs fit the same idiomatic pattern as *recommend*. Among the most common are *admit, contribute, dedicate, demonstrate, describe, distribute, explain, introduce, mention, propose, reveal, speak, state,* and *suggest.* Note, however, that with several of these verbs, if the direct object is itself a noun clause, it usually follows the prepositional phrase:

> He admitted to me <u>that he had been lying</u>.

> She explained to me <u>what she intended to do</u>.

set, sit

Set (principal parts *set, set, set*) means "put, place, cause to sit"; it is transitive, requiring an object: "He *set* the glass on the counter." *Sit* (principal parts *sit, sat, sat*) means "rest, occupy a seat, assume a sitting position"; it is intransitive: "The glass *sits* on the counter. May I *sit* in the easy chair?"—though it can be used transitively in expressions like "I *sat* myself down to listen," "She *sat* him down at the desk." (See also **lie, lay**.)

simple, simplistic

Don't use *simplistic* when all you want is *simple*. *Simplistic* means "oversimplified, unrealistically simple":

> We admire the book for its <u>simple</u> explanations and straightforward advice.

> The author's assessment of the war's causes was narrow and <u>simplistic</u>.

Similarly, *fatalistic* does not mean the same as *fatal*.

so . . . as, as . . . as

In strictly formal contexts, use *so* or *so . . . as* with negative comparisons; use *as* or *as . . . as* only with positive comparisons:

> Belinda was almost <u>as tall as</u> he was, but she was not *so* heavy.

> He was not *so* light on his feet as he once was, but he was <u>as strong as</u> ever.

till, until, 'til
Till and *until* are both standard, and have the same meaning. *Until* is probably felt to be somewhat more formal, and (like the two-syllable *although*) is usually preferable at the beginning of a sentence. The contraction *'til* is little used nowadays, except in markedly informal contexts, such as personal letters.

too
Used as an intensifier, *too* is sometimes illogical; if an intensifier is necessary in such sentences as these, use *very:*

> *ww:* I don't like my cocoa <u>too</u> hot.
> *revised:* I don't like my cocoa <u>very</u> hot.

> *ww:* She didn't care for the brown suit <u>too</u> much.
> *revised:* She didn't care for the brown suit <u>very</u> much.

But often you can omit the intensifier as unnecessary:

> She didn't care much for the brown suit.

toward, towards
These are interchangeable, but in North American (as opposed to British) English, the preposition *toward* is usually preferred to *towards,* just as the adverbs *afterward, forward* (meaning *frontward),* and *backward* are to their counterparts ending in *s.*

unique, absolute, necessary, essential, complete, perfect, fatal, equal, (im)possible, infinite, empty, full, straight, round, square, etc.
In writing, especially formal writing, treat these and other such adjectives as absolutes that cannot logically be compared or modified by such adverbs as *very* and *rather.* Since by definition something *unique* is the *only one of its kind* or *without equal,* clearly one thing cannot be "more unique" than another, or even "very unique"; in other words, *unique* is not a synonym for *unusual* or *rare.* Similarly with the others: one thing cannot be "more necessary" than another. Since *perfect* means "without flaw," there cannot be degrees of perfection.

usage, use, utilize, utilization

The noun *usage* is appropriate when you mean customary or habitual use, whether verbal or otherwise ("British usage," "the usages of the early Christians"), or a particular verbal expression being characterized in a particular way ("an ironic usage," "an elegant usage"). Otherwise the shorter noun *use* is preferable. As a verb, *use* should nearly always suffice; *utilize,* often pretentiously employed instead, should carry the specific meaning "put to use, make use of, turn to practical or profitable account." Similarly, the noun *use* will usually be more appropriate than *utilization.* Phrases like *use of, the use of, by the use of,* and *through the use of* tend toward jargon and are almost always wordy.

while

As a subordinating conjunction, *while* is best restricted to meanings having to do with time:

14

> While Vijay mowed the lawn, Honoree raked up the grass clippings.

When it means "although (though)" or "whereas," it can be imprecise, even ambiguous:

> While I agree with some of his reasons, I still think my proposal is better. (*Although* would be clearer.)

> While he does the lawn-mowing, she cooks the meals. (Fuzzy or ambiguous; *whereas* would make the meaning clear.)

ESSENTIALS OF PUNCTUATION

IV

CONTENTS

INTRODUCTION

Good punctuation is essential to clear and effective writing. It helps writers clarify meaning and tone and, therefore, helps readers understand what writers communicate: try removing the punctuation marks from a piece of prose, and then see how difficult it is to read it. Punctuation points to meaning that in spoken language would be indicated by pauses, pitch, tone, and stress. In effect, punctuation helps readers *hear* a sentence the way a writer intends. Commas, semicolons, colons, and dashes help to clarify the internal structure of sentences; often the very meaning of a sentence depends on how it is punctuated.

The conventions of punctuation have come to be agreed upon by writers and readers of English for the purpose of clear and effective communication. Although good writers do sometimes stray from these conventions, they usually do so because they have a sufficient command of them to break a "rule" in order to achieve a desired effect.

Hyphens and *apostrophes* are dealt with in the discussion of mechanics and spelling in Part V: see #32k and #32m, respectively.

15 THE COMMA ,

The **comma** is a light or mild separator. It is the most neutral punctuation mark and the most used mark. A comma makes a reader pause slightly. Use it to separate words, phrases, and clauses from each other when no heavier or more expressive mark is required or desired.

Main functions of commas

Basically, commas are used in three ways; if you know these conventions, you should have little trouble with commas:

1. Generally, use a comma between independent clauses joined by a coordinating conjunction (*and*, *but*, *or*, *nor*, *for*, *yet*, *so*; see #13b):

   > We went to the National Gallery, and then we walked to the Parliament Buildings.

2. Generally, use commas to separate items in a series:

   > Robert Bateman, Emily Carr, and Mary Pratt are three Canadian painters.

   > Painting landscapes can be a relaxing, rewarding, enjoyable experience.

3. Generally, use commas to set off parenthetical elements, such as introductory words, phrases, and clauses; non-restrictive elements; or sentence interrupters:

   > Grasping the remote control firmly, she walked away.

   > Caffè latte, which has always been a popular drink in Europe, is now popular in North America.

   > There are, however, some exceptions.

Other conventional uses of the comma

1. Use a comma between elements of an emphatic contrast:

This is a practical lesson, not a theoretical one.

2. Use a comma to indicate a pause where a word has been acceptably omitted:

    Ron is a conservative; Sally, a radical.

3. Use commas to set off a noun of address:

    Simon, please write a thank-you note to your grandparents.

4. Generally, use commas with a verb of speaking before or after a quotation:

    Then Dora remarked, "That book gave me nightmares."

    "It doesn't matter to me," said Alain laughingly.

5. Use commas after the salutation of informal letters (*Dear Gail,*) and after the complimentary close of all letters (*Yours truly,*). In formal letters, a colon is conventional after the salutation (*Dear Mr. Eng:*).

6. Use commas with dates. Different forms are possible:

    She left on January 11, 2011, and was gone a month. (Note the comma *after* the year.)

    You may also place the date before the month—a style preferred by some writers in Canada and Britain—in which case no comma is required:

    She left on 11 January 2011 and was gone a month.

    Whichever style you choose, make sure you use it consistently.
    When referring only to month and year, you may use a comma or not, but again, be consistent:

    The book was published in March, 2010, in Canada.

    It was published here in March 2010.

15

7. Use commas to set off geographical names and addresses:

> She left Fredericton, New Brunswick, and moved to Hamilton, Ontario, in hopes of finding a better-paying job. (Note the commas *after* the names of the provinces.)

> Their summer address will be 11 Bishop's Place, Lewes, Sussex, England.

 ## 15a The Comma with Coordinating Conjunctions

Generally, use a comma between independent clauses joined by one of the coordinating conjunctions (*and*, *but*, *or*, *nor*, *for*, *yet*, and sometimes *so*):

> The revision of the text proved difficult, and she found herself burning the midnight oil.

> It was a serious speech, but Gordon included many jokes along the way, and the audience loved it.

> Naieli could go into debt for the sports car, or she could go on driving her old jalopy.

> Don knew he shouldn't do it, yet he couldn't stop himself.

If the clauses are short, the comma or commas may be omitted:

> We studied all night so we were ready.

When the clauses are parallel in structure, the comma may often be omitted:

> Art is long and life is short.

When two clauses have the same subject, a comma is less likely to be needed between them:

15

It was windy and it was wet.

The play was well produced and it impressed everyone who saw it.

When the subject is omitted from the second clause, a comma should not be used:

It was windy and wet.

Independent clauses joined by *but* and *yet*, which explicitly mark a contrast, will almost always need a comma, even if they are short or parallel or have the same subject:

It was windy, yet it was warm.

And when you join two clauses with the coordinating conjunction *for*, always put a comma in front of it to prevent its being misread as a preposition:

Amanda was eager to leave early, for the restaurant was sure to be crowded.

The conjunction *so* almost always needs a comma.

15b The Comma with Items in a Series

15

1. Generally, use commas between words, phrases, or clauses in a series of three or more:

   He sells books, magazines, candy, and life insurance.

   She promised the voters to cut taxes, to limit government spending, and to improve transportation.

   Carmen explained that she had visited the art gallery, that she had walked in the park, and that eventually she had gone to a movie.

2. The common practice of omitting the final comma (known as the Oxford comma—found before the conjunction) can be misleading. That final pause will give your sentences a better rhythm, and you will avoid the kind of possible confusion apparent in

sentences like these (try adding the final comma and then reading them again):

> The manufacturers sent us shirts, wash-and-wear slacks and shoes. (The shoes were wash-and-wear?)

> The Speech from the Throne discussed international trade, improvements in transportation, slowing down inflation and the postal service. (Do we need to slow down the postal service?)

3. Use commas between two or more adjectives preceding a noun if they are parallel, each modifying the noun itself; do not put commas between adjectives that are not parallel:

> He is an intelligent, efficient, ambitious officer.

> She is a tall young woman.

> She wore a new black felt hat, a long red coat, and a woollen scarf with red, white, and black stripes.

15

In the first sentence, each adjective modifies *officer*. In the second, *tall* modifies *young woman*; it is a *young woman* who is *tall*, not a *woman* who is *tall* and *young*. In the third, *new* modifies *black felt hat*, *black* modifies *felt hat*, and *long* modifies *red coat*; *red, white,* and *black* all separately modify *stripes*.

But it isn't always easy to tell whether or not such adjectives are parallel. It often helps to think of each comma as substituting for *and*: try putting *and* between the adjectives. If *and* sounds logical there, the adjectives are probably parallel and should be separated by a comma; if *and* doesn't seem to work, a comma won't either. Another test is to change the order of the adjectives. If it sounds odd to say *a felt black hat* instead of *a black felt hat*, then the adjectives probably aren't parallel. A final aid to remember: usually no comma is needed after a number (*three blind mice*) or after common adjectives for size or age (*tall young woman*; *long red coat*; *new brick house*).

15c The Comma with an Introductory Word, Phrase, or Subordinate Clause

Generally, set off an introductory word or short phrase if you want a distinct pause, for example, for emphasis or qualification or to prevent misreading:

> Generally, follow my advice about punctuation.

> Usually, immature people are difficult to work with.

Of the conjunctive adverbs, *however* is most often set off to prevent its being misread, though the others frequently are as well.

Generally, set off a long introductory adverbial phrase with a comma:

> After many years as leader of the union, Jean retired gracefully.

> To get the best results from your ice cream maker, you must follow the instruction manual carefully.

Generally, use a comma between an introductory subordinate clause and an independent (main) clause:

> After I had selected all the items I wanted, I discovered that I had left my wallet at home.

> When the party was over, I went straight home.

When the introductory clause is short and when there would be no pause if the sentence were spoken aloud, you may omit the comma. But if omitting the comma could cause misreading, retain it:

> Whenever I wanted, someone would bring me something to eat.

> After the sun had set, high above the mountains came the fighter jets.

15

Whenever you're not sure the meaning will be clear without it, use a comma.

Always set off an introductory participle or participial phrase with a comma (see #21d):

> Puzzled, Karen turned back to the beginning of the chapter.

> Finding golf unexpectedly difficult, Kevin sought extra help.

Always set off introductory absolute phrases with commas:

> The doors locked and bolted, they went to bed feeling secure.

Note: Absolute phrases need to be set off with commas no matter where they appear in a sentence:

> Timmy went on stage, head held high, a grin spreading across his face.

Also, participles and participial phrases that appear at the end of a sentence almost always need to be set off. Read the sentence aloud; if you feel a distinct pause, use a comma:

> Kevin sought extra help, finding golf unexpectedly difficult.

Occasionally such a sentence will flow clearly and smoothly without a comma, especially if the modifier is essential to the meaning:

> Shirin left the room feeling victorious.

> She sat there looking puzzled.

15d The Comma with Nonrestrictive Elements

Words, phrases, and clauses are nonrestrictive when they are not essential to the principal meaning of a sentence; they should be set off from the rest of the sentence, usually with commas, though dashes and parentheses can also be used. A restrictive modifier is essential to the meaning and should not be set off:

> **restrictive:** Anyone wanting a refund should see the manager.
>
> **nonrestrictive:** Alex, wanting a refund, asked to see the manager.

The participial phrase explains why Alex asked to see the manager, but the sentence is clear without it: "Alex asked to see the manager"; the phrase *wanting a refund* is therefore not essential and is set off with commas. But without the phrase the first sentence wouldn't make sense: "Anyone should see the manager"; the phrase *wanting a refund* is essential and is not set off. The comma-or-no-comma question most often arises with *relative clauses* (see #3f and #7a.4); *appositives*, though usually nonrestrictive, can also be restrictive, and some other elements can also be either restrictive or nonrestrictive.

1. Restrictive and nonrestrictive relative clauses
Always set off a nonrestrictive relative clause; do not set off restrictive relative clauses:

> She is a woman *who likes to travel.* (The relative clause is essential; therefore, no commas.)
>
> Carol, *who likes to travel,* is going to Greece this summer. (The relative clause is not essential; therefore, add commas.)

Consider the following pair of sentences:

> **incorrect:** Students, who are hard-working, should expect much from their education.
>
> **correct:** Students who are hard-working should expect much from their education.

Set off as nonrestrictive, the relative clause applies to all students, which makes the sentence untrue. Left unpunctuated, the relative clause is restrictive, making the sentence correctly apply only to students who are in fact hard-working.

Note: To determine whether a clause is restrictive or non-restrictive, try the following test: If you can use the relative pronoun *that*, you know the clause is restrictive; *that* cannot begin a nonrestrictive clause:

> The book <u>that</u> I wanted to read was not in the library.

Further, if the pronoun can be omitted (see #7a.4) altogether, the clause is restrictive, as with *that* in the preceding example and *whom* in the following:

> The person [whom] I most admire is the one who works hard and plays hard.

2. Restrictive and nonrestrictive appositives
Always set off a nonrestrictive appositive:

> Jan, <u>our youngest daughter</u>, keeps the lawn mowed all summer.

> *King Lear* is a noble work of literature, <u>one that will live in human minds for all time</u>.

> Virginia is going to bring her sister, <u>Vanessa</u>.

In the last example, the comma indicates that Virginia has only the one sister. Left unpunctuated, the appositive would be restrictive, meaning that Virginia has more than one sister and that the particular one she is going to bring is the one named Vanessa.

15e   The Comma with Sentence Interrupters

Sentence interrupters are parenthetical elements—words, phrases, or clauses—that interrupt the syntax of a sentence. Set off light, ordinary interrupters with a pair of commas:

> This document, <u>the lawyer says</u>, will complete the contract. (explanatory clause)

> Thank you, <u>David</u>, for this much needed advice and the martini. (noun of address)

16   THE SEMICOLON ;

The **semicolon** is a heavy separator, often almost equivalent to a period or "full stop." It forces a much longer pause than a comma does. Basically, semicolons have two functions:

1. Generally, use a semicolon between closely related independent clauses that are not joined by one of the coordinating conjunctions (see #13b.1):

    > Tap water sometimes tastes of chemicals; spring water imported from France usually does not.

    > The lab had 20 new laptop computers; however, there were 25 students in the class.

2. Use a semicolon instead of a comma if a comma would not be heavy enough; for example, if the clauses or the elements in a series have internal commas of their own:

    > Their class presentation examined three novels written by Canadian authors and set largely outside Canada: Edeet Ravel's *Look for Me,* which is set in Israel and the Palestinian territory; Michael Ondaatje's *Anil's Ghost,* which takes place primarily in Sri Lanka; and David Bergen's *The Time in Between,* set principally in Vietnam.

16a   The Semicolon with Independent Clauses

To avoid a *comma splice* (see #25a), generally use a semicolon between independent clauses that are not joined with one of the coordinating conjunctions (*and, but, or, nor, for, yet, so*):

> The actual prize is not important; it is the honour connected with it that matters.

> Leanna was exhausted and obviously not going to win; nevertheless, she persevered and finished the race.

16b The Semicolon with Conjunctive Adverbs and Transitions

Be sure to use a semicolon and not just a comma between independent clauses that you join with a conjunctive adverb, including *however* and *therefore*. Here is a list of most of the common ones:

accordingly	finally	likewise	similarly
afterward	further	meanwhile	still
also	furthermore	moreover	subsequently
anyway	hence	namely	then
besides	however	nevertheless	thereafter
certainly	indeed	next	therefore
consequently	instead	nonetheless	thus
conversely	later	otherwise	undoubtedly

The same practice applies to common transitional phrases such as these:

after this	if not	in the meantime
as a result	in addition	on the contrary
for example	in fact	on the other hand
for this reason	in short	that is

16c The Semicolon with Items in a Series

If the phrases or clauses in a series are unusually long or contain other internal punctuation, you may separate them with semicolons rather than commas:

> How wonderful it is to awaken in the morning when the birds are clamouring in the trees; to see the bright light of a summer morning streaming into the room; to realize, with a sudden flash of joy, that it is Sunday and that this perfect morning is completely yours; and then to loaf in a deckchair without a thought of tomorrow.

16

Saint John, New Brunswick; Victoria, British Columbia; and Kingston, Ontario, are all about the same size.

 THE COLON :

Colons are commonly used to introduce lists, examples, and long or formal quotations, but their possibilities in more everyday sentences are often overlooked. A colon is useful because it looks forward or anticipates: it gives readers a push toward the next part of the sentence. In the preceding sentence, for example, the colon sets up a sense of expectation about what is coming. It points out, even emphasizes, the relation between the two parts of the sentence (that is, the second part clarifies what the first part says). A semicolon in the same spot would bring readers to an abrupt halt, leaving it up to them to make the necessary connection between the two parts.

> Vita's garden contained only white flowers: roses, primulas, and primroses.

> Let me add just this: anyone who expects to lose weight must be prepared to exercise.

> It was an unexpectedly lovely time of year: trees were in blossom, garden flowers bloomed all around, the sky was clear and bright, and the temperature was just right.

Don't get carried away and overuse the colon: its effectiveness would wear off if it appeared more than once or twice a page.

Note: One space after a colon is the norm. And only one space follows colons setting off subtitles or in footnotes or bibliographical entries.

17a The Colon with Items in a Series

When used between items in a series, colons can add emphasis because they are unusual, but mainly their anticipatory nature produces a cumulative effect suitable when successive items in a series build to a climax:

> He held on: he persevered: he fought back: and eventually he won out, regardless of the punishing obstacles.

> It blew: it rained: it hailed: it sleeted: it even snowed—it was a most unusual June even for Medicine Hat.

(Note how the dash in the last example prepares for the final clause.)

17b   The Colon Between a Title and a Subtitle

Use a colon between the title and the subtitle of a book, an article, an essay, or any other document. Insert one space between the colon and the first word of the subtitle:

> *Home Words: Discourses of Children's Literature in Canada* (a book)

> "A Residential School Memoir: Basil Johnston's *Indian School Days*" (an article)

> "The State in Question: Hobbes, Rousseau, and Hegel" (an essay)

17c   The Colon in the Salutation of a Business Letter

In a formal business letter, the salutation line ends with a colon:

> Dear Professor Chow:

> Dear Mayor Ford:

17d   The Colon Introducing a Block Quotation

Colons are conventionally used to introduce "block" quotations:

> Jane Austen begins her novel *Pride and Prejudice* with the observation:
>
>> It is a truth universally acknowledged, that a single man in possession of a good fortune must be in want of a wife. However little known the feelings or views of such

17

a man may be on his first entering a neighbourhood, this truth is so well fixed in the minds of the surrounding families, that he is considered as the rightful property of some one or other of their daughters.

18 THE DASH —

The **dash** is a popular punctuation mark, especially in e-mail and other more informal communications. Use a dash only when you have a definite reason for doing so. Like the colon, the dash sets up expectations in a reader's mind. But whereas the colon sets up an expectation that what follows will somehow explain, summarize, define, or otherwise comment on what has gone before, a dash suggests that what follows will be somehow surprising, involving some sort of twist, or at least a contrary idea. Consider the following sentence:

The teacher praised my wit, my intelligence, my organization, and my research—and penalized the paper for its poor spelling and punctuation.

Here the dash adds to the punch of what follows it. A comma there would deprive the sentence of much of its force; it would even sound odd, since the resulting matter-of-fact tone would not be in harmony with what the sentence was saying.

The dash is also handy in some long and involved sentences, for example after a long series before a summarizing clause:

Our longing for the past, our hopes for the future, and our neglect of the present moment—all these and more go to shape our everyday lives, often in ways unseen or little understood.

Even here, the emphatic quality of the dash serves the meaning, though its principal function is to mark the abrupt break.

As with colons, don't overuse dashes. They are even stronger marks, but they lose effectiveness if used often.

18

18a The Dash with Items in a Series

You can emphasize items in a series by putting dashes between them—but don't do it often. The sharpness of the breaks greatly heightens the effect of a series:

> Rising taxes—rising insurance rates—rising gas costs—skyrocketing food prices: it is becoming more and more difficult to live decently and still keep within a budget.

Dashes can also be effective in a quieter context:

> Upon rounding the bend, we were confronted with a breathtaking panorama of lush valleys with meandering streams—flower-covered slopes—great rocks and trees—and, overtopping all, the mighty peaks with their hoods of snow.

18b The Dash with Sentence Interrupters

Use a pair of dashes to set off abrupt interrupters or other interrupters that you wish to emphasize. An interrupter that sharply breaks the syntax of a sentence will often be emphatic for that very reason, and dashes will be appropriate to set it off:

> The increase in enrolment—over 50 per cent—demonstrates the success of our program.

> He told me—believe this or not!—that he would never drink beer again.

Wherever you want emphasis or a different tone, you can use dashes where commas would ordinarily serve:

> The modern age—as we all know—is a noisy age.

Dashes are also useful to set off an interrupter consisting of a series with its own internal commas; set off with commas, such a structure can be confusing:

> *confusing:* Sentence interrupters are parenthetical elements, words, phrases, or clauses, that interrupt the syntax of a sentence.

18

clear: Sentence interrupters are parenthetical elements—words, phrases, or clauses—that interrupt the syntax of a sentence.

19 PARENTHESES ( )

Use **parentheses** to set off abrupt interrupters or other interrupters that you wish to de-emphasize; often interrupters that could be emphatic can be played down to emphasize the other parts of a sentence:

The stockholders who voted for him (quite a sizable group) were obviously dissatisfied with our recent conduct of the business.

Some extreme sports (hang-gliding for example) involve unusually high insurance claims.

By de-emphasizing something striking, parentheses can also achieve an effect similar to that of dashes, though by an ironic tone rather than an insistent one.

Parentheses have three principal functions in nontechnical writing: (1) to set off certain kinds of interrupters (see the preceding paragraph), (2) to enclose cross-referenced information within a sentence (as we do throughout this book), and (3) to enclose numerals or letters setting up a list or series, as we do in this sentence. Note that if a complete sentence is enclosed in parentheses within another sentence (here is an example of such an insertion), it needs neither an opening capital letter nor a closing period. Note also that if a comma or other mark is called for by the sentence (as in the preceding sentence, and in this one), it comes *after* the closing parenthesis, not before the opening one. Exclamation points and question marks go inside the parenthesis only if they are a part of what is enclosed. (When an entire sentence or more is enclosed, the terminal mark of course comes inside the closing parenthesis—as does this period.)

20 QUOTATION MARKS " "

There are two kinds of quotation: dialogue or direct speech (such as you might find in a story, novel, or nonfiction narrative or other essay) and verbatim quotation from a published work or other source (as in a research paper). For the use of **quotation marks** around titles, see #29a and c.

20a Quotation Marks with Direct Speech

Enclose all direct speech in quotation marks:

> I remember hearing my mother say to my absentminded father, "Henry, why is the newspaper in the fridge?"

In written dialogue, it is conventional to begin a new paragraph each time the speaker changes:

> "Henry," she said, a note of exasperation in her voice, "why is the newspaper in the fridge?"
>
> "Oh, yes," he replied. "The fish is wrapped in it."
>
> She examined it. "Well, there may have been a fish in it once, but there is no fish in it now."

Even when passages of direct speech are incomplete, the part that is verbatim should be enclosed in quotation marks:

> After only two weeks, he said he was "fed up" and that he was "going to look for a more interesting job."

20b Quotation Marks with Direct Quotation from a Source

Enclose in quotation marks any direct quotation from another source that you run into your own text:

> According to Anthony Powell, "Books do furnish a room."

1. Prose

Prose quotations of no more than four lines are normally run into the text. Quotations of more than four lines should be treated as "block quotations":

When asked why she writes about food, M.F.K. Fisher answers directly:

> It seems to me that our three basic needs, for food and security and love, are so mixed and mingled and entwined that we cannot straightly think of one without the others. So it happens that when I write of hunger, I am really writing about love and the hunger for it, and warmth and the love of it and the hunger for it . . . and then the warmth and richness and fine reality of hunger satisfied . . . and it is all one.

Do not place quotation marks around a block quotation, but do reproduce any quotation marks that appear in the original:

> Budgets can be important. As Dickens has Mr. Micawber say in *David Copperfield*,
>
>> "Annual income twenty pounds, annual expenditure nineteen nineteen six, result happiness. Annual income twenty pounds, annual expenditure twenty pounds ought and six, result misery."

If you're quoting only a single paragraph or part of a paragraph, do not include the paragraph indentation. If you are quoting a passage that is longer than one paragraph, include the indentations for the second and subsequent paragraphs.

Note: When you write an essay for class, you should indent and double space all block quotations.

2. Poetry
Set off quotations of four or more lines of poetry in the same way. A quotation of one, two, or three lines of poetry may be set off if you want to give it special emphasis; otherwise, run such a quotation into your text. When you run in more than one line of poetry, indicate the line-breaks with a slash mark or virgule—with a space on each side:

> Dante's spiritual journey begins in the woods: "Midway this way of life, we're bound upon / I woke to find myself in a dark wood / Where the right road was wholly lost and gone."

20

20c Single Quotation Marks for a Quotation Within a Quotation ' '

Put single quotation marks around a quotation that occurs within another quotation; this is the only standard use for single quotation marks:

> In Joseph Conrad's *Heart of Darkness*, after a leisurely setting of the scene by the unnamed narrator, the drama begins when the character who is to be the principal narrator first speaks: "'And this also,' said Marlow suddenly, 'has been one of the dark places of the earth.'"

20d Quotation Marks Around Words Used in a Special Sense

Put quotation marks around words used in a special sense or words for which you wish to indicate some qualification:

> What she calls a "ramble" I would call a twenty-mile hike.

> He had been up in the woods so long he was "bushed," as Canadians put it.

Note: Some writers put quotation marks around words referred to as words, but it is sometimes better practice to italicize them:

> The word *toboggan* comes from a Mi'kmaq word for sled.

Don't put quotation marks around slang terms, clichés, and the like. If a word or phrase is so weak or inappropriate that you have to apologize for it, you shouldn't be using it in the first place. And avoid using quotation marks for emphasis; they don't work that way.

20e Other Marks with Quotation Marks

In standard North American practice, periods and commas go inside closing quotation marks; semicolons and colons go outside them:

> "Knowing how to write well," he said, "can be a source of great pleasure"; and then he added that it had "one other important quality": he identified it simply as "hard work."

Question marks and exclamation points go either outside or inside, depending on whether they apply to the quotation or to the whole sentence:

> "What smells so good?" she asked.

> Who said, "Change is inevitable except from a pop machine"?

20f   Ellipses for Omissions . . .

If when quoting from a written source you omit one or more words from the middle of the passage you are quoting, indicate the omission with the three *spaced* periods of an **ellipsis**. For example, if you wanted to quote only part of the passage from Austen quoted at length earlier (#17d), you might do it like this:

> As Jane Austen wryly observes, "a single man in possession of a . . . fortune must be in want of a wife."

Note that you need not indicate an ellipsis at the beginning of a quotation.

When the ellipsis is preceded by a complete sentence, include the period (or other terminal punctuation) of the original before the ellipsis points. Similarly, if when you omit something from the end of a sentence what remains is grammatically complete, a period (or question mark or exclamation point, if either of these is more appropriate) goes before the ellipsis. In either case, the terminal punctuation marking the end of the sentence is closed up:

> As Jane Austen wryly observes, "a single man in possession of a good fortune must be in want of a wife. . . . this truth is so well fixed in the minds of the surrounding families, that he is considered as the rightful property of some one or other. . . ."

Three periods can also indicate the omission of one or more entire sentences, or even whole paragraphs. Again, if the sentence preceding the omitted material is grammatically complete, it should end with a period preceding the ellipsis.

An ellipsis should also be used to indicate that material from a quoted line of poetry has been omitted. When quoting four or more lines of poetry, use a row of spaced dots to indicate that one or more entire lines have been omitted:

> E.J. Pratt's epic "Towards the Last Spike" begins:
>
> > It was the same world then as now—the same,
> > Except for little differences of speed
> > And power, and means to treat myopia.
> > . . . .
> > The same, but for new particles of speech. . . .

Note: Don't omit material from a quotation in such a way that you distort what the author is saying or destroy the integrity of the syntax. Similarly, don't quote unfairly "out of context"; for example, if an author qualifies a statement in some way, don't quote the statement as if it were unqualified.

21 BRACKETS [ ]

Brackets (often referred to as "square brackets," since some people use the term *brackets* also to refer to parentheses) are used primarily to enclose something inserted in a direct quotation:

> She noted that "he [the lead actor] was difficult to work with."

And if you have to put parentheses inside parentheses—as in a footnote or a bibliographical entry—change the inner ones to brackets.

Keep such changes to a minimum, but enclose in square brackets any editorial addition or change you find it necessary to make within a quotation, for example, a clarifying fact or a change in tense to make the quoted material fit the syntax of your sentence:

> The author states that "the following year [2000] marked a turning point in [his] life."

> One of my friends wrote me that her "feelings about
> the subject [were] similar to" mine.

Use the word *sic* (Latin for *thus*) in brackets to indicate
that an error in the quotation occurs in the original:

> One of my friends wrote me: "My feelings about the
> subject are similiar [*sic*] to yours."

22 THE PERIOD .

Use a **period** to mark the end of statements and neutral
commands:

> Canadians use the telephone very often.

> Don't let yourself be fooled by cheap imitations.

Use a period after most abbreviations (note that this rule
applies to *Ms.* even though it is not a true abbreviation):

abbr.	Mr.	Ms.	Dr.	Jr.
Ph.D.	B.A.	St.	Mt.	etc.

Generally use a period in abbreviated place names:

B.C.	P.E.I.	Nfld.	N.Y.	Mass.

But note that two-letter postal abbreviations do not
require periods:

BC	PE	NL	NY	MA

Periods are not used after metric and other symbols
(unless they occur at the end of a sentence):

km	cm	kg	mc^2	ml
kJ	C	Hz	Au	Zr

Periods are often omitted with initials, especially of
groups or organizations, and especially if the initials are
acronyms—that is, words or names made up of initials
(AIDS, NATO, CEGEP):

UN	UNICEF	WHO	RCMP	RAF
CBC	TV	APA	MLA	MP

When in doubt, consult a good dictionary.

Note: Some Canadian writers and publishers follow the British convention of omitting the period after abbreviations that include the first and last letter of the abbreviated word: Mr, Mrs, Dr, Jr, St, etc. (And note in the preceding sentence that a period after an abbreviation at the end of a sentence serves as the sentence's period.)

23 THE QUESTION MARK ?

Use a **question mark** at the end of direct questions:

> When will the lease expire?

Do not use a question mark at the end of an indirect question:

> He asked when the lease would expire.

Note that a question mark is necessary after questions that aren't phrased in the usual interrogative way (as might occur if you were writing dialogue):

> You're leaving so early? (i.e. "Are you leaving so early?")

> You want him to accompany you? (i.e. "Do you want him to accompany you?")

A question appearing as a sentence interrupter still needs a question mark at its end:

> I went back to the beginning—what else could I do?—and tried to get it right the second time.

> The man in the scuba outfit (what was his name again?) took a rear seat.

Since such interrupters are necessarily abrupt, dashes or parentheses are the appropriate marks to set them off.

24 THE EXCLAMATION POINT !

Use an **exclamation point** after an emphatic statement or after an expression of emphatic surprise, emphatic query, or strong emotion:

> He came in first, yet it was only his second time in professional competition!

> Not again!

Occasionally an exclamation point may be doubled or tripled for emphasis. It may even follow a question mark, to emphasize the writer's or speaker's disbelief:

> She said what?!

> You bought what?! A giraffe?! What were you thinking?!

This device should not be used in formal and academic writing.

25 AVOIDING COMMON ERRORS IN PUNCTUATION

 Unwanted Comma Splice

Using only a comma between independent clauses not joined with a coordinating conjunction results in a **comma splice**:

> *cs:* The actual prize is not important, it is the honour connected with it that matters.

> *cs:* He desperately wanted to eat, nevertheless he was too weak to get out of bed.

The easiest way to fix a comma splice is to replace the comma with a semicolon (see #16a). See also #5b.

Unwanted Comma Between Subject and Verb

Generally, do not put a comma between a subject and its verb unless some intervening element calls for punctuation:

> ***no p:*** His enthusiasm for the project and his desire to be of help, led him to add his name to the list of volunteers.

Don't be misled by the length of a compound subject. The comma after *help* in the last example is just as wrong as the comma in the following sentence:

> ***no p:*** Kiera, addressed the class.

But if some intervening element, for example an appositive or a participial phrase, requires setting off, use a *pair* of marks:

> His enthusiasm for the project and his desire to be of help, both strongly felt, led him to add his name to the list of volunteers.
>
> Kiera—the exchange student—addressed the class.

 Unwanted Comma Between Verb and Object or Complement

Although in Jane Austen's time it was conventional to place a comma before a clause beginning with *that*, today this practice is considered an error. Do not put a comma between a verb and its object or complement unless some intervening element calls for punctuation. Especially, don't mistakenly assume that a clause opening with *that* needs a comma before it:

> ***no p:*** Hafiz realized, that he could no longer keep his eyes open.

The noun clause beginning with *that* is the direct object of the verb *realized* and should not be separated from it.

25

Only if an interrupter requires setting off should there be any punctuation:

> Hafiz realized, moreover, that he could no longer keep his eyes open.

> Hafiz realized, as he tried once again to read the paragraph, that he could no longer keep his eyes open.

25d Unwanted Comma After Last Adjective of a Series

Do not put a comma between the last adjective of a series and the noun it modifies:

> *p:* How could anyone fail to be impressed by such an intelligent, outspoken, resourceful, fellow as Jonathan is?

The comma after *resourceful* is incorrect.

25e Unwanted Comma Between Coordinated Words and Phrases

Generally, don't put a comma between words and phrases joined by a coordinating conjunction; use a comma only when the coordinate elements are clauses (see #15a):

> *no p:* The dog and cat circled each other warily, and then went off in opposite directions.

> *no p:* She was not only intelligent, but also very kind.

Sometimes a writer uses such a comma for a mild emphasis, but if you want an emphatic pause a dash will probably work better:

> The dog and cat circled each other warily—and then went off in opposite directions.

Or the sentence can be slightly revised in order to gain the emphasis:

> She was not only intelligent; she was also very kind.

25f Commas with Emphatic Repetition

If the two elements joined by a conjunction constitute an emphatic repetition, a comma is sometimes optional:

> I wanted not only to win, but to win overwhelmingly.

This sentence would be equally correct and effective without the comma. But in the following sentence the comma is necessary:

> It was an object of beauty, and of beauty most spectacular.

25g Unwanted Comma with Short Introductory or Parenthetical Element

Generally, do not set off introductory elements or interrupters that are very short, not really parenthetical, or so slightly parenthetical that you feel no pause when reading them:

> *no p:* Perhaps, she was trying to tell us something.
>
> *no p:* But, it was not a case of mistaken identity.
>
> *no p:* We asked if we could try it out, for a week, to see if we really liked it.

When the pause is strong, however, be sure to set it off:

> It was only then, after the very formal dinner, that we were all able to relax.

Often such commas are optional, depending on the pattern of intonation the writer wants:

> In Canada(,) the change of the seasons is sharply evident.
>
> Last year(,) we went to Quebec City.
>
> As she walked(,) she thought of her childhood in Cabbagetown.

Sometimes such a comma is necessary to prevent misreading:

> **_incorrect:_** After eating the cat Irene gave me jumped out the window.
>
> **_revised:_** After eating, the cat Irene gave me jumped out the window.

See also #15c.

25h   Unwanted Comma with Restrictive Appositive

Don't incorrectly set off proper nouns and titles of literary works as nonrestrictive appositives (see #15d.2). For instance, it's "Dickens's novel _Great Expectations_," not "Dickens's novel, _Great Expectations_." Dickens, after all, wrote more than one novel.

> **_p:_** In her poem, "Daddy," Sylvia Plath explores her complicated relationship with her father.
>
> **_p:_** The home port of the Canadian Coast Guard icebreaker, _Terry Fox_, is St. John's, Newfoundland.

The punctuation makes it sound as though Plath wrote only this one poem and that the _Terry Fox_ is the only icebreaker in the Canadian Coast Guard's fleet. The titles are restrictive: if they were removed, the sentences would not be clear. If the context is clear, the explanatory words often aren't needed at all:

> In "Daddy" Plath explores . . .
>
> The home port of the _Terry Fox_ is . . .

The urge to punctuate before titles of literary works sometimes leads to the error of putting a comma between a possessive and the title.

> **_no p:_** I remember enjoying Elise Partridge's, "To a Flicker Nesting in a Telephone Pole."

25i Unwanted Comma with Indirect Quotation

Do not set off indirect quotations as if they were direct quotations:

> *no p:* In his last chapter the author says, that
> civilization as we have come to know it is
> in jeopardy.

In an indirect quotation, what was said is being reported, not quoted. If the author is quoted directly, a comma is correct:

> If you ask the author she's sure to say, "Civilization as we
> have come to know it is in jeopardy."

See also #20a.

25j Unwanted Question Mark After Indirect Question

Don't put a question mark at the end of indirect questions—questions that are only being reported, not asked directly:

> I asked what we were doing here.

> What he asked himself then was how he was going to
> explain it to the shareholders.

25k Unwanted Semicolon with Subordinate Element

Do not put a semicolon in front of a mere phrase or subordinate clause. Use a semicolon only where you could put a period instead:

> *p:* They cancelled the meeting; being
> disappointed at the low turnout.

25

> *p:* Only about a dozen people showed up; partly
> because there had been too little publicity and
> no free muffins.

Those semicolons should be commas. Similarly, don't put a semicolon between a subordinate clause and an independent clause:

> *p:* After the show, when they got home, tired and
> with their eardrums ringing; Sheila said she
> was never going to another musical again.

> *revised:* After the show, when they got home, tired and
> with their eardrums ringing, Sheila said she
> was never going to another musical again.

25-l Unwanted Colon After Incomplete Construction

Do not use a colon after an incomplete construction; a colon is appropriate only after an independent clause:

> *p:* She preferred comfort foods such as:
> potatoes, bread, and pasta.

25

The prepositional *such as* needs an object to be complete. Had the phrase been extended to "She preferred such foods as these" or ". . . as the following," it would have been complete, an independent clause, and a colon would have been correct.

> *revised:* She preferred comfort foods such as the
> following: potatoes, bread, and pasta.

25m Unwanted Double Punctuation: Comma or Semicolon with a Dash

Avoid putting a comma or a semicolon together with a dash. Use whichever mark is appropriate.

25n Run-on (Fused) Sentences

Failure to put any punctuation between independent clauses where there is also no coordinating conjunction results in a **run-on** or **fused sentence**:

> *run-on:* Philosophers' views did not always meet with the approval of the authorities therefore there was constant conflict between writers and the church or state.

A semicolon after *authorities* corrects this serious error. See #5c.

> *revised:* Philosophers' views did not always meet with the approval of the authorities; therefore, there was constant conflict between writers and the church or state.

ESSENTIALS OF MECHANICS AND SPELLING

V

CONTENTS

INTRODUCTION

Part V offers some practical advice on how to follow standard conventions of mechanics and spelling. By following these conventions, you will add consistency, clarity, and a sense of professionalism to your writing. If you have trouble with spelling, you will find the advice on spelling rules   in section #32—particularly valuable.

26 FORMATTING AN ESSAY

26a Format

Unless directed otherwise, follow these conventions when you are preparing a manuscript for submission:

1. Prepare your manuscript on plain white recycled paper of good quality, 8½ by 11 inches (or 21 by 28 cm). Use only one side of each page.
2. Choose a plain, readable typeface (12-point Times New Roman or 10-point Arial).
3. Double-space your essay throughout and leave margins of about 1 inch (2.5 cm) on all four sides of the page. Word-processed essays should be justified flush left with a ragged (i.e. unjustified) right-hand margin.
4. If you are submitting a handwritten document, as may be the case for an in-class essay or an examination, use medium- to wide-ruled white paper, and write on alternate lines. Do not use paper torn from a spiral notebook. Use black or blue-black ink, not pencil. Write as legibly as possible.
5. Label all pages after a covering title page at the right margin, about half an inch (1.25 cm) from the top. Include your surname before the page number, as a precaution against misplaced pages. Most word-processing software will enable you to generate these "headers" automatically. Page numbers should be set as Arabic numerals, without periods, dashes, slashes, circles, or other decorations.
6. For a long essay or research paper, begin about 1 inch (2.5 cm) from the top, at the left margin, and on separate double-spaced lines put your name, your instructor's name, the course number, and the date of submission; then double-space again and put the title, centred. In some cases, this information will appear on a title page. If you wish or are instructed to use a separate title page, centre the title about 1 inch (2.5 cm) from the top of the first page following the title page.

7. Set the title in standard font size and in upper- and lowercase roman letters, making sure to capitalize the title correctly (see #28k). Do not put the whole title in capital letters or in boldface type, and do not underline it or put a period after it. Do not put your title in quotation marks (unless it is in fact a quotation); if it includes the title of a poem, story, book, etc., or a ship's name, use italics or quotation marks appropriately (see #29). Do not use the title of a published work by itself as your own title. Here are two examples of effective titles:

> Of Pigoons and Wolvogs: Wildlife in *Oryx and Crake*
>
> The Structure of Dennis Lee's "Civil Elegies"

8. Indent the first line of each paragraph one tab length (approximately 5 spaces). Do not leave extra space between indented paragraphs. Indent long block quotations two tab lengths (approximately 10 spaces). Do not leave any additional space before or after a double-spaced block quotation.

9. Leave only one space after any terminal punctuation, and remember to leave spaces before and after each of the three dots of an ellipsis (see #20f). If you are typing, use two unspaced hyphens to make a dash, with no space before or after them; most word-processing software will automatically convert two hyphens to a dash.

10. Never begin a line with a comma, semicolon, period, question mark, exclamation point, or hyphen. On rare occasions, a dash or the dots of an ellipsis may have to come at the beginning of a line, but if possible place them at the end of the preceding line.

11. As you write an essay on a computer, save your work frequently. Create a back-up file, and save all drafts of your paper in that file. Always keep a copy of the final draft of any paper you submit.

12. Print a clear copy of your document, making sure there is plenty of ink or toner in your cartridge.

13. Aim to produce documents with a professional appearance. If after proofreading you decide that you have to make changes to a word-processed document,

26

call up the file, make the appropriate emendations, save the changes, and reprint the page or pages you have revised. To change or delete a word or short phrase in a handwritten document, draw a single horizontal line through it and write the new word or phrase, if any, above it. If you wish to insert a word or short phrase, place a caret (∧) *below* the line at the point of insertion and write the addition *above* the line. If you wish to start a new paragraph where you haven't indented, put the symbol ¶ in the left margin and insert a caret where you want the paragraph to begin. If you wish to cancel a paragraph indention, write "No ¶" in the left margin.

14. Fasten the pages of an essay together with a paper clip. Do not use a staple.

26b Syllabication and Word Division

Generally, do not divide words at the end of a line. One circumstance in which you may need to insert a word break is in a reference to an electronic source identified by its website or network address. When this address (also known as a *URL*, or *uniform resource locator*) is a long one, it may need to be spread over two lines. The most recent edition of the *MLA Handbook* recommends that the break should appear only after one of the slashes in the URL. Introducing a hyphen or other punctuation into a URL is not recommended, for it will introduce ambiguity and make the website difficult for your reader to locate and access:

> To learn more about Sook-Yin Lee, one of CBC Radio's most lively and entertaining broadcasters, consult the entry for her program, *Definitely Not the Opera*, at <http://www.cbc.ca/dnto>.

On the *rare* occasions when you need to divide a word in a handwritten document, insert a hyphen at the end of a line, after the first part of the word, and begin the next line with the rest of the word. You should not begin a new line

26

with a hyphen. Nor should you divide a word at the end of a page or at the end of a paragraph. Divide words only between syllables, and if you are uncertain, check your dictionary for a word's syllabication.

27 ABBREVIATIONS

Abbreviations are expected in technical and scientific writing, legal writing, business writing, memos, reports, reference works, bibliographies and works cited lists, footnotes, tables and charts, and sometimes in journalism. The following relatively few kinds are in common use.

27a Titles Before Proper Names

The following abbreviations can be used with or without initials or given names:

Mr.	(Mr. Eng; Mr. Marc Ramsay)
Mrs.	(Mrs. L.W. Smith; Mrs. Tazim Khan)
M.	(M. Joubert; M. Stéphane Dion)
Mme.	(Mme. Girard; Mme. Nathalie Gagnon)
Mlle.	(Mlle. Stephanie Sevigny; Mlle. R. Pelletier)
Dr.	(Dr. Paula Grewal; Dr. P. Francis Fairchild)
St.	(St. John; St. Beatrice)

27b Titles and Degrees After Proper Names

David Adams, M.D. (*but not* Dr. David Adams, M.D.)

Claire T. McFadden, D.D.S.

Martin Luther King, Jr.

Academic degrees not following a name may also be abbreviated:

Amir is working on his M.A. thesis.

27c Standard Words Used with Dates and Numerals

720 B.C. (*or* 720 B.P., *or* 720 B.C.E.)

A.D. 231(*or* 231 C.E.), the second century A.D. (*or* the second century C.E.)

7 a.m. (*or* 7 A.M.), 8:30 p.m. (*or* 8:30 P.M.)

no. 17 (*or* No. 17)

Note that *A.D.* precedes a date whereas *B.C.* follows one. Note also that some people now use *B.P.* ("before the present") or *B.C.E.* ("before the common era") and *C.E.* ("of the common era"), both following the date, instead of *B.C.* and *A.D.*, respectively.

27d Agencies and Organizations Known by Their Initials (see also #22)

Capitalize names of agencies and organizations commonly known by their initials:

UNICEF   CAW   CBC   CNN   RCMP   NATO   WHO

27e Scientific and Technical Terms Known by Their Initials (see also #22)

Some scientific, technical, or other terms (usually of considerable length) are commonly known by their initials:

BTU   URL   DDT   DNA   FM

ISBN   HTML   MP   GST   ISP

27f Latin Expressions Commonly Used in English

i.e. (that is)   etc. (and so forth)

e.g. (for example)   vs. (versus)

cf. (compare)   et al. (and others)

In formal writing, it is better to spell out the English equivalent.

Note: If you use *e.g.*, use it only to introduce the example or list of examples; following the example or list, write out *for example*:

> Some provinces—e.g., Manitoba, Saskatchewan, and New Brunswick—supported a single national standard for homecare programs.

> Some provinces—Manitoba, Saskatchewan, and New Brunswick, for example—supported a single national standard for homecare programs.

If you introduce a list with *e.g.* or *for example* or even *such as*, it is illogical to follow it with *etc.* or *and so forth*.

Terms in Official Titles

Capitalize abbreviated terms used in official titles being copied exactly:

> Johnson Bros., Ltd.   Ibbetson & Co.
>
> Smith & Sons, Inc.   *Quill & Quire*

CAPITALIZATION

Generally, capitalize proper nouns, abbreviations of proper nouns, and words derived from proper nouns.

28a Names and Nicknames

Capitalize names and nicknames of real and fictional people and individual animals:

> Nelson Mandela   Margaret MacMillan   Tiger Woods
>
> Colin Firth   Clarissa Dalloway   Rumpelstiltskin
>
> Cinderella   Barack Obama   Sidney Crosby
>
> King Kong   Elmo   Washoe

28b Professional and Honorific Titles

Capitalize professional and honorific titles when they directly precede and thus are parts of names:

> Professor Tamara Jones (*but* Tamara Jones, professor at Mount Allison)
>
> Rabbi Samuel Singer (*but* Mr. Singer was rabbi of our synagogue.)

Normally titles that follow names aren't capitalized unless they have become part of the name:

> Stephen Harper, prime minister of Canada
>
> Roméo Dallaire, the senator
>
> > *but*
>
> Catherine the Great
>
> Smokey the Bear

Some titles of particular distinction are customarily capitalized even if the person isn't named:

> The Queen vacationed in Scotland.
>
> On Easter Sunday, the Pope will address the crowd gathered in St. Peter's Square.
>
> The university was honoured with a visit by the Dalai Lama.

28c Place Names

Capitalize place names—including common nouns (*river, street, park,* etc.) when they are parts of proper nouns:

Active Pass	Alberta	the Amazon
Vancouver Island	Banff	Buenos Aires
Hudson Bay	Japan	Lake Ladoga
Niagara Falls	Québec	Rivière-du-Loup
the Gobi Desert	Asia	Trafalgar Square

28

the Miramichi River	the Andes	Moose Jaw
the Suez Canal	Mt. Etna	Yonge Street
Kootenay National Park		

As a rule, don't capitalize *north*, *south*, *east*, and *west* unless they are part of specific place names (North Battleford, West Vancouver, the South Shore) or designate specific geographical areas (the frozen North, the East Coast, the Deep South, the Northwest, the Wild West, the Far East).

Since writers in Canada usually capitalize *East*, *West*, *North* (and sometimes *South*) to refer to parts of the country (the peoples of the North, the settlement of the West), it makes sense to capitalize *Eastern*, *Western*, *Northern*, and *Southern* when they refer to ideas attached to parts of the country (Northern peoples, Western settlement). Otherwise, except for cases when they appear as parts of specific place names (the Eastern Townships), these adjectives should not be capitalized. This practice applies even to cases such as northern Canada, eastern Canada, and western Canada, which are not specific place names but descriptions of geographic regions.

28d Months, Days, and Holidays

Capitalize the names of the months (January, February, etc.) and the days of the week (Monday, Tuesday, etc.), but not the seasons (spring, summer, autumn, fall, winter). Also capitalize holidays, holy days, and festivals (Christmas, Canada Day, Remembrance Day, Hanukkah, Ramadan).

28e Religious Names

Capitalize names of deities and other religious names and terms:

the Holy Ghost	God	the Virgin Mary
the Bible	the Torah	the Talmud
the Dead Sea Scrolls	Islam	Allah
the Prophet	the Qur'an	Apollo
Jupiter	Vishnu	Taoism

Note: Some people capitalize pronouns referring to a deity; others prefer not to. Either practice is acceptable as long as you are consistent.

28f Names of Nationalities and Organizations

Capitalize names of nationalities and other groups and organizations and of their members:

Canadian, Australian, Malaysian, Scandinavian

New Democrats, the New Democratic Party

Bloquistes, the Bloc Québécois, the Bloc

Roman Catholics, the Roman Catholic Church

Teamsters

the Vancouver Canucks, the Toronto Blue Jays

28g Names of Institutions and Sections of Government, Historical Events, and Buildings

Capitalize names of institutions; sections of government; historical events, periods, and documents; and specific buildings:

McGill University, The Hospital for Sick Children

the Ministry of Health, Parliament, the Senate, the Cabinet, the Opposition

the French Revolution, the Great War, World War I, the Gulf War, the Cretaceous Period, the Renaissance, the Magna Carta, the Treaty of Versailles, the Charter of Rights and Freedoms, the Ming Dynasty

the British Museum, the Museum of Civilization, Westminster Abbey

28

28h Academic Courses and Languages

Capitalize specific academic courses, but not the subjects themselves, except for languages:

> Philosophy 101, Fine Arts 300, Mathematics 204, English 112, Food Writing, Humanities 101

> an English course, a major in French (*but* a history course, an economics major, a degree in psychology)

28i Derivatives of Proper Nouns

Capitalize derivatives of proper nouns:

> French Canadian, Haligonian, Celtic, Québécoise

> Confucianism, Christian

> Shakespearean, Keynesian, Edwardian, Miltonic

28j Abbreviations of Proper Nouns

Capitalize abbreviations of proper nouns:

PMO	TVA	CUPE	CUSO
P.E.I	B.C.	the BNA Act	

Note that abbreviations of agencies and organizations commonly known by their initials do not need periods (see #27d), but that non-postal abbreviations of geographical entities such as provinces usually do. When in doubt, consult your dictionary. See also #22.

28k Titles of Written and Other Works

In the titles of written and other works, including student essays, use a capital letter to begin the first word, the last word, and all other important words; leave uncapitalized only articles (*a, an, the*) and any conjunctions and prepositions less than five letters long (unless one of these is the first or last word):

The Blind Assassin	"The Dead"
Pan's Labyrinth	"O Canada"
"The Metamorphosis"	"Open Secrets"
Paris 1919	*In the Skin of a Lion*
Roughing It in the Bush	

But there can be exceptions; for example the conjunctions *Nor* and *So* are usually capitalized, and the relative pronoun *that* is sometimes not capitalized (*All's Well that Ends Well*).

If a title includes a hyphenated word, capitalize the part after the hyphen only if it is a noun or adjective or is otherwise an important word:

Self-Portrait

The Scorched-Wood People

Murder Among the Well-to-do

Capitalize the first word of a subtitle, even if it is an article:

Beyond Remembering: The Collected Poems of Al Purdy

See #29b for the use of italics in titles.

28-1 First Words

1. Capitalize the first word of a quotation that is intended as a sentence or that is capitalized in the source, but not fragments from other than the beginning of such a sentence:

   When he said "Let me take the wheel for a while," I shuddered at the memory of what had happened the last time I had let him "take the wheel."

If something interrupts a single quoted sentence, do not begin its second part with a capital:

> "It was all I could do," she said, "to keep from laughing out loud."

2. Capitalize the first word of an independent sentence in parentheses only if it stands by itself, apart from other sentences. If it is incorporated within another sentence, it is neither capitalized nor ended with a period.

> She did as she was told (there was really nothing else for her to do), and the tension was relieved. (But of course she would never admit to herself that she had been manipulated.)

3. An incorporated sentence following a colon may be capitalized if it seems to stand as a separate statement, for example if it is itself long or requires emphasis; the current trend is away from capitalization.

> There was one thing, she said, which we must never forget: No one has the right to the kind of happiness that deprives someone else of deserved happiness.

> It was a splendid night: the sky was clear except for a few picturesque clouds, the moon was full, and even a few stars shone through. (The first *The* could be capitalized if the writer wanted particular emphasis on the details.)

28

28m Personification or Emphasis

Although it is risky and should not be done often, writers who have good control of tone can occasionally capitalize a personified abstraction or a word or phrase to which they want to impart a special importance of some kind:

> In his quest to succeed, Greed and Power came to dominate his every waking thought.

Sometimes the slight emphasis of capitalization can be used for a humorous or ironic effect:

> He insisted on driving His Beautiful Car: everyone else preferred to walk the two blocks without benefit of jerks and jolts and carbon monoxide fumes.

And occasionally, but rarely, you can capitalize whole words and phrases or even sentences for a special sort of graphic emphasis:

> When we reached the excavation site, however, we were confronted by a sign warning us in no uncertain terms to KEEP OUT—TRESPASSERS WILL BE PROSECUTED.

29 TITLES (SEE ALSO #28K)

29a Quotation Marks for Short Works and Parts of Longer Works

Put quotation marks around the titles of short works and of parts of longer works, such as short stories, articles, essays, short poems, chapters of books, songs, and individual episodes of television programs:

> Leonard Cohen's "Joan of Arc" and "Democracy" are songs featured in this documentary about the music of Canada.

> "A Wilderness Station" is an Alice Munro story that begins in Ontario in the 1850s.

> Of the ten episodes in the CBC documentary *Hockey: A People's History,* I enjoyed the first one, "A Simple Game," the best.

There can be exceptions, however. Some works, for example Coleridge's *The Rime of the Ancient Mariner,* E.J. Pratt's *Towards the Last Spike,* and Conrad's *Heart of Darkness,* although originally parts of larger collections, are fairly long and have attained a reputation and importance as individual works; most writers feel justified in italicizing their titles.

 Italics for Whole or Major Works

Use italics (see #30) for titles of written works published as units, such as books, magazines, journals, newspapers, and plays; films and television programs; paintings and sculptures; and musical compositions (other than single songs), such as operas and ballets:

> *Paradise Lost* is Milton's greatest work.
>
> *The New Yorker* is a weekly magazine.
>
> The scholarly journal *Canadian Literature* is published quarterly.
>
> I prefer *The Globe and Mail* to the *National Post*.
>
> *The Passionate Eye* is a CBC program featuring the best in current documentaries.
>
> One tires of hearing Ravel's *Bolero* played so often.
>
> Picasso's *Guernica* is a disturbing representation of the Spanish Civil War.

Note that instrumental compositions may be known by name or by technical detail, or both. A title name is italicized (Beethoven's *Pastoral Symphony*); technical identification is usually not (Beethoven's Sixth Symphony, or Symphony no. 6, op. 68, in F major).

Note that MLA documentation style, which once required titles of works to be underlined, now recommends italics. (See #37a.)

 Titles Within Titles

If an essay title includes a book title, the book title is italicized:

> "Things Botanical in *The Lost Garden* and *A Student of Weather*"

If a book title includes something requiring quotation marks, retain the quotation marks and italicize the whole thing:

> *From Fiction to Film: James Joyce's "The Dead"*

If a book title includes something that itself would be italicized, such as the name of a ship or the title of another book, either put the secondary item in quotation marks or leave it in roman type (i.e., not italicized):

> *The Cruise of the "Nona"*
>
> *D.H. Lawrence and* Sons and Lovers: *Sources and Criticism*

Note: Double-check in the titles you cite for the role of the definite article, *the*: italicize and capitalize it only when it is actually a part of the title: Margaret Laurence's *The Stone Angel*; Yann Martel's *Life of Pi*; Roman Polanski's *The Pianist*; the *Partisan Review*; *The Canadian Encyclopedia*; the *Atlas of Ancient Archaeology*.

Try to refer to a newspaper the way it refers to itself—on its front page or masthead: the Victoria *Times Colonist*; the Regina *Leader-Post*; *The Vancouver Sun*; the *Calgary Herald*; *The Globe and Mail*.

30 ITALICS

Italics are a special kind of slanting type that contrasts with the surrounding type to draw attention to a word or phrase, such as a title (see #29). The other main uses of italics are discussed below. In handwritten work, such as an exam, represent italic type by underlining.

30a Names of Ships and Planes

Italicize names of individual ships, planes, and the like:

the *Golden Hind*   *Spirit of St. Louis*

the *Bonaventure*   *Mariner IX*

30b   Non-English Words and Phrases

Italicize non-English words and phrases not yet sufficiently common to be entirely at home in English. English contains many terms that have come from other languages but that are no longer thought of as non-English and are therefore not italicized, for example:

moccasin	prairie	genre	tableau
bamboo	arroyo	corral	sushi
chutzpah	spaghetti	goulash	eureka

There are also words that are sufficiently Anglicized not to require italicizing but that usually retain their original accents and diacritical marks, for example:

cliché   naïf   fête   façade   Götterdämmerung

But English also makes use of many terms still felt by many writers to be sufficiently non-English to need italicizing, for example:

Bildungsroman	*au courant*	*coup d'état*
chez	*joie de vivre*	*jihad*
raison d'être	*savoir faire*	

30c   Words Referred to as Words

30

Italicize words, letters, numerals, and the like when you refer to them as such:

The word *helicopter* is formed from Greek roots.

There are two *r*'s in *embarrass*. (Note that only the *r* is italicized; the *s* making it plural stays roman.)

The number *13* is considered unlucky by many otherwise rational people.

Don't use *&* as a substitute for *and*.

See also #20d. For the matter of apostrophes for plurals of such elements, see #32m.

30d For Emphasis

On rare occasions, italicize words or phrases—or even whole sentences—that you want to emphasize, for example, as they might be stressed if spoken aloud:

> One thing he was now sure of: *that* was no way to go about the task.

> If people try to tell you otherwise, *don't listen to them.*

Like other typographical devices for achieving emphasis (boldface, capitalization, underlining), this method is worth avoiding, or at least minimizing, in academic and other formal writing.

31 NUMERALS

Numerals are appropriate in technical and scientific writing, and newspapers sometimes use them to save space. But in ordinary writing certain conventions limit their use.

31a Time of Day

Use numerals for the time of day with *a.m.* or *p.m.* and *midnight* or *noon*, or when minutes are included:

> 3 p.m. (*but* three o'clock, three in the afternoon)

> 12 noon, 12 midnight (these are often better than the equivalents, *12 p.m.* and *12 a.m.*, which may not be understood)

> 4:15, 4:30 (*but* a quarter past four; half past four)

31b Dates

Use numerals for dates:

> September 11, 2001, *or* 11 September 2001

The year is almost always represented by numerals, and centuries written out:

> 2000 was the last year of the twentieth century, not the first year of the twenty-first century, wasn't it?

Note: The suffixes *st*, *nd*, *rd*, and *th* go with numerals in dates only if the year is not given; or the number may be written out:

> May 12, 1955   May 12th
>
> the twelfth of May   May twelfth

31c Addresses

Use numerals for addresses:

> 2132 Fourth Avenue; 4771 128th Street; P.O. Box 91

31d Technical and Mathematical Numbers

Use numerals for technical and mathematical numbers, such as percentages and decimals:

> 31 per cent   31%
>
> 37 degrees Celsius   37°C
>
> 2.54 centimetres   2.54 cm

31e Pages and Chapters

Use numerals for page numbers and other divisions of a written work, especially in documentation (see #37):

> page 27, p. 27, pp. 33–38   line 13, lines 3 and 5, ll. 7–9
>
> Chapter 4, Ch. 4, chapter IV   section 3, section III
>
> Part 2   Book IX, canto 120 (IX, 120)
>
> 2 Samuel 22: 3, II Samuel 19: 1

(Note that books of the Bible are not italicized.)

31f   Parts of a Play

Use numerals for acts, scenes, and line numbers of plays (some readers may prefer that you use Roman numerals for acts and scenes):

> In act 4, scene 2, . . .

> See act IV, scene ii, line 77.

> Remember Hamlet's "To be, or not to be" (3.1.56) or (III.i.56).

31g   Fractions

Spell out numbers when they are expressed as compound fractions:

> one-third; one-half; five thirty-seconds

31h   Numbers of More Than Two Words

Generally, spell out numbers that can be expressed in one or two words; use numerals for numbers that would take more than two words:

> four; thirty; eighty-three; two hundred; seven thousand; 115; 385; 2120

> three dollars, $3.48; five hundred dollars, $517

Note: If you are writing about more than one number, say for purposes of comparison or giving statistics, numerals are usually preferable:

> Enrolment dropped from 250 two years ago, to 200 last year, to only 90 this year.

Following this convention will help you to avoid mixing numerals and words in the same context.

31i Commas with Numerals

Commas have long been conventional to separate groups of three figures in long numbers:

    3,172,450   17,920

In the metric system, however, along with the rest of SI (Système Internationale, or International System of Units), groups of three digits on either side of a decimal point are separated by spaces; with four-digit numbers a space is optional:

    7723   *or*   7 723

    3 172 450

    3.1416   *or*   3.141 6 (*but* 3.141 59)

There are two exceptions to this convention: amounts of money and addresses. Use commas to separate dollar figures preceding a decimal into units of three:

    $3,500   £27,998.06   ¥30,000

Street addresses of four or more figures are usually not separated by commas or spaces:

    18885 Bay Mills Avenue

For further information about SI consult the *Canadian Metric Practice Guide,* published by the Canadian Standards Association.

32 SPELLING RULES AND COMMON CAUSES OF ERROR

Good spelling comes with practice; taking the time to look up a word now will help you remember its proper spelling the next time you need to use it.

English spelling isn't as bizarre as some people think, but there are oddities. Sometimes the same sound can be spelled in several ways (*fine, offer, phone, cough*; or *so, soap, sow, sew, beau, dough*), or a single element can be pronounced in several ways (*cough, tough, dough, through, bough, fought*). When such inconsistencies occur in longer and less familiar words, sometimes only a dictionary can help us.

In Canada, we contend with the influence of British and American spelling. Broadly speaking, Canadian conventions—whether of spelling, punctuation, usage, or pronunciation—are closer to American than to British, and where they are changing, they are changing in the direction of American conventions. Many of us, when we see the word *lieutenant*, still say "leftenant" instead of "lootenant," but we say and spell *aluminum* rather than *aluminium*. The alphabet still ends in *zed* rather than *zee* for most of us, though the distinction may be fading. Most Canadians write *centre* and *theatre* rather than *center* and *theater*; but we write *curb* rather than *kerb*, and "skedule" is replacing "shedule" as the pronunciation of *schedule*. Endings in *our* (colour, honour, labour, etc.) exist alongside those in *or*; either spelling is conventional in Canada. The same is true of endings in *ise* or *ize*, though the latter is clearly preferred. We have the useful alternatives *cheque* (bank), *racquet* (tennis), and *storey* (floor); Americans have only *check, racket,* and *story* for both meanings. But *draught* is losing ground to *draft*, and *program* and *judgment* are rapidly replacing *programme* and *judgement*.

Where alternatives exist, either is correct. But be consistent. If you choose *analyze*, write *paralyze* and *modernize*; if you choose *centre*, write *lustre* and *fibre*; if you spell *honour*, then write *humour*, *colour*, and *labour*. But if you do choose the *our* endings, watch out for the trap: when you add the suffixes *ous, ious, ate* or *ation*, and *ize* (or *ise*), you must drop the *u* and write *humorous*, *coloration*, *vaporize*, *laborious*, and there is no *u* in *honorary*.

Many spelling errors fall into clear categories. Familiarizing yourself with the main rules and the main sources of confusion will help you avoid these errors.

32a *ie* or *ei*

The old jingle should help: use *i* before *e* except after *c*, or when sounded like *a* as in *neighbour* and *weigh*.

ie:	achieve, believe, chief, field, fiend, shriek, siege, wield
ei **after** *c:*	ceiling, conceive, deceive, perceive, receive
ei **when sounded like** *a:*	eight, neighbour, sleigh, veil, weigh

When the sound is neither long *e* nor long *a*, the spelling *ei* is usually right:

> counterfeit, foreign, forfeit, height, heir, their

But there are several exceptions:

> *ei:* either, neither, leisure, seize, weird
>
> *ie:* financier, friend, mischief, sieve

32b Final *e* Before a Suffix

When a suffix is added to a root word that ends in a silent *e,* certain rules generally apply. If the suffix begins with a *vowel* (*a, e, i, o, u*), the *e* is usually dropped:

desire + able = desirable	forgive + able = forgivable
sphere + ical = spherical	argue + ing = arguing
come + ing = coming	allure + ing = alluring
continue + ous = continuous	desire + ous = desirous

(*Dyeing* retains the *e* to distinguish it from *dying.* If a word ends with two *e*'s, both are pronounced and therefore not dropped: *agreeing, fleeing.*)

If the suffix begins with *a* or *o,* most words ending in *ce* or *ge* retain the *e* in order to preserve the soft sound of the *c* (like *s* rather than *k*) or the *g* (like *j* rather than hard as in *gum*):

> notice + able = noticeable   outrage + ous = outrageous

32

(Note that *vengeance* and *gorgeous* also have such a silent *e*.) Similarly, words like *picnic* and *frolic* require an added *k* to preserve the hard sound before suffixes beginning with *e* or *i*: *picnicked, picnicking, frolicked, frolicking, politicking*. (An exception to this rule is *arc: arced, arcing*.) When the suffix does not begin with *e* or *i*, these words do not require an added *k*: *tactical, frolicsome*.

If the suffix begins with a *consonant*, the silent *e* of the root word is usually not dropped:

> awe + some = awesome
>
> effective + ness = effectiveness
>
> definite + ly = definitely
>
> hoarse + ly = hoarsely
>
> immediate + ly = immediately
>
> mere + ly = merely

(But note a common exception: awe + ful = awful.)

And there is a subgroup of words whose final *e*'s are sometimes wrongly omitted. The *e*, though silent, is essential to keep the sound of the preceding vowel long:

> completely   extremely   hopelessness   livelihood
>
> loneliness   remoteness   severely   tasteless

But such an *e* is sometimes dropped when no consonant intervenes between it and the long vowel:

> due + ly = duly   true + ly = truly
>
> argue + ment = argument

32c Final *y* After a Consonant and Before a Suffix

When the suffix begins with *i*, keep the *y*:

> baby + ish = babyish   carry + ing = carrying
>
> try + ing = trying   worry + ing = worrying

(**Note:** Words ending in *ie* change to *y* before adding *ing*: die + ing = dying; lie + ing = lying.)

When the suffix begins with something other than *i*, change *y* to *i*:

happy + er = happier	duty + ful = dutiful
happy + ness = happiness	silly + est = silliest
harmony + ous = harmonious	angry + ly = angrily

But here are some exceptions: *shyly, shyness; slyer, slyly; flyer* (though *flier* is sometimes used); *dryer* (as a noun—for the comparative adjective use *drier*).

32d Doubling of a Final Consonant Before a Suffix

When adding a suffix, *double* the final consonant of the root if all three of the following apply:

(a) that consonant is preceded by a single vowel,
(b) the root is a one-syllable word or a word accented on its last syllable, and
(c) the suffix begins with a vowel.

One-syllable words:

bar + ed = barred	bar + ing = barring	
fit + ed = fitted	fit + ing = fitting	fit + er = fitter
hot + er = hotter	hot + est = hottest	

Words accented on last syllable:

allot + ed = allotted	allot + ing = allotting
commit + ed = committed	commit + ing = committing
occur + ed = occurred	occur + ing = occurring
	occur + ence = occurrence

But when the addition of the suffix shifts the accent of the root word away from the last syllable, do not double the final consonant:

infer + ed = inferred	infer + ing = inferring BUT inference
prefer + ed = preferred	prefer + ing = preferring BUT preference
refer + ed = referred	refer + ing = referring BUT reference

32

Do not double the final consonant if it is preceded by a single consonant (sharp + er = sharper) or if the final consonant is preceded by two vowels (fail + ed = failed, stoop + ing = stooping) or if the root word is more than one syllable and *not* accented on its last syllable (benefit + ed = benefited, parallel + ing = paralleling) or if the suffix begins with a consonant (commit + ment = commitment).

32e The Suffix *ly*

When *ly* is added to an adjective already ending in a single *l*, that final *l* is retained, resulting in an adverb ending in *lly*. If you pronounce such words carefully you will be less likely to misspell them:

accidental + ly = accidentally	cool + ly = coolly
incidental + ly = incidentally	mental + ly = mentally
natural + ly = naturally	political + ly = politically

If the root ends in a double *ll*, one *l* is dropped: full + ly = fully, chill + ly = chilly, droll + ly = drolly.

Note: Many adjectives ending in *ic* have alternative forms ending in *ical*. But even if they don't, nearly all add *ally*, not just *ly*, to become adverbs—as do nouns like *music* and *stoic*. Again, careful pronunciation will help you avoid error:

alphabetic, alphabetical, alphabetically

basic, basically

cyclic, cyclical, cyclically

drastic, drastically

scientific, scientifically

symbolic, symbolical, symbolically

An exception: *publicly*.

32f Troublesome Word Endings

Several groups of suffixes, or word endings, consistently plague weak spellers and sometimes trip even good spellers. There are no rules governing them, and pronunciation is seldom any help; one either knows them or does not. The following examples will at least alert you to the potential trouble spots:

able, ably, ability; ible, ibly, ibility
It should be helpful to remember that many more words end in *able* than in *ible*; yet it is the *ible* endings that cause the most trouble:

-able		-ible	
advisable	inevitable	audible	inexpressible
comparable	laudable	contemptible	irresistible
debatable	noticeable	deductible	negligible
desirable	quotable	eligible	plausible
immeasurable	respectable	flexible	responsible
indubitable	veritable	incredible	visible

ent, ently, ence, ency; ant, antly, ance, ancy

-en-		-an-	
apparent	independent	appearance	flamboyant
coherent	permanent	blatant	irrelevant
consistent	persistence	brilliant	maintenance
excellent	resilient	concomitant	resistance
existence	tendency	extravagant	warrant

tial, tian; cial, cian, ciate

-tia-		-cia-	
confidential	influential	beneficial	mathematician
dietitian	martial	crucial	mortician
existential	spatial	emaciated	physician

ce; se

-ce		-se	
choice	fence	course	expense
defence	presence	dense	phrase
evidence	voice	dispense	sparse

32

Note: Canadian writers tend to follow the British practice of using the *-ce* forms of *practice* and *licence* as nouns and the *-se* forms *practise* and *license* as verbs:

> We will <u>practise</u> our fielding at today's slo-pitch <u>practice</u>.

> Are you <u>licensed</u> to drive?
> Yes, I've had my driver's <u>licence</u> since I was sixteen.

American writers tend to favour the *-ce* spelling of *practice* and *-se* spelling of *license* regardless of whether each is being used as a noun or a verb.

Note also that Canadian as well as British writers generally prefer the *-ce* spelling for *offence* and *defence*, while American writers tend to use the *-se* spellings of these words.

ative; itive

-ative		-itive	
affirmative	informative	additive	positive
comparative	negative	competitive	repetitive
imaginative	restorative	genitive	sensitive

cede, ceed, or *sede*
Memorize if necessary: the *sede* ending occurs only in *supersede*. The *ceed* ending occurs only in *exceed*, *proceed*, and *succeed*. All other words ending in this sound use *cede*: *accede, concede, intercede, precede, recede, secede*.

32

32g Changes in Spelling of Roots

Be careful with words whose roots change spelling, often because of a change in stress, when they are inflected for a different part of speech, for example:

clear, clarity	maintain, maintenance
curious, curiosity	prevail, prevalent
despair, desperate	pronounce, pronunciation
exclaim, exclamatory	repair, reparable
generous, generosity	repeat, repetition
inherit, heritage, *but* heredity, hereditary	

32h Faulty Pronunciation

Here is a list of words some of whose common misspellings could be prevented by careful pronunciation:

academic	disgust	insurgence	prevalent
accelerate	disillusioned	interpretation	pronunciation
accidentally	elaborate	intimacy	quantity
amphitheatre	emperor	inviting	repetitive
analogy	environment	irrelevant	reservoir
approximately	epitomize	itinerary	sacrilegious
architectural	escape	larynx	separate
athlete	especially	lightning	significant
authoritative	etcetera	limpidly	similar
biathlon	evident	lustrous	strength
camaraderie	excerpt	mathematics	subsidiary
candidate	February	negative	suffocate
celebration	film	nuclear	surprise
conference	foliage	optimism	temporarily
congratulate	further	original	triathlon
controversial	government	particular	ultimatum
definitely	governor	peculiar	village
deteriorating	gravitation	permanently	villain
detrimental	hereditary	phenomenon	visible
dilapidated	hurriedly	philosophical	vulnerable
disgruntled	immersing	predilection	wondrous

Note: Don't omit the *d* or *ed* from such words as *used* and *supposed*, *old-fashioned* and *prejudiced*, which are often pronounced without the *d* sound. And be careful not to omit whole syllables that are near duplications in sound. Write carefully, run a spell check when possible, and proofread, sounding the words to yourself. Here are some examples of such "telescoped" words that occur frequently:

Right	Wrong	Right	Wrong
convenience	~~convience~~	institution	~~instution~~
criticize	~~critize~~	politician	~~politian~~
examining	~~examing~~	remembrance	~~rembrance~~
inappropriate	~~inappriate~~	repetition	~~repition~~

32i   Confusion with Other Words

Don't let false analogies and similarities of sound lead you astray.

A writer who thinks of a word like:	May spell another word **wrong**, like this:	Instead of **right**, like this:
air	~~ordinairy~~	ordinary
breeze	~~cheeze~~	cheese
comrade	~~comraderie~~	camaraderie
democracy	~~hypocracy~~	hypocrisy
desolate	~~desolute~~	dissolute
diet	~~diety~~	deity
exalt	~~exaltant~~	exultant
familiar	~~similiar~~	similar
ideal	~~idealic~~	idyllic
knowledge	~~priviledge~~	privilege
prize	~~surprize~~	surprise
religious	~~sacreligious~~	sacrilegious
restaurant	~~restauranteur~~	restaurateur
sink	~~zink~~	zinc
size	~~rize~~	rise
solid	~~solider~~	soldier
summer	~~grammer~~	grammar
young	~~amoung~~	among

32

32j Homophones and Other Words Sometimes Confused

1. Be careful to distinguish between **homophones** (or homonyms) that are pronounced alike but spelled differently. Here are some that can be troublesome; consult a dictionary for any whose meanings you aren't sure of; this is a matter of meaning as well as of spelling (and see #14d):

aisle, isle	its, it's
alter, altar	led, lead
assent, ascent	manner, manor
bear, bare	meat, meet
birth, berth	past, passed
board, bored	patience, patients
boarder, border	piece, peace
born, borne	plain, plane
break, brake	pore, pour
by, buy, bye	pray, prey
capital, capitol	presence, presents
complement, compliment	principle, principal
council, counsel	rain, rein, reign
course, coarse	right, rite, write
desert, dessert	road, rode, rowed
die, dye; dying, dyeing	sight, site, cite
discreet, discrete	stationary, stationery
forth, fourth	there, their, they're
hear, here	to, too, two
heard, herd	whose, who's
hole, whole	your, you're

32

2. There are also words that are not pronounced exactly alike but that are similar enough to be confused. Again, look up any whose meanings you aren't sure of:

accept, except	eminent, imminent, immanent
access, excess	
adopt, adapt, adept	enquire, inquire, acquire
adverse, averse	ensure, insure, assure
advice, advise	envelop, envelope
affect, effect	evoke, invoke
afflicted, inflicted	illusion, allusion
allude, elude	incident, incidence, instant, instance
angle, angel	
appraise, apprise	incredulous, incredible
assume, presume	ingenious, ingenuous
bizarre, bazaar	insight, incite
breath, breathe	later, latter
choose, chose	loose, lose
cloth, clothe	moral, morale
conscious, conscience	practice, practise
custom, costume	quite, quiet
decent, descent, dissent	tack, tact
decimate, disseminate	than, then
device, devise	whether, weather
diary, dairy	while, wile
emigrate, immigrate	

32

3. Be careful also to distinguish between such terms as the following, for although they sound the same, they function differently depending on whether they are spelled as one word or two:

already, all ready	awhile, a while
altogether, all together	everybody, every body

anybody, any body	everyday, every day
anymore, any more	everyone, every one
anyone, any one	maybe, may be
anytime, any time	someday, some day
anyway, any way	sometime, some time

32k Hyphenation

To hyphenate or not to hyphenate? Since the conventions are constantly changing, sometimes rapidly, make a habit of checking your dictionary for current usage. (For hyphens to divide a word at the end of a line, see #26b.) Here are the main points to remember:

1. Use hyphens in compound numbers from *twenty-one* to *ninety-nine.*
2. Use hyphens with fractions used as adjectives:

   A two-thirds majority is required to defeat the amendment.

   When a fraction is used as a noun, you may use a hyphen, though many writers do not:

   One quarter of the audience was asleep.

3. Use hyphens with compounds indicating time, when these are written out: *seven-thirty, nine-fifteen.*
4. Use a hyphen between a pair of numbers (including hours and dates) indicating a range: *pages 73–78, June 20–26.* The hyphen is equivalent to the word *to.* If you introduce the range with *from,* write out the word *to*: *from June 20 to June 26.* If you use *between,* write out the word *and: between June 20 and June 26.*
5. Use hyphens with prefixes before proper nouns:

all-Canadian	pan-Asian	pseudo-Modern
ex-Prime Minister	pre-Babylonian	trans-Siberian

   But there are well-established exceptions, for example:

antichrist	postmodern	postcolonial
transatlantic	transpacific	transnational

32

6. Use hyphens with compounds beginning with the prefix *self*: *self-assured, self-confidence, self-deluded, self-esteem, self-made, self-pity*, etc. (The words *self-hood, selfish, selfless*, and *selfsame* are not hyphenated, since *self* is the root, not a prefix.) Hyphens are conventionally used with certain other prefixes: *all-important, ex-premier, quasi-religious*. Hyphens are conventionally used with most, but not all, compounds beginning with *vice* and *by*: *vice-chancellor, vice-consul, vice-president, vice-regent*, etc., BUT *viceregal, viceroy*; *by-election, by-product*, etc., BUT *bygone, bylaw, byroad, bystander, byword*. Check your dictionary.

7. Use hyphens with the suffixes *elect* and *designate*: *mayor-elect, ambassador-designate*.

8. Use hyphens with *great* and *in-law* in compounds designating family relationships: *great-grandfather, great-aunt, mother-in-law, son-in-law*.

9. Use hyphens to prevent a word's being mistaken for an entirely different word:

   > He recounted what had happened after the ballots had been re-counted.

   > If you're going to re-strain the juice, I'll restrain myself from drinking it now, seeds and all.

10. Use hyphens to prevent awkward or confusing combinations of letters and sounds: *anti-intellectual, doll-like, e-book, e-learning, e-mail, photo-offset, re-echo, set-to*.

11. Hyphens are sometimes necessary to prevent ambiguity:

    > ***ambig:*** The ad offered six week old kittens for sale.

    > ***clear:*** The ad offered six week-old kittens for sale.

    > ***clear:*** The ad offered six-week-old kittens for sale.

    Note the difference a hyphen makes to the meaning of the last two examples.

12. Some nouns composed of two or more words are conventionally hyphenated, for example:

32

free-for-all	half-and-half	jack-o-lantern
runner-up	merry-go-round	rabble-rouser
shut-in	trade-in	two-timer

13. When two or more words occur together in such a way that they act as a single adjective before a noun, they are usually hyphenated to prevent a momentary misreading of the first part:

a <u>well-dressed</u> man   <u>greenish-grey</u> eyes

a <u>once-in-a-lifetime</u> chance   a <u>three-day-old</u> strike

When they occur after a noun, misreading is unlikely and no hyphen is needed:

The man was <u>well dressed</u>.

Her eyes are <u>greenish grey</u>.

But many compound modifiers are already listed as hyphenated words; for example, the *Canadian Oxford Dictionary* lists these, among others:

first-class	fly-by-night	good-looking
habit-forming	open-minded	right-hand
short-lived	tongue-tied	

Such modifiers retain their hyphens even when they follow the nouns they modify:

The tone of the speech was quite <u>matter-of-fact</u>.

Note: Since one cannot mistake the first part of a compound modifier when it is an adverb ending in *ly*, even in front of a noun, do not use a hyphen:

He is a <u>happily married</u> man.

14. Verbs, too, are sometimes hyphenated. A dictionary will list most of the ones you might want to use, for example:

double-click	pan-broil	pole-vault
re-educate	second-guess	sight-read
soft-pedal	two-time	

32

Note: Some expressions can be spelled either as two separate words or as compounds, depending on what part of speech they are functioning as, for example:

> He works <u>full time</u>. *but* He has a <u>full-time</u> job.

> If you get too dizzy you may <u>black out</u>. *but* You will then suffer a <u>blackout</u>.

32-1 Plurals

1. Regular nouns
For most nouns, add *s* or *es* to the singular form to indicate plural number:

> one building, two buildings   one box, two boxes

2. Nouns ending in *o*
Some nouns ending in *o* preceded by a consonant form their plurals with *s*, while some use *es*. For some either form is correct—but use the one listed first in your dictionary. Here are a few examples:

altos	echoes	cargoes *or* cargos
pianos	heroes	mottoes *or* mottos
solos	potatoes	zeros *or* zeroes

3. Nouns ending in *f* or *fe*
For some nouns ending in a single *f* or an *fe*, change the ending to *ve* before adding *s*, for example:

knife, knives	life, lives	shelf, shelves
leaf, leaves	loaf, loaves	thief, thieves

But for some simply add *s*:

beliefs	gulfs	safes
griefs	proofs	still lifes

32

Some words ending in *f* have alternative plurals:

dwarfs *or* dwarves   scarves *or* scarfs

hoofs *or* hooves   wharves *or* wharfs

The hockey team the *Maple Leafs* is a special case, a proper noun that doesn't follow the rules governing common nouns.

4. Nouns ending in *y*
For nouns ending in *y* preceded by a vowel, add *s*:

keys   toys   valleys

For nouns ending in *y* preceded by a consonant, change the *y* to *i* and add *es*:

city, cities   cry, cries

country, countries   family, families

Exception: Most proper nouns ending in *y* simply take *s*:

From 1949 to 1990 there were two <u>Germanys</u>.

But note that we refer to the Rocky Mountains as the *Rockies* and to the Canary Islands as the *Canaries*.

5. Compounds
Generally, form the plurals of compounds simply by adding *s*:

major generals   lieutenant-governors

webmasters   merry-go-rounds

prizewinners   great-grandmothers

But if the first part is a noun and the rest is not, or if the first part is the more important of two nouns, that one is made plural:

governors general   daughters-in-law

passersby   townspeople

6. Irregular plurals

Some nouns are irregular in the way they form their plurals, but these are common and generally well known, for example:

child, children	foot, feet
mouse, mice	woman, women

Some plural forms are the same as the singular, for example:

one deer, two deer	one series, two series
one moose, two moose	one sheep, two sheep

7. Borrowed words

The plurals of words borrowed from other languages (mostly Latin and Greek) can pose a problem. Words used formally or technically tend to retain their original plurals; words used more commonly tend to form their plurals according to English rules. Since many such words are in transition, you will probably encounter both plural forms. When in doubt, use the preferred form listed in your dictionary. Here are some examples of words that have tended to retain their original plurals:

alumna, alumnae	larva, larvae
alumnus, alumni	madame, mesdames
analysis, analyses	medium, media
basis, bases	nucleus, nuclei
crisis, crises	parenthesis, parentheses
criterion, criteria	phenomenon, phenomena
datum, data	stimulus, stimuli
hypothesis, hypotheses	synthesis, syntheses
kibbutz, kibbutzim	thesis, theses

Here are some with both forms, the choice often depending on the formality or technicality of the context:

antenna	antennae (insects) *or* antennas (radios, etc.)
apparatus	apparatus *or* apparatuses

32

appendix	appendices *or* appendixes
beau	beaux *or* beaus
cactus	cacti *or* cactuses
château	châteaux *or* châteaus
curriculum	curricula *or* curriculums
focus	foci *or* focuses (focusses)
formula	formulae *or* formulas
index	indices *or* indexes
lacuna	lacunae *or* lacunas
matrix	matrices *or* matrixes
memorandum	memoranda *or* memorandums
referendum	referenda *or* referendums
stratum	strata *or* stratums
syllabus	syllabi *or* syllabuses
symposium	symposia *or* symposiums
terminus	termini *or* terminuses
ultimatum	ultimata *or* ultimatums

And here are a few that now tend to follow regular English patterns:

bureau, bureaus	sanctum, sanctums
campus, campuses	stadium, stadiums
genius, geniuses (*genii* for mythological creatures)	

 Apostrophes

1. For plurals

An apostrophe and an *s* may be used to form the plural, but only of numerals, symbols, letters, and words referred to as words:

It happened in the 1870's.

Indent all ¶'s five spaces.

Accommodate is spelled with two *c*'s and two *m*'s.

Note that when a word, letter, or figure is italicized, the apostrophe and the *s* are not.

Many people prefer to form such plurals without the apostrophe: *R*s, *7*s, *1870*s, *and*s. But this practice can be confusing, especially with lowercase letters and words, which may be misread:

> *confusing:* How many *s*s are there in Nipissing?
>
> *confusing:* Too many *this*s can spoil a good paragraph.

In cases such as these, it is clearer and easier to use the apostrophe. Keep in mind that it is sometimes better to rephrase instances that are potentially awkward:

> *Accommodate* is spelled with a double-*c* and a double-*m*.

2. To indicate omissions

Use apostrophes to indicate omitted letters in contractions and omitted (though obvious) numerals:

aren't (are not)	they're (they are)
can't (cannot)	won't (will not)
doesn't (does not)	wouldn't (would not)
don't (do not)	goin' fishin' (going fishing)[informal]
isn't (is not)	back in '83
it's (it is)	the crash of '29
she's (she is)	the summer of '96

If an apostrophe is already present to indicate a plural, you may omit the apostrophe that indicates omission: the *20*'s, the *90*'s.

32n   Possessives

1. To form the possessive case of a singular or a plural noun that does not end in *s*, add an apostrophe and *s*:

the car's colour	deer's hide	children's books
the girl's teacher	Emil's briefcase	the women's jobs

32

2. To form the possessive of compound nouns, use *'s* after the last noun:

> The Solicitor General's report is due tomorrow.
>
> Sally and Mike's dinner party was a huge success.

If the nouns don't actually form a compound, each will need the *'s*:

> Sally's and Mike's versions of the dinner party were markedly different.

3. You may correctly add an apostrophe and an *s* to form the possessive of singular nouns ending in *s* or an *s*-sound:

> the class's achievement   an index's usefulness
>
> the cross's meaning   Keats's poems

However, some writers prefer to add only an apostrophe if the pronunciation of an extra syllable would sound awkward:

> Achilles' heel   Moses' miracles
>
> for convenience' sake   Bill Gates' Foundation

But the *'s* is usually acceptable: *Achilles's heel*; *for convenience's sake*; *Moses's miracles*; *Bill Gates's Foundation*. In any event, one can usually avoid possible awkwardness by showing possession with an *of*-phrase instead of *'s* (see number 5, below):

> for the sake of convenience   the poems of Keats
>
> the miracles of Moses

4. To indicate the possessive case of plural nouns ending in *s*, add only an apostrophe:

> the cannons' roar   the girls' sweaters
>
> the Joneses' garden   the Chans' cottage

Note: When forming possessive pronouns, do not use apostrophes:

> hers (NOT her's)   its (NOT it's)
>
> ours (NOT our's)   theirs (NOT their's)
>
> yours (NOT your's)   whose (NOT who's)

32

5. Possessive with *'s* or with *of*: Especially in formal writing, the *'s* form is more common with the names of living creatures, the *of* form with the names of inanimate things:

the cat's tail	the leg of the chair
the girl's coat	the contents of the report
Sheldon's home town	the surface of the desk

But both are acceptable with either category. The *'s* form, for example, is common with nouns that refer to things thought of as made up of people or animals or as extensions of them:

the team's strategy	the committee's decision
the company's employee	the government's policy
the city's bylaws	Canada's climate
the factory's output	the heart's affections

or things that are "animate" in the sense that they are part of nature:

the dawn's early light	the wind's velocity
the comet's tail	the sea's surface
the plant's roots	the sky's colour

or periods of time:

today's paper	a day's work
a month's wages	winter's storms

Even beyond such uses the *'s* is not uncommon; sometimes there is a sense of personification, but not always:

beauty's ensign	at death's door
freedom's light	*Love's Labour's Lost*
time's fool	the razor's edge

For the sake of emphasis or rhythm you will occasionally want to use an *of*-phrase where *'s* would be normal; for example *the jury's verdict* lacks the punch of *the verdict of the jury*. You can also use an *of*-phrase to avoid awkward pronunciations (see above: those who don't like the sound of *Dickens's novels* can refer to *the novels of Dickens*) and unwieldy constructions (*the opinion of the minister of finance* is preferable to *the minister of finance's opinion*).

6. Double possessives: There is nothing wrong with double possessive, showing possession with both an *of*-phrase and a possessive inflection. They are standard with possessive pronouns and can be used similarly with common and proper nouns:

> a favourite of mine a friend of the family
> *or* of the family's
>
> a friend of hers a contemporary of Shakespeare
> *or* of Shakespeare's

And a sentence like "*The story was based on an idea of Shakespeare*" is at least potentially ambiguous, whereas "*The story was based on an idea of Shakespeare's*" is clear. But if you feel that this sort of construction is unpleasant to the ear, you can usually manage to revise it to something like "*on one of Shakespeare's ideas.*" And avoid such double possessives with a *that* construction: "*His hat was just like that of Arthur's.*"

32

PART VI

ESSENTIALS OF RESEARCH: PLANNING, WRITING, AND DOCUMENTING SOURCES

VI

CONTENTS

INTRODUCTION

A paper based on library research should follow the principles governing any good essay. It should represent you as a thinker, and it should contribute your distinctive perspectives on a question of interest to you. Research essays also call upon you to seek out the findings and the views of others who have investigated a topic and to give full credit to those sources and at the same time to your own research efforts in careful documentation of materials both within and following the essay. Part VI discusses and illustrates the stages of writing a research essay and the details to keep in mind to do a good job.

33 THE RESEARCH PLAN

Begin by preparing a **research plan**, a strategy to focus your research and especially to budget the right amount of time to spend on the stages of the assignment. Draft this plan early—that is, no more than a day or two after you first receive the assignment—and then be prepared, if necessary, to revise it as circumstances change.

33a Formulating Research Questions

Your plan should consist first of a **researchable question**. This question should be of sufficient interest and importance to sustain you through the research and writing process. As you move on and gain more insight into the topic, be confident enough to modify the original question.

33b Designing a Timeline

As important as determining the researchable question is establishing a **realistic timeline** for the stages of your project. Consider how your assignment will fit in with other projects and commitments you have. Then ask yourself how much time you will give to each of the following tasks:

- searching for sources,
- evaluating and reading sources,
- notetaking and synthesizing sources,
- organizing and planning the first draft,
- writing and revising second and subsequent drafts, and
- editing and polishing the final draft.

Try as much as possible to set a firm date for the end of your research and the beginning of your writing, and give yourself at least a week if possible for the writing and polishing of the drafts of your assignment.

33c Identifying and Evaluating Sources

Doing effective research means learning your way around your library and its website. It isn't ordinarily enough to do your research solely on the Internet. Consider following an online tutorial with a conducted tour of your library building(s). Or, on your own, explore the library's layout, its reference facilities, its other holdings, its catalogues, its whole system. And don't be afraid to ask librarians for help. Given good, specific questions from library users, reference librarians can provide invaluable help as you find your way through the myriad of non-electronic and electronic resources available to researchers in this information age. Once you feel reasonably at home in what may be a vast and complex building or group of buildings and databases, you can begin to use the library as it is intended to be used.

1. The catalogues

Most college, university, and public libraries in Canada store information about their holdings in computer catalogues. Searches for information typically follow the paths discussed in the remainder of this section.

A SIMPLE SEARCH

You may search an online catalogue for a book, a periodical (a newspaper, a magazine, a journal), an audio or video recording, or a DVD actually housed in your library. In this **simple search**, as it is called, you can look for a book using one of four pieces of information: the last name of the author, the book's title, key words in the title, or the subject of the book. When you find a source in this way, the detailed catalogue entry will include a **call number**, which will allow you to locate the item in the library system.

AN ARTICLE SEARCH

You may look for relevant articles in a periodical source (a newspaper, a magazine, a print-based or electronic journal) by searching the indexes and databases listing the scholarly papers and popular essays published each year in Canada and around the world. The best way to conduct this kind of search is by using the key word or phrase identifying your topic or sub-topic. Indexes are located in electronic databases, and library websites will provide directions for using the index to search for an article. Once

33

you have identified an article of interest, you may be able to access it online if your library has its periodical collections in *e-form*; otherwise you may need to do a simple search to determine the call number and location of the print-based periodical on the library shelf.

A REFERENCE-RESOURCE SEARCH

You may find valuable information on your topic by consulting reference materials. Libraries increasingly store their own reference materials electronically and subscribe to large electronic databases of reference materials (bibliographies, dictionaries, indexes, encyclopedias, and so on). Not only will learning how to access, evaluate, and use these materials put you in touch almost instantaneously with information and scholarship from around the world, it will make you a stronger, more well-read researcher. Keep in mind that one source leads to another. As you explore reference sources, you will often find that an article in an encyclopedia or a book on a given subject will include its own bibliographical information; by following these leads or links you can save much of the time you might otherwise spend searching for sources.

AN INTERNET SEARCH

Through links in your library's online catalogue you may access the search engines to which your library subscribes (such as Google Scholar, Google, Infomine, or Yahoo). These will enable you to do keyword searches for information in the seemingly limitless number of websites that are part of the World Wide Web.

2. Evaluating Internet sources

The Internet is a largely unregulated source of information. Thus, you need to evaluate carefully and critically the websites you locate in your research. Keep in mind the following suggestions in your use of the Internet:

a. Look for authoritative information on websites maintained by recognized researchers and scholars or by public and private institutions. Anonymous and personal websites and sites such as Wikipedia are not considered authoritative sources for scholarly research.

b. Look for the credentials (the accomplishments and publications) of the identified authors of the website and consider these when weighing the research value of the site.

c. Peer-reviewed materials are considered to be very credible sources of information for academic purposes. Consider using such search sources as Academic Search Complete and Google Scholar, databases that identify peer-reviewed articles online and in print form.

d. Check that the websites you plan to use are current—that is, recently updated—and that claims and evidence offered on the site are supported with detailed and accurate documentation.

e. Avoid using a website whose links to other sites are broken, as it may not be well maintained or particularly reliable in its content.

33d   Producing a Preliminary Bibliography

Once you have decided on a researchable question, designed a timeline, and established criteria for identifying and evaluating sources, the first major step in gathering information is to compile a **preliminary bibliography**. As you consult various sources (for example, periodical indexes, essay indexes, general and particular bibliographies, encyclopedias and dictionaries, your library's own catalogues, and the Internet), make a list of books, articles, websites, and so on that may be useful sources of information about your topic. Next, look in the appropriate part of the catalogue to find out which books and articles on your list are available in your library, and record the call number of each one; list relevant websites with their URLs.

When you access a periodical article or website on the Internet, note the specific date of your access, as this information must be included in the MLA works-cited entry for

33

the source. Materials posted online are often updated, and so the date of your access will help to explain to a reader why the content of a source may have changed between the time the research is conducted and the time the paper is submitted and read.

When you begin looking at the actual books, articles, websites, and other sources on your preliminary list, study and evaluate the book or article to see how useful it looks, and note its likely value as a source. Decide whether the source is scholarly and credible, whether it is promising or appears to be of little or no use, whether it looks good for a particular part of your project, or whether one part of it looks useful and the rest not.

33e Notetaking

Once you have compiled your working bibliography and begun consulting the items it lists, reading and taking notes will become a priority for you. Initially, your notes will likely focus on brief descriptions of sources and of their relevance.

Taking notes about what you read is by far preferable to cutting and pasting together materials you have duplicated or downloaded from the Internet, for it involves you actively from the beginning of the research process in filtering source material and in recording it as much as possible in your own terms. In fact, copying, cutting, and pasting at this stage delays your synthesis of sources and increases the risk of recording someone else's thoughts without any note of the original source. Whether inadvertent or not, the inclusion of such unfiltered material in finished essays without proper acknowledgement constitutes plagiarism and breaches academic integrity.

Your preliminary research should explore your subject, investigating and weighing its possibilities, and attempting to limit it as much as necessary to meet the demands of time and especially the length stipulated for the project. At some point during this early stage you should be able to construct a **preliminary outline or plan**, subject to change as you go along.

33

Following are some tips for good notetaking:

1. **Label each note carefully with information about the source.**
2. **Be as brief as possible.**
3. **Distinguish carefully between direct quotation and paraphrase or summary**. Generally, quote only when you feel strongly that the author's own way of putting something will be especially effective in your essay. When you do quote directly, be careful: your quotation must accurately reproduce the original, including its punctuation, spelling, and even any peculiarities that you think might be incorrect. Set quotes apart from your own words by surrounding them with quotation marks and by typing them in different font styles, sizes, and colours from the rest of your notes.
4. **Enclose your own ideas in square brackets and label them with the phrase MY OWN IDEA.**
5. **Use your own words as much as possible.**
6. **Quote from the original source.** When you quote, or even paraphrase or summarize, do so from the original source if possible. Second-hand quotations may be not only inaccurate but misleading as well.
7. **Distinguish between facts and opinions.** If you are quoting or paraphrasing a supposed authority on a subject, be careful not to let yourself be unduly swayed. Rather than note that "aspirin is good for heart and stroke patients," say that "Dr. Jones claims that aspirin is good for heart and stroke patients." In research-based writing, the credibility of your own presentation depends on such matters of attribution. A research paper missing such attributions is ineffective.
8. **Be careful to record the correct page numbers.**
9. **Enclose explanatory material in square brackets.** Whenever you insert explanatory material (for example, a noun or noun phrase to explain a pronoun) in a quotation, use square brackets.
10. **Use [*sic*].** When there is something in a quotation that is obviously wrong, whether a supposed fact or in the writing, such as a spelling error, insert [*sic*] after it.

33

11. **Indicate ellipses.** Whenever you omit a word or words from a quotation, use three spaced periods to indicate the ellipsis.

34 WRITING THE ESSAY

When your research is complete and all the notes you intend to use are organized to fit into your working outline, you are ready to begin writing the essay. As you write your first draft, include in your text the information that will eventually become part of your documentation. That is, at the end of each quotation, paraphrase, summary, statistic, graphic, or direct reference, enclose in parentheses the last name of the author and the relevant page number or numbers—and also at least a short title if you are using more than one work by the same author. Similarly, if two or more authors have the same surname, you will also include the appropriate first name, or just an initial.

If you are using a system of parenthetical documentation, such as that of the MLA, which is the principal system illustrated in this text (see #37a), or that of the APA (see #37b), the final form of your notes will be the same as, or similar to, these parenthetical notes in your drafts.

If you are using the system of *The Chicago Manual of Style*, which calls for footnotes (or endnotes) and an alphabetized bibliographical list at the end (see #37c), do the same, converting to numbered footnotes or endnotes when you are preparing the final draft.

35 ACKNOWLEDGING SOURCES

The purpose of acknowledging sources through documentation is four-fold:

1. It demonstrates that you, the writer, are a genuine researcher who has done the considerable work of investigating authorities and experts in the field(s) assumed in your researchable question.

2. It acknowledges your indebtedness to particular sources.
3. It lends weight to your statements and arguments by citing experts and authorities to support them.
4. It enables an interested reader to pursue the subject further by consulting cited sources, or possibly to evaluate a particular source or to check the accuracy of a reference or quotation, should it appear questionable.

It is not necessary to provide documentation for facts or ideas or quotations that are well known or "common knowledge"—such as the fact that Shakespeare wrote *Hamlet*, or that Hamlet said "To be or not to be," or that Sir Isaac Newton formulated the law of gravity, or that the story of Adam and Eve appears in the book of Genesis in the Bible, or that the moon is not made of green cheese. But if you are at all uncertain whether or not something is "common knowledge," play it safe: it is far better to over-document and appear a little naive than to under-document and engage in the unethical practice of plagiarism.

If a piece of information appears in three or more different sources, it qualifies as "common knowledge" and need not be documented. For example, such facts as the elevation of Mt. Logan, the current population of the world, or the date of the execution of Louis Riel can be found in dozens of reference books. But it can be risky for a student, or any non-professional, to trust to such a guideline when dealing with other kinds of material. For example, there may be dozens of articles, websites, and books referring to or attempting to explain something like a neutrino, or the red shift, or black holes, or discoveries at the Olduvai Gorge, or Jungian readings of fairy tales, or the importance of the human genome project, or deep structure in linguistic theory, or warnings about bio-terrorism, or neo-Platonic ideas in Renaissance poetry, or the nature and consequences of the great potato famine, or the origin of the name *Canada*; nevertheless, it is unlikely that a relatively non-expert writer will be sufficiently conversant with such material to recognize and accept it as "common

35

knowledge." If something is new to you, and if you have not thoroughly explored the available literature on the subject, it is best to acknowledge a source. And when in doubt, check with your instructor.

36 QUOTATION, PARAPHRASE, SUMMARY, AND ACADEMIC INTEGRITY

Quotation must be exact. A well-documented **paraphrase**, on the other hand, reproduces the content of the original, but in different words. Paraphrase is a useful technique in research-based writing because it enables writers to refer to source material while still using their own words and thus to avoid too much direct quotation. But a paraphrase, to be legitimate, should give clear credit *at its beginning* to the source and should not use significant words and phrases from an original without enclosing them in quotation marks. In other words, begin your paraphrase by identifying your source in an attribution (for example, "Biographer John English suggests . . ." or "John English, Pierre Trudeau's biographer, argues . . ."). End the paraphrase with an in-text parenthetical reference (or a note, if you are using the Chicago style of documentation) indicating the page number(s) for the material you have presented. A paraphrase will usually be shorter than the original, but it need not be. A **summary**, however, is by definition a condensation, a boiled-down version in one's own words expressing the principal points of an original source. It is often the best evidence of a writer's effective synthesis of secondary-source material.

Direct quotation must be documented: a reader of a passage in quotation marks will expect to be told who and what is being quoted. But some writers make the serious mistake of thinking that only direct quotations need to be documented; on the contrary, it is important to know and remember that *paraphrase and summary must also be fully documented*. Failure to document a paraphrase or summary is a breach of **academic integrity** known as

plagiarism, a form of intellectual dishonesty and theft for which there are serious academic penalties. To familiarize yourself with your institution's policies on academic integrity and on plagiarism, consult your institution's most recent academic calendar.

To illustrate the differences between a legitimate and an illegitimate use of source material, here is a paragraph, a direct quotation, from Rupert Brooke's *Letters from America,* followed by

a. legitimate paraphrase,
b. illegitimate paraphrase,
c. combination paraphrase and quotation,
d. summary, and
e. a comment on plagiarism.

> Such is Toronto. A brisk city of getting on for half a million inhabitants, the largest British city in Canada (in spite of the cheery Italian faces that pop up at you out of excavations in the street), liberally endowed with millionaires, not lacking its due share of destitution, misery, and slums. It is no mushroom city of the West, it has its history; but at the same time it has grown immensely of recent years. It is situated on the shores of a lovely lake; but you never see that, because the railways have occupied the entire lake front. So if, at evening, you try to find your way to the edge of the water, you are checked by a region of smoke, sheds, trucks, wharves, storehouses, "depôts," railway-lines, signals, and locomotives and trains that wander on the tracks up and down and across streets, pushing their way through the pedestrians, and tolling, as they go, in the American fashion, an immense melancholy bell, intent, apparently, on some private and incommunicable grief. Higher up are the business quarters, a few skyscrapers in the American style without the modern American beauty, but one of which advertises itself as the highest in the British Empire; streets that seem less narrow than Montreal [sic], but not unrespectably wide; "the buildings are generally substantial and often handsome" (the too kindly Herr Baedeker). Beyond that

36

the residential part, with quiet streets, gardens open to the road, shady verandahs, and homes, generally of wood, that are a deal more pleasant to see than the houses in a modern English town. (Brooke 80–81)

The parenthetical reference for this block quotation, which is given in MLA style, begins one space after the final punctuation mark. It includes the author's surname and the page numbers on which the original appeared. The complete bibliographical entry for Brooke's work would appear in the list of "Works Cited" as follows:

Brooke, Rupert. *Letters from America*. London: Sidgwick and Jackson, 1916.

36a Legitimate Paraphrase

During his 1913 tour of the United States and Canada, Rupert Brooke sent back to England articles about his travels. In one of them, published in the 1916 book *Letters from America*, he describes Toronto as a large city, predominantly British, containing both wealth and poverty. He says that it is relatively old, compared to the upstart new cities further west, but that nevertheless it has expanded a great deal in the last little while. He implies that its beautiful setting is spoiled for its citizens by the railways, which have taken over all the land near the lake, filling it with buildings and tracks and smell and noise. He also writes of the commercial part of the city, with its buildings which are tall (like American ones) but not very attractive (unlike American ones); one of them, he says, claims to be the tallest in the British Empire. (He pokes fun at Baedeker for being over-generous with his comments about the city's downtown architecture.) The streets he finds wider than those of Montreal, but not too wide. Finally, he compares Toronto's attractive residential areas favourably with those of English towns (80–81).

36

This is legitimate paraphrase. Even though it uses several individual words from the original (*British*, *railways*, *tracks*, *American*, *British Empire*, *streets*, *residential*, *English town[s]*), they are a small part of the whole; more important, they are common words that would be difficult to replace with reasonable substitutes without distorting the sense. And, even more important, they are used in a way that is natural to the paraphraser's own style and context. Paraphrase, however, does not consist in merely substituting one word for another, but rather in assimilating something and restating it in your own words and your own syntax.

Note that the writer has carefully kept Brooke's point of view apparent throughout by including him in each independent clause (a technique that also establishes good coherence): *Rupert Brooke, he describes, He says, He implies, He also writes, he says, He pokes fun, he finds, he compares.*

36b Illegitimate Paraphrase

An illegitimate paraphrase of Brooke's paragraph might begin like this:

> Brooke describes Toronto as a <u>brisk</u> kind of city with nearly <u>half a million inhabitants</u>, with some <u>Italian faces popping up</u> among the British, and with both <u>millionaires and slums</u>. He deplores the fact that the <u>lake front</u> on which <u>it is situated</u> has been <u>entirely occupied by the railways</u>, who have turned it into a <u>region of smoke and storehouses</u> and the like, and <u>trains that wander back and forth, ringing their huge bells</u> (80–81).

The parenthetical reference at paragraph's end does *not* protect the writer from the charge of plagiarism, for too many of the words and phrases and too much of the syntax are Brooke's own. The words and phrases underlined are all "illegitimate": they still have the diction, syntax, and stylistic flavour of Brooke's original, and therefore they constitute plagiarism.

Had the writer put quotation marks around the underlined words, the passage would no longer be plagiarism—but it would still be illegitimate, or at least very poor, paraphrase, for if so substantial a part is to be left in Brooke's own words and syntax, the whole might as well have been quoted directly.

36

36c Paraphrase and Quotation Mixed

A writer who felt that a pure paraphrase was too flat and abstract, who felt that some of Brooke's more striking words and phrases should be retained, might choose to mix some direct quotation into a paraphrase:

> In *Letters from America*, Rupert Brooke characterizes Toronto as a "brisk," largely British city having the usual urban mixture of wealth and poverty. Unlike the "mushroom" cities farther west, he says, Toronto has a history, though he points out that much of its growth has been recent. He notes, somewhat cynically, that the people are cut off from the beauty of the lake by the railways and all their "smoke, sheds, trucks, wharves, storehouses, 'depôts,' railway-lines, signals, and locomotives and trains" going ding-ding all over the place (80–81).

This time the context is very much the writer's own, but some of the flavour of Brooke's original has been retained through the direct quotation of a couple of judiciously chosen words and the cumulative list quoted at the end. The writer is clearly in control of the material, as the writer of the preceding example was not.

36d Summary

The purpose of a summary is to substantially reduce the original, conveying its essential meaning in a sentence or two. A summary of Brooke's passage might go something like this:

> Brooke describes Toronto as large and mainly wealthy, aesthetically marred by the railway yards along the lake, with wide-enough streets, tall but (in spite of Baedeker's half-hearted approval) generally unprepossessing buildings, and a residential area more attractive than comparable English ones (80–81).

In MLA style, it is appropriate and usually preferable to refer to an author by name in your text—and the first

36

time by full name. If for some reason you do not want to bring the author's name into your text (for example if you were surveying a variety of opinions about Toronto and did not want to clutter your text with all their authors' names), then your text might read in part like this, with the author's surname tucked away in the parenthetical reference:

> Toronto was once described as "brisk," large, and encumbered with railways and tall but ugly buildings (Brooke 80–81).

36e Maintaining Academic Integrity and Avoiding Plagiarism

Had one of the foregoing versions of the passage not mentioned Brooke, nor included quotation marks, nor ended with documentation, it would have been plagiarism. A student doing research is part of a community of scholars (professors, investigators, instructors, other students, and researchers), all of whom are governed by the codes of academic honesty that define effective research and identify plagiarism—whether intentional or accidental—as a serious offence. Your college or university calendar will no doubt include a detailed definition of plagiarism and a statement of policy on the academic discipline (failing marks, suspension, a note on one's academic transcript) arising from a finding of plagiarism. You should review this information and discuss any questions or concerns with your instructors and academic advisers.

When you are working on a research project, keep in mind that you are ethically bound to give credit twice—*in the text* of the written document and *in the works cited list*—to all sources of information you have used (both print-based and electronic). All of the following kinds of material require acknowledgement:

- direct quotations—whether short or long,
- your summaries and paraphrases of sources,
- ideas, theories, and inspirations drawn from a source and expressed in your own words,

36

- statistical data compiled by institutions (for example, think tanks and governmental or non-governmental organizations) and other researchers,
- original ideas and original findings drawn from course lectures and seminars,
- graphic materials (diagrams, charts, photographs, illustrations, slides, film and television clips, audio and video recordings, CD-ROMs, and DVDs), and
- materials drawn from authored or unauthored Internet sites.

Note that giving credit for this kind of material does not diminish your own work: it enhances the credibility of your claims and demonstrates just how much genuine research you have done on your project. It shows you adding your voice and your views to those of the community of scholars and researchers of which you are a part.

One final note. It is possible to commit self-plagiarism. This happens when a writer submits the same work—in whole or in part—for two different courses or assignments. If you are working in the same subject or topic area for two different courses or assignments, it is essential to discuss the ethical issues involved with both instructors to whom the work will be submitted.

36f Integrating and Contextualizing Quotations

When you include quoted material within one of your own sentences, you may well have to alter it in one way or another to incorporate it smoothly. That is, you may have to change the grammar, syntax, or punctuation of a quotation to make it conform to your own grammar and syntax. Note how the writers have altered the quoted material in the following examples.

The original quotation (from Mary Shelley's *Frankenstein; or, The Modern Prometheus*):

> I am by birth a Genevese; and my family is one of the most distinguished of that republic. My ancestors had been for many years counsellors and syndics; and my father had filled several public situations with honour

36

and reputation. He was respected by all who knew him for his integrity and indefatigable attention to public business. He passed his younger days perpetually occupied by the affairs of his country; a variety of circumstances had prevented his marrying early, nor was it until the decline of life that he became a husband and the father of a family.

(a) altered for pronoun reference:

Victor Frankenstein begins his story by stating that "[he is] by birth a Genevese; and [his] family is one of the most distinguished of that republic" (Shelley 31).

The first-person pronouns have been changed to third person in order to fit the third-person point of view in the sentence as a whole. The changed pronouns and the accompanying verb (*is* for *am*) appear in square brackets.

(b) altered for consistent verb tense:

As we first encounter him in the description at the beginning of his son's narrative, Victor's father is a man "respected by all who [know] him for his integrity and indefatigable attention to public business" (Shelley 31).

The verb in square brackets has been changed from past to present tense to conform with the tense established by the *is* of the student's sentence.

(c) altered for punctuation:

The first words of Victor Frankenstein's narrative—"I am by birth a Genevese" (Shelley 31)—reveal a narrator preoccupied with himself, his birth, and his nationality.

The semicolon of the original has been dropped to avoid its clashing with the enclosing dashes of the student's own sentence.

(d) selective quotation:

The first paragraph of Victor's narrative focuses more on Victor's father than on any other member of the

36

Frankenstein family. Victor takes pains to describe him as a man of "honour and reputation . . . respected by all who [know] him for his integrity and indefatigable attention to public business" and "perpetually occupied by the affairs of his country" (Shelley 31). A first-time reader of the novel might well be forgiven for assuming that Victor's narrative will be more a tribute to his father than an account of his own creation of a monster.

Here, the student writer has selected key words and phrases from the opening paragraph of Victor Frankenstein's narrative in order to make a point about the novel's focus. The ellipsis indicates that material has been omitted in the interests of the student's own sentence structure.

37 DOCUMENTATION

To be effective, documentation must be complete, accurate, and clear. Completeness and accuracy depend on careful recording of necessary information as you do your research and take notes. Clarity depends on the way you present that information to your reader. You will be clear only if your audience can follow your method of documentation. Before you begin any research project, investigate the method of documentation you need to use. This section presents three frequently used methods:

1. The *name–page* method, currently recommended by the Modern Language Association (**MLA**) and in wide use in the humanities;

2. the *name–date* method, recommended by the American Psychological Association (**APA**) and used in some of the social and other sciences as well as in education studies; and

3. the *note* method, recommended by *The Chicago Manual of Style* and preferred in some disciplines.

Which method you choose will depend on what discipline (field of study) you are writing in and on the wishes of your audience.

37a The Name–Page Method (MLA Style)

The name–page method is detailed in the seventh edition of the *MLA Handbook for Writers of Research Papers* (2009). This method of citation is simple and efficient. Using this method, you provide a short, usually **parenthetical** or **in-text reference** to each source as you use it in the body of your paper. Then, you provide complete bibliographical information about all the electronic and non-electronic sources you have used at the end of the essay, in a list titled "Works Cited," alphabetized by surnames of authors or editors (or title, when no author or editor is named).

The pages that follow illustrate examples of the most common patterns of MLA documentation: each in-text parenthetical reference is accompanied by its works-cited entry. Note that parenthetical references are usually placed at the end of the sentence in which the citation occurs; but if a sentence is long and complicated, a reference may be placed earlier, immediately after the citation itself.

Note also that in an actual paper, the examples that follow would be **double-spaced** rather than single-spaced.

Print Sources

A book by one author (or editor)

IN-TEXT REFERENCE

> Today, North Americans do less walking than they did fifty years ago. Even if they are travelling only a short distance, they tend to drive or get a ride to their destination. In fact, a recent survey revealed that many Canadian municipalities "did not provide pedestrian amenities at all, and only half, in any way, encouraged their citizens to reach their destinations by foot" (Friedman 136).

When you don't mention the author by name in your sentence, the parenthetical reference includes the author's surname and a page reference, with *no intervening punctuation*. The closing period follows the parenthesis. If you can include the author's name and credentials in your text,

37
MLA

however, the parenthetical reference will be shorter, the context of the quotation clearer, and the credibility of the point stronger:

> Pedestrians are not a priority for today's city planners. Avi Friedman, professor of architecture at McGill University, notes that "a survey of Canadian municipalities found that many did not provide pedestrian amenities at all, and only half, in any way, encouraged their citizens to reach their destinations by foot" (136).

WORKS-CITED REFERENCE

> Friedman, Avi. *A Place in Mind: The Search for Authenticity.* Montreal: Vehicule Press, 2010. Print.

The works-cited reference for a book includes

- the author's name (surname, followed by a comma, and the full first name, followed by a period);
- the full title of the book (italicized), followed by a period; and
- the publication information—city of publication, short name of the publisher (words such as "Company," "Inc.," or "Ltd." are omitted, and a publisher's name can be reduced to a single name or word such as "McClelland"), year, and medium of publication (Web, Print, TV, DVD, etc.). So punctuation here is City: Publisher, Year. Medium.

A book by two or three authors (or editors)

IN-TEXT REFERENCE

> "For researchers in geography, anthropology, philosophy, and politics, for instance, animal and environmental considerations are increasingly seen as the necessary basis for human studies" (Huggan and Tiffin 16).

WORKS-CITED REFERENCE

> Huggan, Graham, and Helen Tiffin. *Postcolonial Ecocriticism: Literature, Animals, Environment.* London: Routledge, 2010. Print.

37
MLA

When you have more than one author or editor in a works-cited entry, the names following the first name appear in first-name–last-name order. When a works-cited entry exceeds one line, the second and subsequent lines are indented by one tab (roughly five spaces) from the left margin.

A book by more than three authors (or editors)

IN-TEXT REFERENCE

> "In early Canada, reading was often predicated upon the dangers of secrets and discovery, both of which are so intimately connected with the colonial condition of being distant, and the resulting precariousness of family history" (Blair et al. xl).

In the parenthetical reference, supply the name of the author or editor whose name appears first on the title page of the work, followed by the Latin abbreviation *et al.* (for Latin *et alii*, "and others").

WORKS-CITED REFERENCE

> Blair, Jennifer, et al., eds. *ReCalling Early Canada: Reading the Political in Literary and Cultural Production.* Edmonton: U of Alberta P, 2005. Print.

Two or more works by the same author

IN-TEXT REFERENCE

If you cite two different works by a single author in your writing, the in-text references must include title information to distinguish the two works. Note that the pattern calls for the author's surname and then a comma, followed by the distinctive word or phrase from the title and then the page number. There is no comma between the title word and the page number. While it is preferable to include all of the required information, the "n. pag." notation can be used when the referenced page is not numbered.

> Both novels—*Stanley Park* and *Story House*—begin with searching looks into the past. *Stanley Park*'s "Author's Note" recalls "January of 1953 [and] the

> skeletal remains of two children . . . found in Stanley Park" (Taylor, *Stanley* n. pag.). *Story House* begins with the cryptic chapter title "17 Years Before the Beginning" (Taylor, *Story* 3).

WORKS-CITED REFERENCE

The two works by Taylor would be listed alphabetically according to the titles. In this case, the title beginning with "Sta" would precede the title beginning with "Sto."

> Taylor, Timothy. *Stanley Park*. Toronto: Knopf, 2001. Print.
>
> ———. *Story House*. Toronto: Knopf, 2006. Print.

Note that the second entry does not repeat the author's name but rather marks it with three consecutive hyphens followed by a period.

A work by a government agency or a corporate author
A government agency is one of the many branches or departments of government at the international, federal, provincial, or municipal level. A corporate author is a group, association, or institute of authors who are not named individually on the title page of a work.

IN-TEXT REFERENCE

> A sixteen-page guide for parents on the immunization of Canada's children has been published in several languages—among them Tagalog, Mandarin, Punjabi, Urdu, and Farsi (Government of Canada).

Here, there is no page number because the reference is to the report as a whole.

WORKS-CITED REFERENCE

> Government of Canada. *A Parent's Guide to Immunization*. Ottawa: Public Health Agency of Canada, 2010. Print.

A work by an anonymous author

IN-TEXT REFERENCE

> When a magician dies, his or her friends and colleagues gather for a service known as "the broken-wand ceremony" ("Mere" 43).

This anonymous essay, entitled "Mere Stick," appeared in *The New Yorker* magazine in August 1993. A short version of the title moves into the position usually occupied by the author's surname in the parenthetical reference; there is no punctuation between it and the page number. In the list of works cited, such items are alphabetized by title.

WORKS-CITED REFERENCE

> "Mere Stick." *New Yorker* 23–30 Aug. 1993: 43–44. Print.

A multivolume work

IN-TEXT REFERENCE

> In an entry dated 3 August 1908, she described her second book as "not nearly so good as *Green Gables*" (Montgomery 1: 338).

When you cite one volume from a work of two or more volumes, include the volume number in the parenthetical reference, followed by a colon and a space, and then the page number.

WORKS-CITED REFERENCE

> Montgomery, Lucy Maud. *The Selected Journals of L.M. Montgomery.* Ed. Mary Rubio and Elizabeth Waterston. 5 vols. Toronto: Oxford UP, 1985–2004. Print.

37
MLA

The "UP" in the publication information is an abbreviation for "University Press." The year "1985–2004" indicates that the first volume of the journals was produced in 1985 and the last volume in 2004.

Quotation at second hand

IN-TEXT REFERENCE

Try as often as possible to quote from primary sources. If you quote from a secondary source, identify it and give a full context (date, name of the speaker, identity of the audience, circumstances of the utterance) for the words you quote:

> In 1918, Reverend M. McGillivray wrote in *King's Own*, a publication of the Presbyterian Church of Canada, about the Red Cross dogs used on the battlefields of France, praising their "feats of sagacity, courage and endurance" (qtd. in Fisher 135).

WORKS-CITED REFERENCE

> Fisher, Susan R. *Boys and Girls in No Man's Land: English-Canadian Children and the First World War.* Toronto: U of Toronto P, 2011. Print.

A work of literature

Many major works of pre-contemporary literature—fictional and non-fictional prose, plays, poems—have been published in several different editions. To enable readers to locate quotations in any edition they may have access to, parenthetical references to such works should include or consist of clear indications of text divisions other than the page numbers of the particular edition you happen to be using. If you begin with a page number, follow it with a semicolon and then add the other information, using clear abbreviations. Some examples:

37
MLA

(a) Prose works

IN-TEXT REFERENCE

> Jane Austen presents readers of *Pride and Prejudice* with the heroine's father, the likable Mr. Bennet, an "odd . . . mixture of quick parts, sarcastic humour, reserve, and caprice" (3; vol. 1, ch. 1); only much later do we learn that these in part contribute to his serious shortcomings as a father.

WORKS-CITED REFERENCE

> Austen, Jane. *Pride and Prejudice*. 1813. Oxford: Oxford
> UP, 2008. Print.

(The year 1813 is the year of the work's first publication.)

(b) A play in prose

IN-TEXT REFERENCE

> In the first moments of the play, Constance asks herself
> this hypothetical question: "What if a Fool were to enter
> the worlds of both *Othello* and *Romeo and Juliet*?" (14;
> act 1, sc. 1).

WORKS-CITED REFERENCE

> MacDonald, Ann-Marie. *Goodnight Desdemona (Good
> Morning Juliet)*. 1990. Toronto: Vintage, 1998. Print.

(c) A play in verse

IN-TEXT REFERENCE

> The final act of *As You Like It* includes a memorable
> discussion about what it means to love. Silvius
> answers this question with these words:
>
> > It is to be all made of fantasy,
> > All made of passion, and all made of wishes,
> > All adoration, duty, and observance,
> > All humbleness, all patience and impatience,
> > All purity, all trial, all obedience[.] (5.2.89–94)

With verse plays, you need not include page numbers at all,
since act, scene, and line numbers clearly locate the citation.

37
MLA

WORKS-CITED REFERENCE

> Shakespeare, William. *As You Like It*. Ed. Roma Gill.
> Oxford: Oxford UP, 2002. Print.

(d) *A poem*

IN-TEXT REFERENCE

> Margaret Atwood's ironic tone is immediately evident in this passage: "The poets hang on. / It's hard to get rid of them, / though lord knows it's been tried" (lines 1–3).

The line number tells a reader precisely where in the work the quotation comes from; no page number is needed. Subsequent references to the same poem need not include the words *line* or *lines*; the number will be enough.

WORKS-CITED REFERENCE

> Atwood, Margaret. "The Poets Hang On." *The Door: Poems.* Toronto: McClelland, 2007. 35–37. Print.

(e) *A long poem with divisions*

IN-TEXT REFERENCE

> Those who find Satan heroic are overlooking Milton's flat statements, for example that the Father of Lies is "in pain, / Vaunting aloud, but racked with deep despair," and that his "words . . . bore / Semblance of worth, not substance" (1.125–26, 528–29).

The second set of line numbers is separated from the first by a comma. Again, no page numbers are needed. When citing a range of numbers in references to lines, list all digits for second numbers up to 99 (for example, *lines 5–88*). When citing second numbers above 99, list only the last two digits unless more are necessary to prevent confusion (for example, *lines 108–22* for a range from 108 to 122, but *lines 385–485* for a range from 385 to 485). (Treat page ranges in citations of other materials in a similar way: *pages 97–99; 275–77; 391–405*.) Note the need for a space before and after the slash mark indicating a line break in the verse.

WORKS-CITED REFERENCE

> Milton, John. *Paradise Lost.* Ed. Scott Elledge. New York: Norton, 1993. Print.

37
MLA

Citing more than one source

IN-TEXT REFERENCE

To cite more than one source in a single parenthetical reference, simply write each in the usual way and separate items with a semicolon:

> The First World War left Canadians "a deeply divided people who had inherited a staggering debt," but it has also been said to have "mark[ed] the real birth of Canada" (Morton 226; Gwyn xxi).

WORKS-CITED REFERENCES

Morton, Desmond. "First World War." *The Oxford Companion to Canadian History*. Ed. Gerald Hallowell. Toronto: Oxford UP, 2004. 226. Print.

Gwyn, Sandra. *Tapestry of War: A Private View of Canadians in the Great War*. Toronto: HarperCollins, 1993. Print.

Using notes as well as parenthetical references

If circumstances demand, you may also use an occasional note along with the name–page method. For example, if you think that a reference requires some comment or explanation, make it an endnote or a footnote rather than an obtrusive parenthetical reference. But keep such notes to a minimum; if you cannot comfortably include such discursive comments in your text, it may be that they aren't relevant after all. Try to limit such notes to (a) those commenting in some useful way on specific sources, such as a "See," "See for example," or "See also" note, and (b) those listing three or more sources, which might be unwieldy as a parenthetical reference.

In the text, insert a superscript numeral where you want to signal the note (usually at the end of a sentence). Begin the note by indenting five spaces, followed by a numeral corresponding with the one in the text, then another space, and then the note. If you use a footnote, put it at the bottom of the page, below your text; the text of the note should be single-spaced, but double space between notes. If you use endnotes, put them on a separate page with the heading *Notes*, following the text and before the list of works cited; they should be double-spaced.

Here are some examples of in-text references and corresponding works-cited listings for other kinds of print sources.

An essay in an edited collection of essays by various authors

IN-TEXT REFERENCE

"What's the Trouble with the Trickster?" ends with Kristina Fagan's speculation: "I wonder what they will be saying about the trickster ten years from now" (16).

WORKS-CITED REFERENCE

Fagan, Kristina. "What's the Trouble with the Trickster?" *Troubling Tricksters: Revisioning Critical Conversations*. Ed. Deanna Reder and Linda M. Morra. Waterloo: Wilfrid Laurier UP, 2010. 3–20. Print.

An article in a journal

IN-TEXT REFERENCE

Sally Chivers notes the place of Terry Fox in Canadian life with the observation that "[a] mountain and a large section of the TransCanada highway are named after him, and he appears on two stamps and two coins. Fox has also had twelve schools named after him" (86).

WORKS-CITED REFERENCE

Chivers, Sally. "Ordinary People: Reading the TransCanadian Terry Fox." *Canadian Literature* 202 (2009): 80–94. Print.

37
MLA

This particular journal uses only issue numbers. Were there a volume number as well, the issue number would follow it in the entry. For example, 19.2 would mean that the article appeared in the second issue of volume 19.

Note that the *MLA Handbook* does not require a journal with continuous pagination throughout a volume and one with separate pagination for each issue to be treated differently. For all journals, regardless of how they are paginated, you must provide both volume and issue numbers if both exist.

An editorial
IN-TEXT REFERENCE

"Largely by leading the first presidential campaign to take full advantage of the Internet, Mr. Obama turned millions of Americans into donors or volunteers" ("Victory" A20).

WORKS-CITED REFERENCE

"A Victory Won with Dignity." Editorial. *Globe and Mail* 5 Nov. 2008: A20. Print.

Newspaper editorials are not ordinarily attributed to a particular writer or editor. Without an author, the title moves into the author position and is used in short form in the parenthetical in-text reference and in full form in the works-cited entry.

A review
IN-TEXT REFERENCE

The reviewer notes that the book provides "a judiciously selective overview of the history of walking and its changing place in urban life" (Joseph 188).

WORKS-CITED REFERENCE

Joseph, Maia. "This City Is Made for Walking." Rev. of *The Walkable City: From Haussman's Boulevards to Jane Jacobs' Streets and Beyond*, by Mary Soderstrom. *Canadian Literature* 205 (2010): 188–89. Print.

A newspaper article
IN-TEXT REFERENCE

Devyani Saltzman evokes a vivid image in her opening comments on the holy rivers of India: "Frigid and tumultuous, the white water of the Ganges sped past a rocky bank where family friends had set up a bonfire and chairs overlooking the river" (T1).

WORKS-CITED REFERENCE

Saltzman, Devyani. "At the Water's Edge." *Globe and Mail* 17 Feb. 2007: T1+. Print.

In this example, the page number T1+ indicates that the article begins on page 1 of section T of the newspaper and then continues not on page 2 but later in the section.

Interviews

This category includes interviews published in news-papers, magazines, books; interviews broadcast on radio or television; and interviews conducted by researchers themselves.

In your text, include a parenthetical reference for a published interview; for a broadcast or for an interview you conduct for your own research include the necessary information, but without page numbers.

In the works-cited entry, indicate the medium through which you heard the interview: radio, television, Web, or other. For an interview you conducted yourself, give the kind of interview: "Personal interview," "Telephone inter-view," or other.

(a) A published interview

IN-TEXT REFERENCE

In an interview with Susan Fisher, Frances Itani recalls the origins of her novel *Deafening* in a 1996 visit she made to the Ontario School for the Deaf, where her grandmother had once lived as a resident (40–41).

WORKS-CITED REFERENCE

Itani, Frances. "Hear, Overhear, Observe, Remember: A Dialogue with Frances Itani." Interview by Susan Fisher. *Canadian Literature* 183 (2004): 40–56. Print.

37
MLA

(b) A broadcast interview

IN-TEXT REFERENCE

> In a CBC interview marking the centennial of International Women's Day, Almas Jiwani, president of the National Committee of UN Women in Canada, took stock of the status of women in Canada and across the world today.

WORKS-CITED REFERENCE

> Jiwani, Almas. Interview by Peter Mansbridge. *Mansbridge One on One*. CBC News Network, Toronto. 12 Mar. 2011. Television.

(c) Your own research interview

IN-TEXT REFERENCE

> Professor Joseph Atkinson reported that ideas of innovation in the teaching of science in British universities are a relatively new concern among his colleagues.

WORKS-CITED REFERENCE

> Atkinson, Joseph. E-mail interview. 12 June 2011.

Here are some examples of works-cited entries for a few other kinds of print and non-print sources. Remember to include the medium marker at the end of each entry.

A book in translation

> Eco, Umberto, and Jean-Claude Carrière. *This Is Not the End of the Book*. Trans. Polly McLean. London: Harvill Secker, 2011. Print.

A lecture

> Thom, Bing. "The Transformative Power of Architecture: The Works of Bing Thom." Vancouver Institute Lecture. University of British Columbia. 2 April 2011. Performance.

37
MLA

A television program

"A Simple Game." *Hockey: A People's History*, Episode 1.
CBC. 17 Sept. 2006. Television.

A sound recording

Obama, Barack. *Dreams from My Father: A Story of Race
and Inheritance*. Random House Audio, 2005. CD.

A film or movie in theatres

Begin with the italicized title (unless you are emphasizing
a particular contributor, such as the writer or director, or
a performer), followed by the director, the distributor, the
date, and the medium:

Midnight in Paris. Dir. Woody Allen. Mongrel Media,
2011. Film.

You may wish to include other information as well—whatever you think relevant to your use of the item:

Allen, Woody, writ., dir. *Midnight in Paris*. Perf. Carla
Bruni. Mongrel Media, 2011. Film.

A recorded film or movie

Away from Her. Dir. Sarah Polley. Mongrel Media, 2006.
DVD.

A painting

Hughes, E.J. *Trees, Savary Island.* 1953. Painting.
Museum of Fine Arts, Montreal.

37
MLA

If you are working from a published photograph rather
than from a visit to Montreal's Museum of Fine Arts to
see the painting, include the necessary data to indicate the
print source in which you have studied the work.

Hughes, E.J. *Trees, Savary Island. 1953*. Photograph.
E.J. Hughes. By Ian Thom. Vancouver: Douglas &
McIntyre and the Vancouver Art Gallery, 2002.
117. Print.

Electronic Sources

IN-TEXT REFERENCE

The in-text reference patterns for electronic sources follow those for print sources. Include the last name of the author and, if it is available, the number of the page in the electronic document. If the document is not paginated, include the paragraph number(s) from which you are quoting, and use "par." or "pars." If the document you are referring to does not have an author, then the in-text reference will begin with a key word from the title of the document.

WORKS-CITED REFERENCE

A website or online scholarly project

> Goldstein, Evan, ed. *Arts and Letters Daily. Chronicle of Higher Education*, 15 May 2011. Web. 24 May 2011.

For an online scholarly project or an entire website, first give the name of the author or editor, followed by the name of the website in italics. Indicate the publisher of the site and the date of publication, followed by the medium of publication marker ("Web" for online sources). Finally, indicate the date you accessed the material.

A home page for a course

> McNeilly, Kevin. English 220/007. Literature in English to the Eighteenth Century: Displaced Persons, Past Presences. Course home page. 2009–10. Dept. of English, U of British Columbia, n.d. Web. 18 Jan. 2010.

Titles here are not italicized. Include "Course home page" or "Dept. home page" and the timeframe in which the course is being offered, followed by the name of the institution. The citation ends with the medium marker ("Web") and the date of access.

An online book

> Grant, Jeannette. *Through Evangeline's Country*. Boston, 1894. *Early Canadiana Online*. CIHM, 2 Feb. 2007. Web. 29 Apr. 2011.

37
MLA

This book on the expulsion of the Acadians from Nova Scotia was originally published in Boston in 1894. CIHM is the acronym for the Canadian Institute for Historical Reproductions, which maintains this website for publications from early Canada.

An online government publication

> Canadian Food Inspection Agency. *Causes of Foodborne Illness*. 2010. Web. 10 May 2011.

An online newspaper or magazine

> MacKinnon, Mark. "Japan Haunted by Spectre of Chernobyl." *Globe and Mail*. Globe and Mail, 12 April 2011. Web. 21 May 2011.

Be aware that some online periodicals may have names different from those of their print versions:

> Faught, Brad. "A History of the Exam." *Macleans.ca*. Rogers Publishing, 13 Nov. 2006. Web. 8 Jan. 2011.

Macleans.ca is the online version of *Maclean's* magazine. The article was first posted in November 2006 and accessed in January 2011.

An online review

> Zakaria, Fareed. "The Convert." Rev. of *A Journey: My Political Life*, by Tony Blair. *New York Times Sunday Book Review*. New York Times Company, 8 Oct. 2010. Web. 20 Dec. 2010.

An article from an online journal

37
MLA

> Golovankha-Hicks, Inna. "Demonology in Contemporary Ukraine: Folklore or 'Postfolklore'?" *Journal of Folklore Research* 43.3 (2006): 219–40. *Project Muse*. Web. 15 Jan. 2011.

> Weisenfeldt, Gerhard. "Dystopian Genesis: The Scientist's Role in Society According to Jack Arnold." *Film & History* 40.1 (2010): 58–74. *MLA International Bibliography*. Web. 2 Feb. 2011.

Griffin, Andrew. "The Banality of History in *Troilus and Cressida*." *Early Modern Literary Studies* 12.2 (2006): 4.1-12. Web. 4 Jan. 2011.

The first two examples refer to journal articles accessed through online databases (Project Muse and MLA International Bibliography). The third example refers to an article that is available in a journal that publishes exclusively online and is available independently.

An online dissertation abstract

Bourrie, Mark. "Between Friends: Censorship of Canada's Media in World War II." Diss. U of Ottawa, 2009. *ProQuest*. Nov. 2010. Web. 18 Mar. 2011.

A posting to an online forum

Dungo, Winnie. "Facebook Backtracks on User Policy." Comment. *Globeandmail.com*. CTVglobemedia Publishing, 18 Feb. 2011. Web. 18 Feb 2011.

37b The Name-Date Method (APA Style)

The name-date system is common in the social sciences; the standard guide is the *Publication Manual of the American Psychological Association*, sixth edition (2010). This system uses parenthetical references in the text to provide the name of the author and the date of publication of the source. The practice is the same whether the source is print-based or electronic. Since in the behavioural and social sciences reference is quite often made to the argument or evidence presented by an entire work, page numbers are not always necessary:

Historians have struggled to pinpoint a date for the beginning of science (Fara, 2009).

But if you refer to a particular part of the source, or if you quote from it, supply the relevant page number or numbers:

Patricia Fara (2009) notes that "Science has no definite beginning, and all historians must . . . choose their own starting point" (p. 5).

37 APA

Note that if you name the author in the text, you don't include the name in the parenthetical reference.

Here are some further examples of name–date parenthetical references, followed by some examples of reference-list entries. Were these examples to appear within an essay, they would be double-spaced.

A work with one author

A fascination with lost musical manuscripts led Eric Siblin (2009) to produce a book on missing cello suites composed by Johann Sebastian Bach.

A work with two or more authors

Although it is true that "the religious and secular customs of the community sometimes helped women who had been assaulted or harassed, nothing could lessen the impact of war on the countryside and its inhabitants" (Anderson & Zinsser, 1988, pp. 115–116).

Note that in APA style an ampersand rather than *and* separates two authors in a reference, that author and date are separated by a comma, that the abbreviations "p." and "pp." are used for "page" and "pages," and that all three digits of the closing page number are included.

If a work has two authors, list both names in each reference you make to the source. If it has three, four, or five authors, list all of them the first time, but only the first and "et al." (not italicized or underlined) thereafter. If it has six or more authors, list only the first and "et al." each time, including the first.

Online sources

When citing electronic sources using APA style, you can follow most of the conventions you use to cite print sources. The one exception is that if your electronic source has no page numbers, identify the paragraph or section

37
APA

number instead. If page, paragraph, and section numbers are not used, identify the section by its heading and count the paragraphs following the heading to assign a number to the paragraph containing the material you are citing:

> Some of Pereira's views have recently been questioned (Freedman, 2004, para. 22).

> This recent development has many analysts perplexed (Hashemi, 2002, Further developments, para. 3).

Sample Reference-List Entries

An entire book

> Siblin, E. (2009). *The cello suites: J. S. Bach, Pablo Casals, and the search for a baroque masterpiece.* Toronto: Anansi.

Note that initials are used instead of the author's full given name or names. Also note the style of capitalization. For book and article titles, capitalize only the first letter of the first word of the title, the first letter of the first word following a colon, and the first letter of a proper noun. For periodical titles, capitalize all key words except for prepositions, articles, and conjunctions. These rules apply to the APA reference list only. In the body of a paper, all titles are treated according to the rule given here for periodical titles.

An article in an edited book

> Gilbert, H. (2009). Contemporary Aboriginal theater. In C. Howells & E.-M. Kroller (Eds.), *The Cambridge history of Canadian literature* (pp. 518–535). Cambridge: Cambridge University Press.

An article in a reference book

> Fernandez, D. (2002). Rice cake of the Philippines. In A. Davidson (Ed.), *The Penguin companion to food* (pp. 792–797). London: Penguin.

37
APA

A multivolume work

Smelser, N. J., & Baltes, P. B. (Eds.). (2001). *International encyclopedia of the social and behavioural sciences* (Vols. 1–26). Amsterdam: Elsevier.

An anonymous article

Canadian dollar at 3-1/2 year high. (2011, 12 April). *The Vancouver Sun*, p. C1.

A republished book

McLuhan, M. (2002). *The mechanical bride: Folklore of industrial man.* Corte Madera, CA: Gingko Press. (Original work published 1951).

A translated work

Fortier, D. (2010). *On the proper use of stars* (S. Fischman, Trans.). Toronto: McClelland & Stewart.

A review

Calder. A. (2010). One good step. [Review of the book *One step over the line: Toward a history of women in the North American wests*, by E. Jameson & S. McManus (Eds.)]. *Canadian Literature, 206*, 149–150.

Wong, L. (2011). [Review of the book *Inside Chinatown: Ancient culture in a new world*, by R. Amos & K. Wong]. *BC Studies, 169*, 157–158.

The first review is entitled "One Good Step." The second review is untitled, as are many reviews appearing in scholarly journals.

An audio recording

Ma, Y. (2007). *Appassionato* [CD]. Toronto: Sony BMG Music Canada.

A television program

Fleming, S. (Producer & Director). (2011, April 10). Raccoon nation [Television series episode]. In *The*

nature of things with David Suzuki. Toronto: Canadian
Broadcasting Corporation.

A video

Barnim, A. (Director). (2011). *Agents of change* [Motion
picture]. Canada: National Film Board of Canada.

A journal article, one author

Ziser, M. (2010). Bioregionalism 2.0: Global climate
change, local environmentalism, and new-media
communities. *Western Humanities Review, 64*(3),
81–84.

A journal article, two or more authors

Weber, B., & Shields, R. (2011). The virtual north: On
the boundaries of sovereignty. *Ethnic and Racial
Studies, 34*(1), 103–120.

A government agency or corporate author

Agriculture and Agri-Food Canada. (2008). *Export
program information: Canada's agri-food and seafood
export market development opportunities guide.*
Ottawa: Agriculture and Agri-Food Canada.

A magazine article

Gladwell, M. (2011, May 16). Creation myth. *The New
Yorker*, 44–53.

A newspaper article, no author

Market and roadside bombs leave 16 dead. (2011, 12
April). *The Vancouver Sun*, p. B3.

37
APA

Electronic Sources

Reference-list entries for electronic sources should
include, in addition to the details you would include for
a print source, the URL (or, if applicable, the digital
object identifier).

An entire website

> Deutsch, A. (2011, May 30). *Psychology Today* [Website]. Retrieved from http://www.psychologytoday.com

In APA style, the name of the person or organization that has provided the content of the site comes first. The date in parentheses is the date the material was last updated. Note that the URL is not contained in angle brackets, and the entry does not conclude with a period.

An article from a journal available online
Use the same format you would for a print version of the article, adding the digital object identifier (DOI) at the end:

> Zielke, S. (2011). Integrating emotions in the analysis of retail price images. *Psychology and Marketing, 28*(4), 330–359. doi:10.1002/mar.20355

If the article has not been assigned a DOI, include the URL:

> Giddens, E. (2010–11). Masculinity and barbarism in *Titus Andronicus. Early Modern Literary Studies, 15*(2), 1–35. Retrieved from http://extra.shu.ac.uk/emls/15-2/giddtitu.htm

An online government publication

> Health Canada. (2009). Prenatal nutrition guidelines for health professionals. Retrieved from http://publications.gc.ca/site/eng/347568/publication.html

A dissertation, from an electronic database

> Ing, N. L. (2002). *Dealing with shame and unresolved trauma: Residential school and its impact on 2nd and 3rd generation adults* (Doctoral dissertation). Available from Theses Canada Portal. (AMICUS No. 27109905).

A webcast, blog post, or online video
For informally published material from online communities, provide the format of the content in square brackets following the title, and include the URL:

37
APA

AgileHProductions. (2009, February 14). Canada goose [Video file]. Retrieved from http://www.youtube.com/watch?v=OQFAtjvDmMO

37c The Note Method (Chicago Style)

The note method uses either footnotes or endnotes and a bibliography. Although it is one traditionally used in some courses in the humanities, many disciplines that have used the note method in the past are moving away from footnotes and endnotes in favour of in-text references, which enable the reader to see the source being cited without having to stop reading to refer to the end of the paper or the foot of the page. The following guidelines are based on the sixteenth edition of *The Chicago Manual of Style*.

Notes—either footnotes or endnotes—should be single-spaced and formatted with either a first-line indent (as in the examples that follow) or a hanging indent. Although the note numbers in the text are superscript, the note numbers preceding each endnote or footnote are not. Notes should contain the name of the author, the name of the source, and the publisher and place of publication, as well as the page, chapter, or table number referred to if appropriate. If you are referring repeatedly to the same source, you can use the abbreviation "Ibid." and the page number for subsequent references, provided that there is no intervening reference to a different source. In cases where a different source intervenes, you can use a shortened citation, which should include enough information to lead the reader to the appropriate entry in the bibliography and normally consists of the last name of the author and a shortened version of the title:

1. Frances W. Kaye, "The Tantalizing Possibility of Living on the Plains," in *History, Literature, and the Writing of the Canadian Prairies*, ed. Alison Calder and Robert Wardhaugh (Winnipeg: University of Manitoba Press, 2005), 25.

2. Ibid., 26.

3. Joan Thomas, *Curiosity* (Toronto: McClelland and Stewart, 2010), 69.

4. Kaye, "Tantalizing Possibility," 27.

37
CHI

All of the sources you have used in an essay, including those you may have consulted but not referred to directly, are listed in a bibliography at the end of the document. A bibliography allows the person reading your essay to see at a single glance all of the sources you have used.

The following examples illustrate the Chicago style for documenting sources in footnotes or endnotes and in the bibliography.

A book by one author

FOOTNOTE OR ENDNOTE

> 5. Kit Dobson, *Transnational Canadas: Anglo-Canadian Literature and Globalization* (Waterloo: Wilfrid Laurier University Press, 2009), 9.

BIBLIOGRAPHY REFERENCE

> Dobson, Kit. *Transnational Canadas: Anglo-Canadian Literature and Globalization*. Waterloo: Wilfrid Laurier University Press, 2009.

A book by two or more authors or editors

FOOTNOTE OR ENDNOTE

If the work you're referencing has two or three authors, list all of the authors' names:

> 6. Geoffrey Leech, Margaret Deuchar, and Robert Hoogenraad, *English Grammar for Today: A New Introduction*, 2nd ed. (London: Palgrave Macmillan, 2006), 66.

If the book has more than three authors, you can use the name of the first author only, followed by "et al.":

> 7. Eva-Marie Kröller et al., eds., *Pacific Encounters: The Production of Self and Others* (Vancouver: Institute of Asian Research UBC, 1997), 126.

BIBLIOGRAPHY REFERENCES

If the book you are referencing has two or more authors, invert the name of the first author only:

37
CHI

Leech, Geoffrey, Margaret Deuchar, and Robert Hoogenraad. *English Grammar for Today: A New Introduction*. 2nd ed. London: Palgrave Macmillan, 2006.

If the book has more than three authors, you may follow the first author's name (inverted) with a comma and "et al." or you may include up to ten names for one book in the bibliography:

Kröller, Eva-Marie, et al., eds. *Pacific Encounters: The Production of Self and Others*. Vancouver: Institute of Asian Research UBC, 1997.

A work by a government agency or a corporate author

FOOTNOTE OR ENDNOTE

8. Health Canada, *Eating Well with Canada's Food Guide: A Resource for Educators and Communicators* (Ottawa: Health Canada, 2007), 35.

BIBLIOGRAPHY REFERENCE

Health Canada. *Eating Well with Canada's Food Guide: A Resource for Educators and Communicators*. Ottawa: Health Canada, 2007.

A book with an editor or translator

FOOTNOTE OR ENDNOTE

If the book you are citing has an editor and no author, give the editor's name first, followed by "ed.":

9. William Toye, ed., *The Concise Oxford Companion to Canadian Literature*, 2nd ed. (Toronto: Oxford University Press, 2010), 644.

If the book has a translator or editor as well as an author, the author's name should come before the title, with the translator's or editor's name following the title:

10. Denyse Baillargeon, *Making Do: Women, Family and Home in Montreal During the Great Depression*, trans. Yvonne Klein (Waterloo: Wilfrid Laurier University Press, 1999), 16.

37
CHI

BIBLIOGRAPHY REFERENCE

If the book has an editor and no author, give the editor's name first, followed by "ed.":

> Toye, William, ed. *The Concise Oxford Companion to Canadian Literature*. 2nd ed. Toronto: Oxford University Press, 2010.

If the book has an editor or translator as well as an author, give the author's name first and give the translator's or editor's name after the title:

> Baillargeon, Denyse. *Making Do: Women, Family and Home in Montreal During the Great Depression*. Translated by Yvonne Klein. Waterloo: Wilfrid Laurier University Press, 1999.

A work in an edited anthology
FOOTNOTE OR ENDNOTE

> 11. Al Purdy, "On the Flood Plain," in *An Anthology of Canadian Literature in English*, 2nd ed., eds. Donna Bennett and Russell Brown (Toronto: Oxford University Press, 2010), 582.

BIBLIOGRAPHY REFERENCE

> Purdy, Al. "On the Flood Plain." In *An Anthology of Canadian Literature in English*. 2nd ed. Edited by Donna Bennett and Russell Brown, 582–84. Toronto: Oxford University Press, 2010.

An article in a journal
FOOTNOTE OR ENDNOTE

37
CHI

> 12. Alison Toron, "The Model Prisoner: Reading Confinement in *Alias Grace*," *Canadian Literature* 208 (2011): 23.

BIBLIOGRAPHY REFERENCE

> Toron, Alison. "The Model Prisoner: Reading Confinement in *Alias Grace*." *Canadian Literature* 208 (2011): 12–28.

A newspaper article

FOOTNOTE OR ENDNOTE

Since a newspaper may have several editions in a given day, and items may be moved or eliminated in various editions, page numbers should be omitted. If the section of the newspaper containing the article is identified, give its name, number, or letter.

> 13. J.B. MacKinnon, "Paradise Lost?: The Great Bear Rain Forest," Travel, *Globe and Mail*, July 26, 2003, sec T.

If the article is unsigned, begin with the title of the article.

BIBLIOGRAPHY REFERENCE

> MacKinnon, J.B. "Paradise Lost?: The Great Bear Rain Forest." Travel, *Globe and Mail*, July 26, 2003, sec. T.

An Internet site

FOOTNOTE OR ENDNOTE

> 14. Evan Goldstein, ed., *Arts and Letters Daily* (2011), accessed June 2, 2011, http://www.aldaily.com.

BIBLIOGRAPHY REFERENCE

> Goldstein, Evan, ed. *Arts and Letters Daily* (2011). Accessed June 2, 2011. http://www.aldaily.com.

An article from a journal available online

FOOTNOTE OR ENDNOTE

> 15. Nicholas B. Mayer, "Catalyzing Prufrock," *Journal of Modern Literature* 34, no. 3 (2011): 188, http://muse.jhu.edu/journals/journal_of_modern_literature/v034/34.3.mayer.html.

37
CHI

BIBLIOGRAPHY REFERENCE

> Mayer, Nicholas B. "Catalyzing Prufrock." *Journal of Modern Literature* 34, no. 3 (2011): 182-98. http://muse.jhu.edu/journals/journal_of_modern_literature/v034/34.3.mayer.html.

APPENDIX:
CHECKLIST FOR USE IN REVISING, EDITING, AND PROOFREADING

As you begin to prepare a piece of your writing for final submission to your reader(s), it is good strategy to ask yourself a series of questions designed to ensure that you have polished your work to the point where you can consider it a finished and appealing discourse. What we have listed here are the kinds of questions we ask ourselves in reading and evaluating students' writing. If you can ask and answer all of the following questions in the affirmative, your essay should be not just adequate, but very good.

1. During and after planning the essay, ask yourself these questions:

Subject

☐ Have I chosen a subject that sustains my interest? (#1a)

☐ If I am doing research, have I formulated a researchable question? (#33a)

☐ Have I sufficiently *limited* my subject? (#1a)

Audience and Purpose

☐ Have I thought about audience and purpose?

☐ Have I written down a statement of purpose and a profile of my audience? (#1b)

Evidence

☐ Have I collected or generated more than enough material/evidence to develop and support my topic well? (#1c)

Organization and Plan

☐ Does my *thesis* offer a focused, substantive, analytical claim about the subject? (#1d)

☐ Is my *plan* or *outline* for the essay logical in its content and arrangement? (#1e)

☐ Considering my plan or outline, do I have the right number of *main ideas*—neither too few nor too many—for the purpose of my essay?

☐ Are my main ideas reasonably *parallel* in content and development?

☐ Have I chosen the best *arrangement* for the main parts? Does it coincide with the arrangement of ideas in the thesis?

2. **During and after your revision of the essay, ask yourself these questions:**

Title

☐ Does the *title* of my essay clearly indicate the subject and topic?

☐ Is the *title* original?

☐ Does the *title* contain something to catch a reader's interest?

Structure

☐ Does my beginning engage a reader's curiosity or interest?

☐ Have I kept the beginning reasonably short and to the point? (#1g)

☐ Have I clearly stated my *subject* (and my *thesis* as well) somewhere near the beginning? (#1g.3)

☐ Does my *ending* bring the essay to a satisfying conclusion?

☐ Have I used the ending to do something other than re-hash ideas already well presented in the rest of the essay?

☐ Have I kept my ending short enough, without unnecessary repetition and summary?

Unity; Development

☐ Is my essay unified? Do all its parts contribute to the whole, and have I avoided digression?

Emphasis

☐ Have I been sufficiently *particular* and *specific*, and not left any generalizations unsupported? (#14b)

☐ Have I devoted an appropriate amount of space to each part?

Paragraphs

☐ Does the first sentence of each body paragraph somehow mention *the particular subject* of the essay? (#2a–b)

☐ Do the early sentences of each body paragraph clearly state the topic, or part of the topic? Or, is the topic sentence, when it isn't among the first sentences, effective where it is placed?

☐ Is each body paragraph *long enough to develop its topic* adequately? (#2d)

☐ Does each paragraph *end* adequately, but not too self-consciously?

Coherence

☐ Do the sentences in each paragraph have sufficient *coherence* with each other? (#2b–c)

☐ Does the beginning of each new paragraph provide a clear *transition* from the preceding paragraph?

☐ Is the coherence between sentences and between paragraphs smooth? Have I revised any unnecessary or illogical transitional devices?

Sentences

☐ Is each sentence (especially if it is compound, complex, or long) internally *coherent*?

☐ Is each sentence clear and sufficiently *emphatic* in making its point? (#4e–i)

☐ Have I used a variety of *kinds, lengths, and structures* of sentences? (#4b–d)

☐ Have I avoided *the passive voice* except where it is clearly necessary or desirable? (#8h)

Diction

☐ Have I used *words* whose meanings I am sure of, or checked the *dictionary* for any whose meanings I am not sure of?

☐ Is my diction sufficiently *concrete* and *specific?* (#14b)

☐ Have I avoided *unidiomatic* usages? (#14e)

☐ Have I weeded out unnecessary repetitions and other *wordiness?* (#14f)

☐ Have I avoided *jargon* and unnecessary *clichés* and *euphemisms*? (#14c, #14a)

☐ Have I avoided unintentional *slang* and *informal* diction, as well as *overformal* diction? (#14a)

☐ Have I avoided inappropriate or confusing *figurative language?*

☐ Have I avoided *gender-biased, sexist language?* (#7e, #14g)

Grammar

☐ Are my sentences *grammatically* sound—that is, free of dangling modifiers, agreement errors, incorrect tenses, faulty verb forms, incorrect articles and prepositions, and the like? (Parts II and III)

☐ Have I avoided *run-on sentences* and *unacceptable fragments* and *comma splices?* (#5a–c, #25a, #25n)

Punctuation

☐ Is the *punctuation* of each sentence correct and effective? (Part IV)

☐ Have I proofread sentences slowly with special attention to the punctuation?

Spelling

☐ Have I checked all my words—reading backwards if necessary—for possible *spelling* errors? (Part V)

☐ Have I used the spell checker in my software package to check the essay?

Mechanics

☐ Have I carefully *proofread* my essay *in hard copy* (not just on the computer screen) and corrected all typographical errors? (#1h)

☐ Is my manuscript neat and legible? Does it conform to all *manuscript conventions* (especially spacing, margins, font size, pagination, and headers)? (#26)

☐ Have I introduced and handled all *quotations* and *references* properly? (#20, #35, #36, #37)

☐ Have I checked all *quotations* for accuracy? (#36)

Acknowledgement

☐ Have I *acknowledged* everything that requires acknowledgement according to the guidelines and rules of my university or college? (#35, #36)

☐ Have I double-checked my *documentation* for accuracy, consistency, and correct form? (#37)

The Last Step

☐ Have I read my essay aloud—preferably to a colleague—as a final check on how it sounds and made adjustments for clarity and emphasis?

INDEX